CW01455396

Dear England

ALSO BY GARETH SOUTHGATE

Anything Is Possible

Dear England

Lessons in Leadership

GARETH SOUTHGATE

C

CENTURY

CENTURY

UK | USA | Canada | Ireland | Australia
India | New Zealand | South Africa

Century is part of the Penguin Random House group of companies
whose addresses can be found at global.penguinrandomhouse.com

Penguin Random House UK,
One Embassy Gardens, 8 Viaduct Gardens, London SW11 7BW

penguin.co.uk

Penguin
Random House
UK

First published 2025
001

Set in 14.2/17pt Fournier MT Pro
Typeset by Six Red Marbles UK, Thetford, Norfolk

Printed and bound by CPI (UK) Ltd, Croydon CR0 4YY

The authorised representative in the EEA is Penguin Random House Ireland,
Morrison Chambers, 32 Nassau Street, Dublin D02 YH68

A CIP catalogue record for this book is available from the British Library

ISBN: 978–1–529–95829–4 (hardback)
ISBN: 978–1–529–95830–0 (trade paperback)

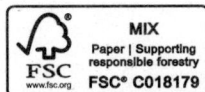

To Alison, Mia and Flynn.
You are the only ones who know fully where this journey has taken us all. Without your strength, love and unwavering support, it wouldn't have been worthwhile, or remotely possible. Thank you for understanding.

Contents

CONTENTS

Introduction

England v. Spain, Final, 2024 Uefa European Football Championship, Olympiastadion, Berlin, 14 July.

It was like a punch in the gut.

The eighty-sixth minute of the match, the ball flying low and hard into our penalty area, the outstretched boot . . . And then the net rippling and a horde of their subs and coaching staff exploding out of the dugout next to ours and chasing off in ecstasy down the touchline.

Two–one to Spain, and time almost up.

There by the pitch, I'm not sure I had ever known disappointment feel so visceral – so much like an actual physical blow. Was this really how it was going to end?

Only a quarter of an hour earlier, we had put ourselves right back into this game. We were 1–0 down and getting forced repeatedly backwards by formidable opponents, and I had already made the decision after sixty-one minutes to withdraw our captain, Harry Kane, and send on Ollie Watkins up front. I then changed things again and brought on the young Chelsea forward Cole Palmer in the seventieth minute.

Cole had been menacing defenders all tournament as an impact sub and, in the previous game, he had made Ollie's winning goal. I felt sure the pair of them would make the difference here. It would mean playing our attacking midfielder Jude Bellingham a little further back, and it would risk making us less stable when Spain had the ball, which was often. But it would increase our goal threat. And we were going nowhere, obviously, without a goal.

And almost immediately the change paid off – after just 142 seconds, to be exact. Under pressure in Spain's penalty area, and with Ollie distracting defenders in the centre, Jude laid the ball back to Cole. From twenty yards out, the freshest player on the pitch calmly stroked it into the bottom corner. It was the fastest-ever goal by an England substitute. More importantly, we were level with Spain, and our fans, banked in the stadium's west stand, could start to believe again.

And why not? Weren't resurrections a bit of a theme for England in these Euros? We certainly had some recent history in this area. In each of our knockout matches in this tournament, we had come back to win from a goal down. Now we just needed to do it again; to fight the fatigue, find the belief and make one last comeback, here in the final.

Game on, then. For the next ten minutes, the match see-sawed. The speed of Spain's passing remained relentless, but we were now finding the composure we needed to mount counter-attacks and create moments of our own. And like the fans thunderously encouraging us, I genuinely felt that we could do this – score again, complete the turnaround, win the trophy and start a national party that had been waiting to kick off since 1966. Given the decision I had recently made in private about my own future, I was as desperate as anyone in that stadium that we should make it happen.

Then the eighty-sixth minute came, and that stomach punch – Marc Cucurella's raking pass, Mikel Oyarzabal's sliding lunge . . .

I've always been an optimistic person – have always tried to dig deep for positivity when things start going against me. I did so now, striding out to the touchline, urging my players to get up and go again, to keep pushing. I wanted them to remember that we had come back from the brink before – with even less time left on the clock, in fact. There were still whole minutes here in which to equalise. There would be another chance.

And there was. Right in the dying seconds we forced a corner. This was the moment, surely, the moment to send the game into extra-time and keep the dream alive.

I watched the ball float into the penalty area – saw Declan Rice rise above the jostling pack to meet it. What followed was a chaotic flurry, something which, from fifty yards away, looked closer to volleyball than football. I saw Declan's header get pushed back out with a flailing arm by the Spanish keeper. I saw Marc Guéhi jump at the rebound, saw the ball heading for the goal again, only to be blocked on the line. With each of these actions my own body involuntarily jerked. And then I saw the ball come out to Declan again, saw his reflex header loop up and over the bar and fly away.

At that point, my assistant coach and I turned to each other as we had so many times before. Steve Holland and I had navigated our way through more than a hundred England games together. Our working relationship ran deep. He knew what I was thinking and feeling. We had worked every day for eight years towards this dream of a trophy. But we knew it was fading.

Seconds later, with the referee's final whistle, it was gone.

Football offers few moments as raw as the immediate aftermath of a final you've lost. And if you've lost it to a late goal, it's about as bad as football gets. Glory has been within touching distance, only to be snatched away. There's so much invested in these campaigns: all the hours of preparing and training, all the personal sacrifices made, all the hope built up over time, all of the focus on this one thing. And then it's over and all the air goes out of you, every last bit. Everyone in our team, players and staff, looked hollow. Meanwhile, Spain danced in front of their supporters and got ready to receive the trophy. At that moment, I wanted to be anywhere but on that pitch. We all felt the same.

Yet some kind of autopilot kicked in. I had to set my personal feelings aside. I was the manager. I had duties. I needed to congratulate our opponents, thank the officials, and console my players. Most importantly of all, and with the team joining me, I needed to cross the pitch to applaud our supporters, the thousands of them who had arrived so hopefully in Germany but were now as floored as we were.

This may have been the rawest moment of them all. Looking up into the crowd, I could see faces painted red and white – was close enough to make eye contact with some of them individually, with children, women and men draped in the flag of St George; families and friends from different generations who had made the trip and were now united in disappointment. There was also some disgruntlement, no question.

But I genuinely shared their pain and their anguish at that point. Not only had I narrowly missed a genuine opportunity to transform our fortunes and bring home the trophy that had eluded our country for so long, I also knew I wouldn't get another. Later that evening, I was going to tell my bosses at the Football Association that I was stepping down as England manager.

Before then, though, my sole focus was on throwing my arms around my players and staff. Our bid to become champions was over, but my responsibility to the team went beyond chasing bits of silverware. Some were in tears. Others were just numb. I did my best to find the right words but sometimes there aren't any.

It would be some time before I could look back on that 2024 final with any objectivity – and even longer before I could put it in perspective with all the other moments and milestones in my eight years in charge of the England team. In other words, it would be a while before I could sit down and write this book. But now I can see that, right until the end, on that pitch in Berlin, and in the moments afterwards when we were finally able to retreat to the dressing room, I was learning lessons in leadership. And perhaps that's one of the fundamental facts about such lessons: that, while you're a leader, they never really stop.

I was learning those lessons in extraordinary circumstances all along, in high-pressure situations, often with the whole nation watching and with millions of people deeply, emotionally invested in the outcome. I was learning them in what I think most people will agree is, however you look at it, an extraordinary role. Actually, I think there might be no job quite like managing England.

That said, I've spoken to all kinds of leaders over the years, from all walks of life; have taken every chance to seek them out, in fact, in order to pick their brains and share experiences and find out what I could learn. And, no matter what their field was, or how different from mine, we've nearly always found some common ground.

As my career took shape – as a player and then afterwards in coaching and management – leadership was always the subject that really fascinated me. What kind of people become great leaders? What are the qualities required to become one? What life experiences, skills and lessons do they learn along the way?

In my professional life, I had the chance to observe and be led by leaders of many different sorts – the shouters and screamers, the quiet types, the inspirational figures . . . you name it. And I eventually had the opportunity to carve my own path through leadership's many and sometimes wildly unpredictable challenges, and work out my own way of being a leader. That's the journey I'm going to try to describe in this book.

———

My field has always been football of course, and a critical part of preparing a football team is the tactical detail. An inordinate amount of my time as England manager was spent with my staff, studying and working through the best way to maximise our strengths and hide our weaknesses on the pitch. Systems, formations and patterns of play are constantly evolving and, in working at the highest level of the game, we needed to be across every innovation. That is the 'technical detail' of the business of football, a unique operating and information index, which every business will have in relation to their own sector or industry.

These technical and tactical components, of course, don't easily translate to other fields of play. So, for the purposes of this book, we are focusing on my leadership and management experiences – which, I believe, will resonate way beyond the football pitch. The way I see it, many of us find ourselves called upon to be leaders at some point in our lives. It might be in business. It might be in a charity. It could be in a school or in a community group. Or we find ourselves having to take on leadership roles in our families. There are so many situations where what's suddenly called for is some leadership.

So my hope is, whatever meaning leadership has for you, or whatever form it comes to take in your life, the stories I tell in these pages about my own learnings as a leader will also occasionally chime with your own experiences, and maybe even in some cases offer you some guidance.

That match against Spain in Euro 24 was the last time you saw me on the touchline as England manager. It ended in defeat, and that night the pain of losing was all I could think about. But there was a whole journey leading up to that moment whose lessons would endure – a journey that I came to realise was transformative in ways the simple, brutal fact of that final scoreline could not destroy.

Or, to put it another way, that final was the end of the story. But it was by no means the whole story. Let me tell you the whole story.

CHAPTER I

Finding My True North

On building resilience and defining values

Positive influences

On the eve of the 2020 Euros, I composed an open letter to fans. It began 'Dear England . . .' and it set out some ideas I had about national identity and unity and what it means in the twenty-first century to come together proudly as a country, and how football can help us do that. I wrote it from the heart, not just as a football manager but as a proud Englishman, and also as someone who really wanted to make a difference and who believed that, through football, he could do so. It came from my deeply held values: integrity, courage, empathy, resilience and accountability. But to tell you where those values came from, I need to take you right back to my childhood.

Like every child, there were men and women in my life who influenced me greatly. None of them were famous or 'influencers' in the modern meaning of the term but, fortunately for me, they were people whose example has meant a lot and shaped the way I try to go about things. They were, in effect, leaders in my life and I still feel their presence today.

There was my grandfather, my mum's dad. Football was at the centre of my world from the start, and it was my grandfather who took me to the park to practise. He was a veteran of the Second World War and he carried himself with quiet dignity: kind-hearted, morally anchored, always immaculately dressed – a shirt and tie every day. When I stayed over, I would watch him wet-shave every morning and polish his shoes. Like so many men of his generation, he had his standards of decency and he kept to them, raising his hat to say good morning to people as he passed them. Sometimes he'd buy me sweets on the way home, but I wouldn't be allowed to eat them in the street. He believed in the idea that the way you do the small things reflects who you are. And even though I'd be absolutely desperate to tuck into those sweets, I came to admire him enormously for that attitude. I was lucky to have my grandfather in my life.

Then there was my mum, a dinner lady who also worked in the classroom, helping children to read, and who swallowed her disappointment when I announced that I wouldn't be taking A levels after all, but would be quitting school for a highly uncertain life in football instead. Not that my mum didn't value sport. She had been a hurdler in her youth, and she was still good at overcoming obstacles in her later life. She was quietly competitive, not least when it came to family board games. And in crazy golf on holiday, there were no gimmies. 'No dinner if you don't win tonight,' she would say when I had a game after school. And I think some kids thought she was serious. I know she wasn't. Well, she may have been semi-serious I guess.

Then there was my dad, who had a steady job with IBM and coached at a local athletics club in his spare time. In fact, that's how my mum and dad met, through athletics, both representing Hertfordshire at the English Schools trials. So competitive sport was always in the family. My dad was a humble man – he stood quietly at the side of the pitch, never criticised the ref, encouraged me but never grilled me on the way home if I'd played badly. He responded to wins and losses in the same way: with dignity. I tried to follow him in that.

From my dad I also learned how generosity of spirit could promote loyalty and trust, and how it could help to fuel morale. I remember visiting him at his workplace one day after football training. Watching him mill around the office, I was struck by how popular he seemed to be with his colleagues. He was just a decent guy who got along with everyone around him. It made a big impression on me, and from that day forward informed how I set out to relate to the people I met.

In everything I did, my parents expected that I would try, and they had high hopes for me. That said, they were supportive and never pushy. And looking back, my parents provided the love and stability that my sister and I needed to make a solid start, and they made it possible for me to speak very casually later in life about having had 'an ordinary childhood'. It's not until you have children of your own that you understand exactly how much work and sacrifice goes into producing a childhood that's 'ordinary'. I so appreciate what they did for me.

Then there was Alan Smith, my coach at Crystal Palace when I was an apprentice player there, aged sixteen. I was struggling, and he knew it. Like all the apprentices, I was on a small wage, but, at least in theory, I was living the dream: getting paid to play football! In reality, I was hating it. In a group of mostly outgoing and confident kids, I stood out as the quiet one and found it really hard to fit in. Plus, there was the job itself, which included such glamorous activities as cleaning the first-team squad's boots, not to mention a large amount of toilet-scrubbing and floor-mopping.

And then there was the two-train commute every day from Crawley in West Sussex, which saw me setting out early and getting home late every day. All in all, it was quite a lot for a kid who was fresh out of school to adapt to. Alan, as the man in charge of overseeing my progress, recognised something in me but felt I needed to show my harder edge, if indeed I had one, in order to make it as a professional footballer. He took a dim view, for example, of the fact that whenever we lost a game I made a point of congratulating the opposition and shaking their hands. Not that I wasn't gutted; I was. But I buried that disappointment publicly and dealt with it later in the privacy of the dressing room, where, in those days, and throughout my time at Crystal Palace, the team's disgruntlement would often spill over into arguments, stand-offs and even punch-ups.

However, that public show of respect would drive Alan mad and, after one moment of despair, he took me aside and said, 'Gareth, you're a lovely bloke, but if I were you, I'd think about becoming a travel agent.'

Now, I love a holiday, the same as anyone, but at that point my dream was football and I had no ambition to go into the flight-booking business, so Alan's reassessment of my future course rather threw me off. I left his office feeling well and truly sorry for myself.

Today, though, I look back and consider Alan's remark a turning point, something I'll always be grateful to him for. What he was doing was challenging me, trying to shake me awake to something very important for my development: that I was going to need to exhibit some steel. It didn't mean that I had to reinvent myself overnight as the kind of player who stormed off the pitch like a spoilt child every time we lost. I could still be myself and still shake hands, win or lose (something I would continue to do for the rest of my career, and something I believe demonstrates both courtesy and the ability to keep your emotions in check). But I needed to be tougher and not come over quite so readily as a soft touch. Point taken.

My grandfather, my parents, Alan Smith: they were all crucial influences in their own different ways on my development as a person, and, by extension, as the kind of player and coach that I turned into. And consequently, at some level, these people will always be part of what I mean when I talk about leadership.

Making a leader

Are leaders born or made? That's an enduring question. Are effective leaders the product of nature or nurture? Or are they the result of both of those things in some combination? The view I've come to is that there are particular personal qualities that are essential for leadership. Traits that are built over time, but timeless. Values that are easy to talk about but hard to live by. For me, as I've mentioned, integrity, courage, empathy, resilience and accountability are values I try to embrace and stand by. They are how I try to live my life. And they are the foundations of how I try to lead.

They are by no means the only values to have to be an effective leader. There are many others that work. But whatever values you accrue, or aspire to, they will likely be forged over time, by the challenges you face. And they will not necessarily be dependent on your personality type, be it extrovert or introvert (for the record, it may or may not surprise you to learn that I place myself in the latter category).

Right from the beginning, from my earliest days playing organised football, I found I was being asked to take charge on the pitch. This was at primary school and in the team I turned out for at my Cub Scout troop. (Yes, I went to Cubs, and I don't mind saying I was a very proud wearer of the woggle.) In other words, before I even really knew what a captain was or did, coaches started picking me to be captain.

I can think of two reasons for this, and they're slightly contradictory. First, it was clear to anyone that I was bound-lessly enthusiastic about the game – a football-mad, sticker-collecting kid who punted a ball around the park, the garden, the playground and anywhere else he got the chance to. And passion was obviously important in a coach's eyes.

But, diametrically opposed to that, I was also considered to be quite sensible, and that was probably a slightly rarer commodity at that age. And when it came to captaincy, level-headedness, rather than passion, was probably the quality that clinched it for me with the coaches.

So suddenly I was a kid who was learning captaincy on the job and finding out how it worked. I noticed how the coaches would communicate with me, as captain, in a slightly different way to how they communicated with other players. I understood to some degree that I was the coach's representative out on the pitch. I mean, this was Cub football, so obviously there was no mind-blowingly complex, data-driven game-plan going on. But essentially it was down to me to lift the team if our heads dropped and it was down to me to thank the referee at the end of the game. It wasn't the biggest job in the world, then. Yet it gave me some responsibility for others, not just myself. It made me see that being captain went beyond how I performed as a player and became a matter of what I represented. And it showed me quite quickly that I could influence and galvanise people if I was given the chance. For someone who was naturally quite introverted, and certainly not a big noise-maker by comparison with the other kids, that was a major revelation.

Decency and respect

To some of my teammates, I was the posh boy, and surely too middle-class for football. And given first impressions count,

I can forgive them for thinking that, as I was the kid who, on his first day of duty as a Crystal Palace apprentice, turned up in his school shirt and trousers to find everyone else in casual-wear. (Look, I thought we'd be expected to come smart and those were the smartest clothes I had. Where was the memo?)

I suppose 'nice' was the label people put on me in those days, the inference being I was 'too nice to make it'. That just made me dig deeper to prove them wrong – a harder tackle, standing up to bravado, practising for hours on end. And if doing that while showing decency, manners and respect, on and off the pitch, is still 'too nice', then I'm guilty as charged. But given I went on to represent England more times as a player and manager combined than anyone else in the history of English football, I guess I wasn't too nice to make it. In fact, as I have developed as a leader, the inference in football, and sometimes in life, that in order to have a winning mentality you have to be nasty, aggressive or divisive is exactly the opposite of how I see it – and exactly the opposite of how I was raised to see it.

For me, there were no contradictions between being determined to win, prepared to challenge people and fully capable of making tough decisions while also showing decency and respect for others. On the contrary those values – the values which had been instilled in me all my life – would shape my leadership style and end up giving it strength. They were the place of authenticity from which I would lead. And let's face it, if you asked most of the players I have dropped from my squads or teams over the years, I doubt they would describe me as nice. Probably quite the opposite.

Building resilience

However nice I was, or wasn't, that had no bearing on the lessons in resilience I, and every player I knew, learned in order to make it as a professional. My journey began at the age of twelve when I was given the opportunity to join Southampton's youth programme, training with them once a week at their Centre of Excellence in Crawley.

I loved it. I was a late developer, and inevitably found myself pitted against bigger, stronger boys in that setting. But it forced me to raise my game and I improved as a player massively. It was the best fun, and I thought I was already on my way to achieving my childhood dream of becoming a professional footballer.

And then after three years, when I was fifteen, they let me go.

'Dear Gareth Southgate,' said the letter. The 'dear' was typed. My name was handwritten. This perhaps gives you a sense of the personal nature of this communication. It went on: 'On behalf of Southampton Football Club, I am writing to inform you that we will not be offering your son a place on our Centre of Excellence.'

My *son*?

It was gutting – and not just because of the tactless nature of the dismissal, though that didn't help. The fact is, I could have been flattened altogether by that rejection and given up on the ambition. It certainly tested my faith in myself at that tender age. But I was determined. I kept plugging away,

17

kept striving to be a better player. Eventually, I was invited to train with Crystal Palace Under-18s. I was only fifteen, but quite used to playing with an older cohort, so it was another brilliant opportunity to stretch myself. One year later, I was offered my apprenticeship.

On my first day at Crystal Palace, I was lapped in a twelve-minute run at the end of training and had to perform an extra lap as a 'reward'. Still skinny for my age, I quickly realised that I would need to get physically stronger – but also that it was mostly my mind that had previously limited me in tests of endurance. Slowly, through painful practice, I realised that I could run a yard further, and then 200 metres further, and then a mile, and soon I would be up and down another two hill runs. This exertion helped me to build stores of mental fortitude that I believe I've drawn on ever since. Maybe my team-mates and I should have used the ball more in training in those days, but I believe the physical and mental strength we were building was a huge factor in my staying fit throughout a career that would eventually span 700 matches. This exertion also stood me in good stead for the many trials I would later experience in my career.

That mental fortitude was essential to make it through the youth system and into the professional game. There were eight other apprentices alongside me at Crystal Palace and only two, maybe three, would be offered a contract. So I realised I needed to work harder, and be better, than my team-mates to make it. The moments that could build resilience were constant and relentless. Every day you were competing, not just with your opponents, but with your own team-mates.

If there was a place up for grabs, it had to be yours. That was the pact in football and it was cut-throat. Looking back, I realise it's incredibly hard to make it as a professional player.

Determination was the trait that got me through those years. I had a constant desire to improve and a strong work ethic, allied to self-reliance. If I fell short, I believed it was on me to recognise the reasons why and fix them. It was a matter of mindset as much as anything. When there were setbacks I would try to rise against them and learn from them, rather than be sunk by them. I honed the ability to bounce back and that resilience stood me in good stead. For it was only after five years of travelling up and down the country playing for Crystal Palace's reserves that I finally broke into the first team. By the time I did so, most of my mates that I had joined up with had fallen by the wayside. But I kept at it, and I hung in there, and I came through.

If resilience and belief were the keys to me making it as a player, they were not traits that appeared overnight. This is something I always try to explain to young people, especially those who meet with rejection in some form for the first time and are immediately driven to despair. I understand that the strength to continue in the face of adversity is built, step by step, experience by experience, through grit and determination, over time. This is the consequence of meeting rejection, getting beyond it and keeping going, until you have deep reserves of those qualities that you can easily reach for when you need them. And then you are a stronger person.

These cumulative encounters rapidly built up as I turned professional. Twice a week I played matches. I won, I drew,

I lost. I pushed myself physically and mentally to the limit. If there were five minutes to go in a game, 1–0 up away from home, and the ball was flying into our penalty area, I was fighting to defend our lead with every scrap of my energy. My defeats or individual errors soon became public. They were highlighted on television. I was taunted by opposition fans. Sometimes I would crawl into bed bruised and battered after a game, mentally exhausted. Like my fellow professionals, I had to find the strength to go again the following morning.

As the stakes got higher, I continued to be (to use the interesting phrase) 'captaincy material'. At Crystal Palace I was made captain at the young age of twenty-three. The manager who gave me the job? Alan Smith. Clearly, for Alan, I had finally lost the 'travel agent' tag. It was no secret that some of the older players in the squad at that time felt the role should have been theirs, quite reasonably, and that was potentially an awkward hurdle for me to negotiate. I could only apply myself to the task and work on it until those older players accepted my authority. That year we won the First Division title – the Championship, as it is now. Later I would move on to Aston Villa and then to Middlesbrough, and I would captain both those sides too. I had become someone who could be relied upon to lead.

My worst moment

My England debut was against Portugal on 13 December 1995. It was one of the proudest days of my life, and it would begin a period of representing my country that lasted for the best part of a decade. But that rarefied air I was now breathing as an England player also brought with it the noxious fumes of pressure and attention. Most acutely, I would have to draw heavily on my supplies of resilience and belief following my penalty miss in the semi-finals of Euro 96. Without question, that was a watershed moment for me. Four years earlier, a still-uncapped 21-year-old who had just completed his first full season with Palace, I had been on holiday with mates in Portugal, watching Euro 92 (which was in Sweden that year) in bars – and watching England fail to win a game. Nevertheless, I'd found myself turning to one of my friends and saying, 'Wouldn't it be great to be involved in that next time?'

I wasn't wrong. The first major football tournament hosted in our country since the World Cup in 1966 took place in conditions of high national fervour, and an exciting and richly talented England team rode the wave. Terry Venables had accelerated me into the side and there I was, less than a year after my international debut, a starter in defence. Everybody in the country seemed to be watching and sharing the mounting hope and excitement. Bobby Charlton described my performance as 'world class'. Truly heady times.

And then Germany at Wembley. Ninety thousand people in the ground and millions watching at home. Ten penalties, all perfect, and I make the long walk from the centre circle as the first taker outside the designated five, my head already repeating the worst question I could have been asking myself at that point: 'What if I miss?' My unconvincing penalty is saved, Andreas Möller scores the winner, and in that handful of minutes my life is turned completely upside down.

A countrywide party had come to an anguished halt because of me. I was centre-stage. I'd never been centre-stage before in my career, and now I was – for ending a nation's dream. Back in the dressing room, I felt broken, overcome by the sense of having let down not just myself and the team, but everyone in the land. I was comforted by Terry Venables and by the captain, Tony Adams, who did their absolute best for me. But I was inconsolable at that point. I felt like I had just done something that was going to overshadow everything I did forever afterwards, something truly irreversible from which there would never be any escape. It was suffocating, and it was a feeling that would stay with me for a very long time. Arriving home the following day, the press already camped on my front lawn, I admit the thought came to me, 'How am I ever going to recover from this?'

Eventually, though, I was able to begin to turn it around. The recovery began with invaluable advice from my friend and team-mate Stuart Pearce. Stuart had missed a critical penalty in a shoot-out during the 1990 World Cup in Italy. Not only had he survived, he had remained an important member of the England squad, so that was encouraging in itself. Less encouragingly, he was able to warn me about the sleepless nights I would face, the kind of newspaper headlines I would read and the abuse that would be hurled at me in the streets for years to come. And all of those things he was absolutely right about. But he was also able to suggest a way for me to begin processing the incident.

Stuart pointed out that, in football, nothing would likely ever be as painful for me again as that Wembley experience.

In other words, just about the worst thing that could possibly happen to me on a football pitch, short of dire injury (and possibly even including that), had happened, and was over. As Stuart had found out for himself – and as I would duly discover – accepting that reality was a motivating force going forward. I was now able to see that I still had a choice at that point. I could choose to be permanently floored by that moment. Or I could get back up and keep going. The way in which that moment defined me was still within my power to control. I could, by my own actions, turn it to my advantage and use it to make me even stronger. Even though away fans would ridicule me for years, even though people would shout out of vans as I walked down the street, and even though I would be introduced as 'the guy that missed the penalty' for about two decades, I would build fortitude.

I would learn that setbacks and failures are the inevitable consequence of striving to perform at the highest level. That doesn't mean they don't hurt – that they aren't even traumatic sometimes. But with the right, positive mindset and the will to learn, they have the potential to deepen our reserves, increase our resilience, and inform and shape the personal style with which we then lead.

Listening and learning

When I became a manager, I had already seen the many forms that effective leadership from the side of the pitch could take.

In fact, you could say I'd had a fast-track education in that subject.

For example, there was Steve Coppell, my first manager at Crystal Palace. Steve was young and forward-thinking – a university graduate, which made him pretty much unique in football management at the time. He was way ahead of the game in seeing how data could help him make informed decisions. Yet perhaps his biggest strength was how attuned he was to the players and their different personalities, and how well he accommodated that variety in the group. He allowed the creative types a little more leeway, providing encouragement in different quantities and at different volumes according to which player needed it, and was firm when it mattered. He was particularly good at giving a chance to players who had a point to prove. In that team, we were all either from the youth system, or from the lower leagues. Most of us had been rejected somewhere along the line. In some ways, we were a team of highly motivated misfits. We trained unbelievably hard to compensate for the feeling that we were catching up, which meant that we became an athletic, powerful team to play against. Steve was clear about this identity for our team. He recognised a great leadership truth, that getting the best out of people was first and foremost about understanding their characters. When I thought back on my time under Steve, I realised that he had shown me a lot about the value of emotional intelligence and reading the room.

Then there were the four England managers I played under. There was Terry Venables, for whom I had enormous respect – and not just because he was the manager who first put me in the England team. So much about Terry impressed me as a coach and as a man manager. Even though I only really worked with him for a few weeks, during one international season, his way of going about things left a deep impression.

I was struck by his immense personal assurance as a leader. Of course, when he took the England job, he had already been the manager of Barcelona, so there was no question about his ability to handle the pressure of a job like England. He had that quiet confidence about him, generally relaxed and smiling whenever you saw him around the camp. The 'big players' liked and respected him, because his tactical knowledge was clear, and he was equally adept at pulling you quietly to one side for a reassuring word or a gee-up. During Euro 96, he demonstrated his tactical prowess by switching the system we played in games several times during the tournament, which was unusual, and not always successful. But when we beat Holland 4–1, it was a coaching masterstroke.

Terry's all-round assuredness was particularly impressive in tough moments. As I later came to understand very well, the pressure on an England manager to be forever changing things is immense. Every time something goes wrong or there's some kind of setback, the world around you seems to be demanding a reaction – is screaming at you, sometimes, to rip up the plan and start again. Shutting out the noise and sticking to your path in that circumstance, as Terry did, requires the highest degree of self-belief. Whether it was on the touchline, on the training ground or in the press conference, Terry always appeared to be in control, an aspiration for any leader.

Terry also had the good sense and humility to have excellent staff around him. His assistants, Don Howe and Mike Kelly, were two of the finest coaches in the country in their individual roles at the time. Terry once told me he wanted to employ people who were better than him, in order to make himself better and to challenge his own thinking. I've sometimes witnessed the opposite when managers surround themselves with 'yes men' who never say a word against them. I wouldn't say Don and Mike were 'better' than Terry; that was Terry being generous with his praise. But they were elite – they understood the level we needed to reach with England, and they were skilled in the areas that balanced Terry's strengths.

And then there was Kevin Keegan. Very different from Terry, Kevin was a 'big picture' manager. He could sell a vision, tell a story, excite people about what was possible. And he could make players feel ten feet tall. I remember, on his first game in charge of England – a Euros qualifier against Poland in 1999 – listening to him, in the dressing room, telling Paul Scholes exactly how brilliant he was. Scholes immediately went out and scored a hat-trick. Under Kevin, I witnessed the potential power of the great motivator, binding a team to a narrative about itself. I was rarely first choice for Kevin, but even despite that, I enjoyed playing for him, and he was someone personally who I wanted to do well for. His warmth and his style of wearing his heart on his sleeve were inspiring.

Glenn Hoddle, by contrast, was a details manager – incredibly clear on tactics and how he wanted to play, interested at a granular level in the physical preparation of the team, and bringing with him new thinking on diet and fitness which he had picked up while playing in France with Monaco. In Glenn, I saw an openness to innovation and a belief in the potential importance of even the littlest things.

The final England manager I played under was Sven-Göran Eriksson. Sven was a decorated trophy winner on the domestic and European stage with IFK Göteborg, Benfica and Lazio, with a much quieter and understated style of managing. Dressing room doors were most definitely safe in his presence. In 2002, I was on the bench when England under Sven faced Brazil in the quarter-final of the 2002 Korea/Japan World Cup. Formidable opponents, high stakes. An early goal from Michael Owen gave us hope, but Brazil gradually worked their way back into the match and stunned us with an equaliser in injury time just before the interval. When the team returned to the dressing room they had clearly had the belief momentarily knocked out of them.

Yet when Sven addressed the players, he did so very calmly. His message was, essentially, 'hold your nerve', and he delivered it in his usual even tone. I remember sitting there and feeling, in the circumstances and given what was on the line here, that he might have taken a more demonstrative approach in that moment – might have banged the drum or rattled the rafters or gone in for something a bit more Churchillian. When Brazil's Ronaldinho scored from a free kick early in the second half – a goal that would send us all home – I felt silently vindicated.

I've come to see that moment completely differently

now. I can appreciate that, under the greatest pressure, he was courageously staying true to himself and playing to his unique strengths. Sven's approach was measured, pragmatic and, above all, thought-through. It wasn't simply that noisy oratory and battle cries weren't his thing; he didn't think they were the *right* thing. He thought our best chance in that particular moment, against that particular opponent, was to go into the second half and play with composure. And to communicate that, he remained composed himself.

We didn't win against a top-class side who would go on to lift the trophy in that tournament. But it was a defeat by the narrowest margin, and who knows how long we would have been able to stay in the game if the team had gone charging into that second half like soldiers flinging themselves over the top, and lost their composure?

All of these managers, and many others, provided reference points for me when I began to carve my own path as a leader. And yet perhaps the most striking thing, when I thought back over the various leaders I had witnessed in my playing career, was that each of them was so very different. They each operated unswervingly in accordance with their own personal values, and in absolute keeping with their personalities, their characters and their authentic selves.

And perhaps this was the most important lesson that their example could teach: that the best leadership comes from an individual place of authenticity. I should qualify that statement by saying that not every 'authentic' individual makes a good leader. But when the right values, authentically rooted in a leader's personal history, meet the right challenge, I believe great leadership can develop (we'll be exploring my personal values in action in the course of this book).

To think of it another way, there's an ancient saying: 'Knowing yourself is the beginning of all wisdom.' It's clearly the beginning of all effective leadership, too. So, even while looking to role models for valuable inspiration and ideas, the question I realised I was eventually going to have to ask myself was: who am *I* as a leader? What kind of leader am *I* going to be?

It was the question I was still asking myself when I stepped into my first job in management, at a point where I still had so many lessons to learn – and some painful experiences to go through in order to learn them. 'Sink or swim' was about to take on a whole new order of meaning. Nothing could have fully prepared me for the journey I was about to go on.

SUMMARY
Finding My True North
On building resilience and defining values

- Before leading others, you must first lead yourself. This can only start when you are clear about your values. These will act as your compass and are the foundation of all effective leadership.

- Think about the formative figures in your early life, or leaders in your life now. What is it about these people that inspires you? What did you learn from them, and what qualities would you be proud to replicate in front of others?

- Identify the experiences that have shaped your life so far. Values are often formed from the tougher moments you endure. These 'origin' stories create personal learnings that help to make up who you are, and what you stand for.

- If someone doubts you, listen with humility and be open to change. But never be defined by another person's criticism, or allow their thoughts to limit your potential. The best leaders channel their energies into proving others wrong, and use challenges to develop personal qualities that compound over time.

- Accept and embrace obstacles if you want to be a leader. They are real, they are inevitable, and they are constant. There is no shortcut to building resilience and, by association, there is no shortcut to leadership.

- Setbacks or 'failures' are the inevitable consequence of striving to perform at the highest level. While they may be painful, they are also temporary, and with a positive mindset you have the potential to respond, and, in fact, to harness the power of these moments, in order to shape the personal style with which you lead.

- Always be a student of leadership. Be curious and hungry to improve. Listen and learn from others. And, no matter what your situation is in life, surround yourself with great leaders to help you achieve your goals.

CHAPTER 2

Driving the Team Bus

On learning lessons the hard way

Getting the call

It was the summer of 2006 and I was on holiday with the family in Florida. I was sitting on the balcony of our hotel room, idly watching the waves roll in under the evening sun and bracing myself in readiness to make one of those big decisions that – no matter how much you try to guard against them – inconsiderately creep up on you at these moments of downtime: whether to have a glass of wine or a cold beer from the fridge before getting showered and going down to dinner.

That was when my phone rang. It was Steve Gibson, the chairman and owner of Middlesbrough FC.

'Gareth,' he said, 'how would you feel about taking the role of manager at the club?'

Talk about getting blindsided. I did wonder for a split-second whether this was a wind-up or some kind of prank call. But there was nothing in Steve's tone of voice to suggest he wasn't actually Steve, and nothing in his tone of voice, either, to suggest that he was anything other than serious. He told me I had earned his trust as captain of the club for these past four seasons, and he thought I could do it again in charge of the team.

I liked and strongly admired Steve. This was the man who had pretty much single-handedly saved Middlesbrough from going into administration. He'd then put all of his energy into building the club into a thriving Premier League outfit. Two weeks before his call, we had finished our season with an appearance in the final of the Uefa Cup, now the Europa League, playing Sevilla in the Philips Stadium in Eindhoven. True, Sevilla had crushed us 4–0, but getting all the way to a European final was still a remarkable achievement for a club that hadn't even qualified for Europe at any point in its history until two years previously. Even with that distraction, we had also managed to finish comfortably mid-table in the Premier League. Middlesbrough in that period were well set up.

However, we were officially short of a manager. Steve McClaren's bold work piloting Middlesbrough deep into a European competition hadn't gone unnoticed by the FA, who had asked him to replace Sven-Göran Eriksson in charge of England. So I'd gone on holiday assuming that Steve Gibson would be spending his summer working through his list of preferred managerial candidates. I never for one moment thought he would get so far down that list that he would end up offering *me* the job. Actually, at that time, I wouldn't have thought you could make a list that long.

At the same time, I was at a pivotal moment in my professional life. I was thirty-five and I had just one year left on my contract. I was loving playing as much as ever, but I knew that I was coming to the end of the road in that regard. I'd made my last appearance in the England team two years beforehand. I had seen the grim signs that nearly all footballers ignore until it becomes impossible to do so: the incremental loss of pace, the longer recovery times after matches, the protracted efforts to get over knocks and injuries.

I had certainly started thinking about what the next phase of my career was going to look like – and was already figuring that coaching and management were going to be at the centre of it. I'd definitely already let Steve know that was my plan. In fact, part of me had wondered whether, when Middlesbrough appointed their next boss, I might talk to Steve and see whether I could become an assistant manager. That would have been the perfect next step – a chance to spend time learning alongside a qualified boss at a club I was already familiar with. And, meanwhile, I could continue studying for my coaching badges, which I'd made a start on but which is something it's hard to find the time to do when you're still playing regularly.

This phone call on the Florida balcony, though, was obviously dangling a whole other deal in front of me. This would be walking into a significant managerial job with no experience of that role whatsoever; with no official qualifications, even. (We would run into some trouble over my absent certificates a little further down the line, as you'll see.) Moreover, I'd be following Steve McClaren in the wake of an unprecedentedly successful European campaign – an achievement that brought both excitement and enormous expectation. Whatever else you wanted to say about it, this was an enormous leap of faith on the chairman's part; and it was asking for an enormous leap of faith on my part too, to accept his offer.

The obvious answer, then, was: 'Thank you, Steve, so much for thinking I could do this – but no.'

And then I should go and have dinner with the family and think no more about it.

On the other hand . . .

Was this not just the most amazing opportunity? How could I even *conceive* of turning it down? Steve and I already had a solid working relationship – there were no problems in that direction. And I knew as well as I knew anything that I wanted to be a manager: wasn't this just the chance to press the fast-forward button – cut to the chase and leave out all of the tiresome build-up? Steve's call was a summoning. Wasn't this a moment when I should back myself and step up?

Also, frankly, if I turned this offer down, when was the next opportunity to manage a Premier League club likely to come flying past my hotel balcony?

Because I'm a sensible person (as my former school and Cub Scout coaches will tell you – see earlier), I asked Steve at the end of our conversation if I could have a little time to think about it. But I was kidding myself. I knew it, and I think Steve knew it. There was only ever going to be one answer.

Answering the call

Nearly two decades later, I can look back knowing that heeding Steve Gibson's call and accepting the manager's role

35

at Middlesbrough in the summer of 2006 was simultaneously one of the best and one of the worst decisions I ever made. It was my first step on a journey into football management that would ultimately lead me to the England post. At the same time, it set me on a learning curve, which, far from carefully graded, proved both exhaustingly steep and treacherously slippery. It was too much too soon.

On reflection, I should have been more aware of what a daunting task I faced when Middlesbrough had to secure special dispensation from the Premier League Board to permit me to become manager before I'd completed my qualifications. When the League Managers Association (LMA) lodged an official challenge to that decision, supported vocally by Sir Alex Ferguson, I was just annoyed that they would seek to block my opportunity. Their protest was overruled, but the upshot was that I had to study for my Uefa A Licence and then my Pro Licence while simultaneously getting to grips with my new job. If I thought completing my coaching badges was tricky enough in combination with being a full-time player, I now found that it was even worse while trying to manage a Premier League club for the first time. It created a lot of additional stress for me at a point when stress was not exactly in short supply.

So thanks very much for getting involved, Sir Alex.

It was only later, with experience under my belt, that I came to appreciate that Sir Alex was right. Indeed, it was a principle that he and I would agree upon in conversations many years later, when I became honorary president of the LMA. There *should* be a minimum qualification for any manager before they take control of a top-flight team.

Quite apart from the risk of exposing someone to a role that they're not ready for (and I'm holding my hand up here), to argue otherwise is really to devalue the job and suggest that anyone just in off the street could do it.

But I had to learn that the hard way.

Here was my problem: I didn't know what I didn't know. In my professional playing career, I'd served under a string of coaches, including some of the most famous names in football: Terry Venables, Sven-Göran Eriksson, Kevin Keegan and Glenn Hoddle at England, Steve Coppell at Crystal Palace, Brian Little and John Gregory at Aston Villa, Steve McClaren at Middlesbrough. I'd seen them work, from a position very close to them, and I thought I knew what they did. From my first day in charge at Middlesbrough, however, it became abundantly clear to me that being a footballer had only exposed me to a fraction of what a manager has to get up to in his working day. I'd been on the receiving end of plenty of team-talks. I knew how to personally prepare myself for games and captain a team on the pitch. But everything else was new to me – and there was so much else to it. The job, it turned out, was multi-disciplinary to a degree that I had barely imagined.

Instead of a life dedicated tidily to training from 9 a.m. until 2 p.m., I was now in a job where the working hours seemed to expand almost indefinitely. Straight away, then, I was seeing less of my family and was unavailable to them to a degree that I had never been before – a massive change in my life that I had to instantly adapt to. And even when I was at home, I couldn't necessarily switch off. One time, I went into the garden to kick a ball about with my son, who was then five. And then my phone rang (almost certainly an agent) and I got into a conversation. I had been walking up and down the garden for quite some time when I eventually looked up and saw my son, his shoulders slumped, trudging back indoors. If there's one thing children crave sometimes it's the undivided attention of their parents. I felt mortified with guilt.

Then there were all these new responsibilities. I found myself expected to chair meetings, to communicate with the board, to work with financial spreadsheets . . . None of these things had formed any part of my life as a footballer, and now I was having to learn how to handle them all in a rush.

Take transfer business, for instance, which it now fell to me to make decisions about. Obviously I knew what a good player looked like. But Middlesbrough weren't in a position to buy the best, so 'valuing' a player became a highly complex matter of assessing a player's physical, psychological and technical attributes relative to the available budget. There were constantly trade-offs to be made: do we go for this younger player who may develop, or this older player with flaws? It didn't help that Middlesbrough's scouting network was not as broad as some other clubs'. It certainly didn't help that I was coming to all this without experience.

Today I would be far clearer, able to make the required calculations, analyse the player in the context of the team's needs, and so forth. Back then, though, I made some poorly informed judgements around identifying players at the right level, and vetoed some candidates that I didn't feel were a good fit for the team, but who, on reflection, would have been. Even worse, the impact of those decisions only became slowly and agonisingly apparent as the season progressed. In any business, once you recruit the wrong people, it can be a long and costly business to 'manage them out', and football clubs are certainly no less reluctant than any other kind of company to take a big financial hit on a person appointed in error.

One example of what I got wrong was allowing our senior goalkeeper, Mark Schwarzer, to leave the club. I should have put up much more of a fight to keep him. I knew his value, both as a player and as a top professional. However, at the time we had two young goalkeepers showing real promise, and Mark was thirty-six, seemingly coming to the end of his career and making the club reluctant to offer him a two-year contract. Assessing the decision while staring at a spreadsheet, it may have appeared entirely logical to let Mark go. But I placed too much faith in those younger – and more affordable – goal-keepers. I assumed they would be good enough to get us through the following season while we developed them to sell on. Ultimately, though, neither of them was at Mark's level. Plus, we lost Mark's leadership, experience and professional-ism, qualities that didn't have a line item on that spreadsheet we were staring at, but did have a tremendous impact when we were looking to build the right culture at the club.

The ultimate irony was that Mark went on to play out-standingly for Fulham for another five (yes, five) years. As for the two goalkeepers we had hoped would become assets, both eventually moved on free transfers, so Middlesbrough didn't even get to cash in. We lost out all round.

Then there was dealing with players' agents. In today's world, a club's director of football would be the agents' primary point of contact. Back then, it was the manager who got the call. As a result, it seemed that every hour of every day, someone would be ringing to try to sell me a player they represented. Fearing that I might miss out on a great signing, muggins here would have the conversation, almost without exception. Of course, football agents are savvy. Given the opportunity, they're skilled at getting inside your head. They also know how to chat. Boy, do they know how to chat . . . Eventually, I learned to screen their calls, but for a long period all that communication and ear-bending became a drain on my time and energy.

I found myself in a constant scramble to learn. Every room I walked into seemed to contain a number of plates spinning on sticks and it was up to me to stop them crashing to the floor. There were many times, I confess, when it left me exhausted and overwhelmed. I had a huge sense of responsibility to Steve Gibson, who had trusted me with this opportunity, and to the club that I had captained, and I rose to the many challenges as best I could. But I never truly felt like I had things under full control.

Because I wanted to become a good manager, I found myself doing the things I believed good managers did. For instance, I made sure I was first at the training ground every morning. Classic good-manager behaviour, no? Right out of the good-manager instruction manual.

What I had yet to learn was how best to manage the time that stretched ahead of me. Frequently, not only was I the first to arrive, but also the last to leave, with my day having run away from me. I'd work until the early hours on everything from training schedules to team selection – I worked when I should have been asleep, frankly. Was this also in the good-manager manual? Probably not, actually, because in practice I was frequently knackered and nowhere near as effective as I wanted to be.

There is a great phrase that's used about senior leaders and their time: 'All the things you could do as opposed to all the things only you can do.' I had yet to learn about that, clearly. I had a personal assistant, of course – something else entirely new to me. Catherine's role was (the clue was in the job title) to assist me, and yet, naively, I continued to do everything myself. If I had to attend meetings away from the North East, I'd book my own travel and accommodation. It hadn't fully occurred to me that by delegating those administrative tasks I could manage my time and my diary more productively. Poor Catherine must have felt pretty unfulfilled in her responsibilities to me. I wasn't letting her do her job!

My players were supportive, even though we all found it hard to adjust to the fact I'd been their captain the previous season. That's a difficult line to cross in any circumstance – a total shift in the social dynamic. But in this case I assumed the authority of manager over the players only six weeks after I had been sitting in the dressing room next to them. I'd effectively gone out one door as their team-mate, whom they could address as an equal, and come in another as their boss, with a huge influence over their careers.

The full awkwardness of this situation came home to me almost immediately. Not long after I started, I was faced with telling Jimmy Floyd Hasselbaink that his contract would not be renewed. Jimmy and I had been equal partners on the pitch the previous season; now I was tasked with moving him on. Budgets had tightened, the club were spoiled for players in that position, and the chief executive made it very clear to me that we should let Jimmy go (of course, in hindsight my boss had his own financial targets to deliver). With experience, I might well have used the opportunity to analyse what Jimmy's departure would mean for the team or push for more budget to retain him. Lacking that insight and self-certainty, I just had to focus on how I was going to break it to Jimmy. By then, sensing the outcome, Jimmy was already calling me for updates. I broke the news as considerately as I could, but in some ways it felt like the worst kind of role-play.

I'd always hated having difficult conversations, and I'd always stepped around them when I could. Avoid confrontation, maintain good relations, be the nice guy, stay popular . . . that had basically been my way of going about things. But that wasn't going to work, I quickly realised, as a manager. The difficult conversations were now officially on me.

It was Middlesbrough FC's staff who were my saviours. They helped me find my way. My coaching squad had years of experience between them. I could rely on them for help and advice when things got tough and when I didn't have the knowledge to fall back on – and I did so. The staff were my guides, really. But I knew this wasn't the right way round. Ultimately, the manager is supposed to be guiding his staff, not the staff guiding the manager.

However, I need to stress that we did some good work in those years. In top-flight football, a team's wage bill is often used to estimate its eventual league position. Bigger wages mean better players, more or less. Using wage expenditure as a metric for success, analysts can to some extent predict the league's order before the season begins. In 2006–07, my first season as Middlesbrough manager, we finished twelfth in the Premier League, which was two places higher than the previous year and close to our predicted wage-bill position. The following season, the team dropped a place to thirteenth, but still performed more or less in accordance with the budget prediction. In the realms of what was reasonably possible, those seasons were a clear success.

But then the 2008–09 season began. Budgets tightened still further and players departed. As I mentioned, Mark Schwarzer was allowed to go, and we also sold George Boateng, Lee Cattermole and Luke Young, without recruiting suitable replacements. Nevertheless, we started brilliantly, beating Tottenham and then coming agonisingly close to defeating Liverpool at Anfield, where we led until the eighty-fifth minute.

Sadly, that was about as good as it got. Starting in mid-November we went fourteen games without a win. In the second half of the season, we suffered twelve consecutive away defeats, equalling the Premier League record. Just to make things worse, we earned an FA charge after the players reacted to a sending-off by surrounding the referee, Mark Halsey, and jostling him enough that he dropped one of his cards. And, after drawing at home to Portsmouth, I had to respectfully ask our fans to desist from singing 'We've only got one player', a) because it wasn't factually true; and b) because I really didn't think it was helpful at that juncture.

The ups, then, and the downs . . . I'd been Premier League Manager of the Month for August. We were relegated in May.

And relegation was a horrendous thing to go through – and not just for the obvious football reasons. Relegation meant redundancies – actual job losses around the staff at Middlesbrough. It hit me hard. People's livelihoods had been resting on the decisions I made.

Many people assumed I would be forced out over the summer, and I was one of them. But Steve Gibson continued to stand by me. Alas, our transition to life in the Championship was less than smooth, and we lost three early home games, including getting a horrible 5–0 thrashing from West Bromwich Albion, and, at that point, I could sense even Steve's faith in me ebbing way.

Things seemed to steady, though, and when we beat Derby at home in late October, we went fourth in the league, just one point off the top. But it was too late. Ironically, if you had asked me straight after that Derby game how I was doing, I would have told you that I was finally finding my feet as a manager. Two hours later, I was sacked and replaced by Gordon Strachan. Driving home, feeling numb and miserable and preparing myself to break the news to the family, I was so distracted that I drove right across the middle of a mini-roundabout. I did this in full view of a policeman, who pulled me over. Fortunately, he let me get away with a quiet talking-to.

I wasn't ready. That's the bottom line. I was over-promoted and in at the deep end. In my first job in senior management, I found out what it was like to be in a high-profile, high-pressure leadership role for which I wasn't properly prepared. It's a mistake I still see being made today. And I was determined never to be in that position again.

Twenty years on, there are far fewer gaps in my knowledge, having managed at the very top level and having been involved in some of the biggest matches in world football. Even so, looking back at my time at Middlesbrough, and reflecting on the specific circumstances of the appointment, those twelfth- and thirteenth-place finishes in the league in my first two seasons were creditable. In fact, if a current Premier League player coming to the end of his career at a mid-table team stepped straight up into management, and kept the team up for two seasons, I'd say they were doing pretty well.

And even when I left Middlesbrough, in the midst of the disappointment, uncertainty and mortification, I was confident I had what it took to manage at the very top level. Because the personal qualities that I'd built over my time as a player, and through the baptism of fire in my first management role, were still ingrained. In fact, my drive, determination and desire to bounce back were strengthened as a result of the experience.

But I also now knew there was no leaping ahead, no jumping straight in at the top. There was knowledge to be acquired and a journey to go on in the meantime. And if I could make that journey then maybe, eventually, I would be in a position to step back up to a leadership position.

What leadership looks like

Part of that journey, I believe, has to involve understanding the art and science of leadership. For me that has involved studying leaders and visiting all kinds of high-performance

environments in search of wisdom and enlightenment – from
the factory of the Mercedes Formula 1 team to the offices of
Google, from access to senior leaders with the All Blacks
to the home of the Royal Ballet, from the headquarters of
British Cycling to various US sports franchises, among many
others. But perhaps nowhere have I found a clearer strategy
for the assessment of leadership candidates than at the Royal
Military Academy Sandhurst, where the British Army trains
its officers.

During one of a number of information-gathering visits,
I sat in on a selection panel where candidates were being
rigorously assessed for promotion to the next level on their
Army career paths. And it was there that I was introduced
to something called the British Army Leader Competency
Framework. I wish I had known about it sooner. Indeed, I
wish I'd had it to hand in 2006 when that call came through
to my hotel from Steve Gibson. Certainly, I know of no
framework that so clearly offers, for recruiters and potential
leaders alike, a set of criteria by which readiness to lead can
be measured.

There are a lot of layers to this model, but the graphic
version reproduced on p. 51 is a sharp, shareable summary of
how the Army addresses suitability for leadership, beginning
with its crisp definition of leadership itself:

> *Army leadership is a combination of character,*
> *knowledge and action that inspires others to succeed.*

The framework then engages with three fundamental questions, which I realised I'd been thinking about and seeking

answers to since Middlesbrough and my own first steps into leadership.

What are leaders?

What do leaders do?

And what do leaders know?

What leaders are

Some people have said to me that I proved Steve Gibson wrong by going from being sacked to managing at the game's highest level. I would actually say that I proved him right. Steve saw in me the qualities that he believed essential in a manager – qualities like integrity, moral courage and self-discipline. And to the extent that I went on to manage England for eight years, I would maintain that he wasn't wrong.

The attributes listed by the Army under this heading are the raw ingredients for leadership, likely to be formed early in a person's life and less likely to be developable later. When people say leaders are born, not made, I would suggest it's these kinds of traits they are thinking about – responsibility, integrity, humility. I would argue that none of them are there at birth, but rather emerge in early years, affected by the environment you grow up in and key influencers shaping your world view and your values.

But without these raw materials, however and whenever they arrive, it's going to be much more challenging to earn the respect required to lead. And without these real-life timeless leadership traits and values, it's almost impossible to build a culture that is strong and enduring. To put it another way, if

I was recruiting a leader today, their character would be the first assessment I would make. It is the foundation stone from which everything else in leadership is built on.

What leaders know

Having played 700 matches, including more than fifty at international level, I casually assumed that 'what I know' would have been the least of my worries when transitioning to management.

It's true that, at thirty-five, I knew who I was – something the Army's leadership framework suggests is important. I was confident in my own skin and had developed the emotional intelligence to operate as captain, and lead players on the pitch. Equally, I felt I knew my team-mates and our relationships were strong. We fought together on the pitch (and sometimes off it!) week in, week out. We had each other's backs. Again, I thought I could tick that box.

But what I didn't know was how to teach. How to coach players technically and tactically to improve their individual – and the team's – performance. Or how to mentor them, as a leader should, to be the best they could be. My task as a manager wasn't to play any more, and that called for an entirely new set of skills.

Even the simplest of examples highlights the gap. As a player, one of my biggest strengths was said to be my ability to 'read' the game. This came naturally to me after so many years watching the ebb and flow of a game unfold from the back, even when attackers were desperately trying to distract me. That's all I had to do. Anticipate danger. Keep them out. Rally the team. Do my job.

As a manager, however, I was standing in a completely different spot on the side of the pitch, looking at the game from a completely different angle, and looking for totally different things. I was now assessing whole-team patterns of attacking and defending, focusing on the relative performance of players, on tactical changes and substitutions, as opposed to where I was going to run or who I was marking. It was completely alien to me. It was the same ninety minutes, but the game was different.

And that was just on the pitch, without considering the many facets of management off it: from recruitment, to chairing meetings, to overseeing budgets, to media relations and stakeholder management. And this is where I fell short in the Army model. I didn't fully know my trade. I didn't have the context. I didn't understand the operating environment. In fact, I didn't know much at all. It was 'sink or swim' rather than step in confidently and make your mark.

What I continue to find fascinating about the Leadership Competency Framework is the emphasis the Army puts on 'emotional intelligence' and creating 'psychological safety' as vital skills for any leader. I did not expect to see these terms used in the context of a military environment, where life and death is the field of play. This has made me realise that these are more courageous and harder-edged traits to develop and deploy than many people give them credit for. And these are traits I feel fortunate to have had in my locker as a leader.

What leaders do

What you 'know' as a leader gives you the best possible chance to make the right decisions. And what you 'do' – and more importantly, the 'way' that you do it – is definitely leadership in action. It's a true-ism that actions speak louder than words.

Despite Steve Gibson believing I had the right personal qualities to lead, without the knowledge, my actions fell short. For example, my 'trade' was not in developing players at that point. To be honest, I was busy enough developing myself (and fighting fires), rather than purposely delivering a plan for improving the players. Acquiring and practising that know-how in incremental phases – becoming a coach at youth level, assisting an experienced manager, managing at a lower level – in which I could have more gradually stretched myself, would have been a far better way to prepare me for that moment.

That said, while I lacked the full trade secrets, I felt I was good at delivering the knowledge I did have in an authentic and consistent way. I could have talked to my players all day about playing with freedom and not worrying about making mistakes. But if I then stood on the sidelines and threw my arms in the air as soon as someone gave the ball away, then I would have instantly contradicted myself and shattered their trust. My attitude and actions were, I hope, consistent, and that was something to build on.

And as I began to master the knowledge leading up to and throughout my England reign, the way in which I delivered that know-how became synonymous with my leadership style.

The British Army
Leader Competency
Framework (LCF)

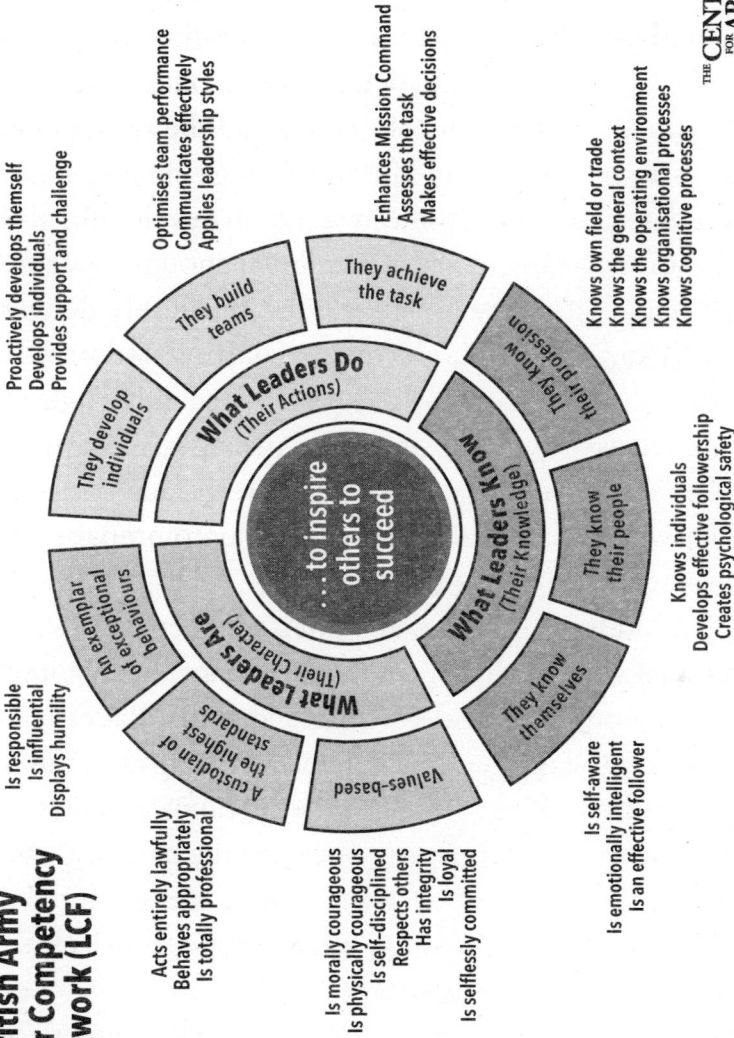

THE CENTRE FOR ARMY LEADERSHIP | ARMY

What Leaders Do (Their Actions)

They build teams
- Optimises team performance
- Communicates effectively
- Applies leadership styles

They achieve the task
- Enhances Mission Command
- Assesses the task
- Makes effective decisions

They develop individuals
- Proactively develops themself
- Develops individuals
- Provides support and challenge

What Leaders Know (Their Knowledge)

They know their profession
- Knows own field or trade
- Knows the general context
- Knows the operating environment
- Knows organisational processes
- Knows cognitive processes

They know their people
- Knows individuals
- Develops effective followership
- Creates psychological safety

They know themselves
- Is self-aware
- Is emotionally intelligent
- Is an effective follower

What Leaders Are (Their Character)

An exemplar of exceptional behaviours
- Is responsible
- Is influential
- Displays humility

A custodian of the highest standards
- Acts entirely lawfully
- Behaves appropriately
- Is totally professional

Values-based
- Is morally courageous
- Is physically courageous
- Is self-disciplined
- Respects others
- Has integrity
- Is loyal
- Is selflessly committed

...to inspire others to succeed

I understood that the way I interacted with staff or supporters or hotel workers or anybody that we came into contact with would set a tone for the rest of the group. For instance, when we got back from matches in the early hours of the morning, the kit van would frequently arrive sometime after us, and it always heartened me to see that large numbers of our staff hung around to help unload it. Everyone was knackered, but everyone also recognised the significance of pulling together. Great camaraderie was built in those moments, and I made sure I was there unpacking the van with everybody else.

All in all, I think of the Army's leadership framework as a superb diagnostic tool. Using it in my own case, I can now assess with enormous clarity the degree of my readiness to step up into management back in 2006 – where I approached the mark, and where I fell short of it. It's clear to me that I was confident in my understanding of what a leader represented. I recognised the importance of values and setting high standards. What I lacked was that all-important craft knowledge. And only further experience was going to bring me that – in the right place and at the right pace.

Stepping back up

The first time I was offered the chance to put myself forward for the England job, I turned it down. That was in the summer of 2016, when the FA asked me if I would apply to take over from Roy Hodgson.

As I hope you'll already know about me from what you've

been reading here, this was the dream invitation – nothing less than the culmination of my hopes and ambitions in management. If you're a proud Englishman and a football manager, there can be no greater honour than being asked to step up and lead the country's side. It would have been an absolute privilege.

And yet I declined.

You're bound to ask why – especially given that, just two months later, the FA would ask me again, and this time I would say yes. So let me explain what was going through my mind in those extraordinary weeks.

After my time at Middlesbrough came to an end in 2009, I stepped away from club football and joined the FA in a development role. I'll say more in the next chapter about what that work involved, but suffice it to say here that the experience I gained in that period was a valuable grounding for what lay ahead. Then, in 2013, my friend and former England team-mate Stuart Pearce stood down as manager of the England Under-21 side and urged me to apply for the job. He thought I would enjoy it, and he was right: I absolutely loved it, in fact. I got a lot of energy from working with the younger players – watching them improve, helping them fulfil their potential. What's more, extremely satisfyingly, the investment of time and thought in that area had started to yield a tangible return on the pitch. The Under-21 team had qualified for the 2015 European Championship, and though we went out in the group stage of that tournament I believed we were creating a really productive environment in which to bring on England's best young players. It was great to be at the heart of that.

The future looked bright, in other words, and the present

was an exciting challenge. And accordingly, when the FA sounded me out about the bigger job, my immediate feeling was that I would be terribly reluctant to come out of that under-21 role just when things there were coming together so positively.

But that wasn't the only reason why I wasn't biting anybody's hand off for the chance to be interviewed. The FA at the time was under a fiercely critical spotlight concerning the England team's direction and performance. 'Well, when *isn't* the FA under the spotlight?' you might say. But this was directly in the wake of England getting beaten by Iceland in the first knockout round of the 2016 Euros, an outcome that was widely regarded as a humiliation, and the critical spotlight was glowing hot, even by FA standards.

Now, given my work with the junior teams, I knew I would be considered a viable candidate and looked on pretty positively by the FA if I put my application in. But it was also clear, given the broader mood, that whoever the FA appointed was straight away going to step into a cauldron. And it seemed likely to me that a promotion from within the organisation would only intensify the heat.

So that was another factor that dissuaded me from putting myself forward at that point. But there was a bigger one: my own story.

Specifically, my own story as an England player. Two whole decades had passed, but I was well aware that, in many quarters, I was still regarded as that bloke who missed the penalty in the shoot-out against Germany in the Euro 96 semi-final. And if that was the case, then my currency with the fans and critics wasn't going to be high enough to stave off the inevitable hammering that was going to be coming the way of the next England manager. In fact, it was going to make me a massive target for it, with a big flashing light on my head. Particularly because I had witnessed growing up, and then as a player, enough England managers with big flashing lights on their heads to go around. Bobby Robson, Graham Taylor, Glenn Hoddle and Kevin Keegan were all highly skilled managers. But they had all endured awful periods of abuse in the job. It was a position that seemed to leave scars, and a role that seemed hard to recover from if things went south. I was, of course, assuming the worst, rather than thinking positively.

So I thanked my bosses at the FA and told them that, on reflection, I was happy where I was and that this time around I would resist the temptation to apply. Soon after that, the FA gave the job to Sam Allardyce.

My own decision nagged at me, though, over that summer. Had I stepped back for the right reasons? Could I have been bolder? *Shouldn't* I have been bolder? Was I still allowing myself to be held back by an event that had happened twenty years ago?

Missing that penalty in 1996, and then enduring the aftermath, was, it goes without saying, an absolutely traumatic experience for me: life-changing, I can definitely say. But I did genuinely think that I was out the other side of it at this stage. I had worked very hard to turn it around and use it to build resilience – the resilience I had been able to call upon when I moved into management. I was, I felt very confident in saying, a stronger person for that gruesome episode in my life.

Yet, clearly, here I was, still thinking about it and still allowing it at some level to influence my decision-making. Was some small part of me still, even now, all these years later, caught up in that one moment and frightened of failing?

Not long after this, I was at home watching football on the telly with my son, who was then thirteen. And up on the screen came one of my old Crystal Palace team-mates, Chris Coleman. Chris was managing Wales at the time and he was being interviewed, with a very happy expression on his face, after his team had won. Seeing him in that position really chimed with me because Chris had also faced challenges as a coach, including getting sacked by a Championship side. The experience had knocked his confidence, as he said in the interview, and yet he'd found the courage to keep going and step up, and now here he was, steering his national team to success.

Towards the end of the interview, Chris was asked what advice he could give to anyone in a similar situation to him, and his reaction was very simple and straightforward. 'Don't be afraid of going for things in life,' he said.

At that moment, Chris might as well have been talking straight into my sitting room and directly to me. I looked across at my son. It struck me that Chris's message about simply throwing yourself into things was something I was constantly encouraging my son to do. 'Grab the chance! Don't be afraid! Go for it!' As a parent, you find yourself saying those kinds of things all the time. But I didn't seem to be acting on that philosophy myself.

Two months later, after making some unguarded remarks to an undercover newspaper reporter from the *Daily Telegraph*,

Sam Allardyce agreed to step down as England manager. He'd been in the role just sixty-seven days. His departure came less than a week before an important international training camp, so suddenly the FA were urgently looking for someone to lead that camp and make the selection for the 2018 World Cup qualifier that would follow it. I was pretty sure I would be asked to fill in. It made sense: I was already in the building and I already knew quite a few of the players. Indeed, a number, including Harry Kane and John Stones, had risen through the England youth ranks. Sure enough, the FA called me in and proposed that I act as a caretaker manager for the next four matches while they looked for a permanent replacement.

So, another invitation to step up. But this time, unlike two months previously, I would at least be stepping up in a way that put me more in control of the process – via a probationary period for everyone involved. In the worst-case scenario, I would be in charge for a handful of fixtures, and if things didn't work out then I could move on knowing I had given it my best shot.

Make a positive impression in those games, however, and I would be strongly in the running for the permanent position, having already proven myself. There was going to be a lot of media attention, of course. But it wouldn't be impossible, surely, to keep my head down and focus on the job, and the initially limited timescale somehow seemed to make the prospect of the media attention less daunting too.

Whatever happened, I certainly wasn't going to be using that media spotlight to further my claim to the job in the long term. I'd seen coaches in caretaker positions make a play for the permanent position in this way before, and I never believed it helped them. If the FA wanted to discuss things in that regard, then great. But we would do it behind the scenes in a controlled way and not through me setting my stall out in a press conference.

All in all, weighing everything up, I could see that this was a fantastic chance to find out if I was capable of leading the national team, and to discover whether everyone – the FA, the players, the public, the media – bought into the idea of me in the role. It was pretty perfect, actually. The risks, as I saw it, had been wonderfully minimised.

And somebody needed to drop everything and run that camp.

With Chris Coleman's little piece of post-match wisdom still echoing in my mind, I told the FA I would do it.

The decision to lead

So, how can we be sure that we know enough to be competent before we make the commitment to step up into a leadership role? When the opportunity arose for me to take on the England team on a temporary basis, I was at a very different point in my life from when I was a 35-year-old player invited to become a Premier League club manager. I was ten years older and a bit wiser, and with a better understanding of myself. I knew my strengths and weaknesses as a leader, and I recognised the kinds of support and processes I needed around me to deliver to the best of my abilities.

Because I was in a better place in that respect, those external considerations and incentives that had led me to accept my first managerial position were no longer as pressing. Back in 2006, facing some uncertainty as my playing days came to an end, the offer on the table spoke loudest to the ambitious part of me. I was flattered simply to have been approached, and aware that the offer was an extremely rare one for someone in my position. By contrast, when the England proposition arose, I already had a fulfilling position with the under-21s. I also knew that other opportunities would almost certainly come my way if my period as caretaker manager ended up going pear-shaped.

Those things gave me the confidence to focus on the one thing that really matters when it comes to considering a leadership role. What would be in it for me was immaterial. I was able to make an informed judgement based on what would be in it for the team.

Sometimes, of course, as prospective leaders we *should* pass up an opportunity in cases where the timing or circumstance isn't right, or because it's clear we don't have the right skills in that moment. That's not timidity. It could be that we're committed to establishing that groundwork first, in which case another opportunity will come. We're still backing ourselves to get there eventually.

Of course, even if we feel ready there will always be those invitations to lead that shine so brightly we fail to see the reality behind the dazzle. In a sport where management positions often appear to be established on a revolving-door basis and vacancies regularly arise, I've been approached with big, enticing offers that were seriously hard to resist. Every time,

I've come away from the meeting feeling excited and energised. Let's face it, no organisation is ever going to open one
of those conversations with me by saying, 'Listen, Gareth –
just between us, this job is going to be an absolute nightmare.'
On the contrary, the people doing the pitch have, naturally,
shone a golden light on all the upsides and the wonderful pos-
sibilities, and I've allowed myself to be thrilled by the mere
fact of my candidacy – that they're considering me as the
person who has what it takes to assume control.

Over time, however, I've learned to look beyond the
headline, as it were, and investigate the story. Here are some
of the questions that I've found it useful to ask in order to
unpack some of the complexities and distractions that can
surround the offer of a job in management and reach a
decision with conviction.

What could go right?

Every leadership opportunity or promotion arrives with
unknowns. You won't have perfect information to inform your
decisions, and some learning will happen on the job, which for
some people, like me, could take place in public. Before taking
the England role, I accepted there would be situations I hadn't
encountered or moments I couldn't predict. What mattered
was not eliminating uncertainty but knowing I possessed the
skills to face those challenges constructively. Most importantly,
I thought about where I could create meaningful improvement.
In other words, what specifically could I do, especially in the
early days, to make a difference? It's a good exercise to make

a list of these controllables, because this approach and positive mindset will stop you obsessing about what might go wrong, and help you to focus your energy on what may go right.

What shape is the business in?

When I took over at Middlesbrough, the club had just enjoyed a European high point. Expectations were buoyant. Under the surface, the picture was very different: a reduced budget and an ageing squad that had likely peaked. A seasoned manager would have addressed those realities and either negotiated for investment or walked away. I did neither. Hindsight is a wonderful thing, of course, but given my experience I really should have declined the job, even though I ended up learning an enormous amount in the process and became a more accomplished manager for it. But the perceived failure is quite a weighty thing to carry around on your CV afterwards – remarkably, even today I still occasionally notice people using those three seasons at Middlesbrough as an exclusive measure of my likely capabilities, and it was sixteen years ago. So if the underlying trend for a team or business is down and resources are shrinking, realise that you are not inheriting momentum – you are absorbing risk.

What is the mandate, and who grants it?

Change is easier when people know the status quo isn't working. In 2016, England were looking back at several disappointing tournaments marked by high hopes and underachievement. Combined with the circumstances of my predecessor's sudden departure, I arrived to find an enormous willingness to make a fresh start. That gave me the authority and space to reset behaviours and standards. Before stepping up to a role that requires some sort of transformation, a leader should ask: *Is there a real mandate for this change or is the business just paying lip service? Who actually wants this new direction?* In my case at England, the answer lay with stakeholders, including the CEO, the board, the players, the fans and, yes, even the media. And finally, consider this crucial question: *How long will this mandate last once the hard decisions start to bite?*

Do I have the 'craft' for this job today – or a plan to acquire these skills in time?

Leadership depends on values and judgement, but delivery depends on craft. At Middlesbrough I did not yet possess the technical coaching skills or management experience to develop players and staff while still developing myself. If you don't have the craft, back yourself and develop it purposefully, because your time will come if you are determined, and you will be more likely to be successful when the moment arrives.

Will I get joy or satisfaction from this new role?

We should always question what we will be giving up in order to take on a new role. Promotion always involves compromise. A chef who runs a restaurant may spend more time managing people than practising the passion of cooking which drew them to the profession in the first place. Ask which parts of the work must remain central for you to thrive. Which new demands may displace your core interests? Are you prepared for the resulting identity shift? If not, renegotiate the role – or decline it.

Who will tell me what I don't want to hear?

Before major decisions I now assemble a small, trusted 'brains trust', a term I think I first heard to describe a group of players having a discussion over a free-kick in a dangerous position, but which I now know was coined in 1932 for the group of US academics that President Franklin D. Roosevelt assembled to help him form policy. This brains trust should be people with different vantage points who can be brutally honest with you. Their value is not to agree, but to challenge your assumptions and test for blind spots. Good counsel won't make the choice for you, but it will lead to a more informed choice.

If I say yes, what will the first hundred days prove?

A final discipline: write down three outcomes that would validate your decision within a hundred days – behaviours you will see, decisions you will have taken and improvements you can show evidence for. If you cannot define these outcomes, you are not ready to accept the role. If you can, you have both a test and a plan.

SUMMARY
Driving the Team Bus
On learning lessons the hard way

- Excellence as a practitioner does not mean excellence as a leader. Both require different skillsets and both take time, effort and learning to master.

- If you want to assess your own, or someone else's, readiness to lead, consult the British Army Leader Competency Framework and, specifically, the core characteristics of integrity, selflessness, humility and emotional intelligence.

- Every leader, no matter how accomplished, needs support. Identify your development areas and demonstrate that you are humble enough to work with people who complement your skills and challenge your thinking.

- Leadership has real-world consequences. Poor decisions affect the performance of the team and consequently people's jobs, families and livelihoods. An awareness of this focuses the mind when tough calls have to be made.

- Protect your time and energy. Focus on the work that only you can do and delegate the rest. Create a detailed schedule and factor in personal time.

- Perform an honest assessment of the opportunity before accepting a new role. Do your due diligence and find out what is really going on behind the scenes. Is this the right role for you? Is your leadership style the right fit for the position? Has success been clearly defined? What are the risks involved?

CHAPTER 3

Changing the Script

On transforming England's culture

The golden goal

'The trouble with not having a goal is that you can spend your life running up and down the field and never score.'

— *Bill Copeland, cricket umpire*

The clock brought things sharply into focus. It was on the wall in the office at St George's Park National Football Centre, the shiny, new, state-of-the-art 330-acre complex the FA had recently built in the Staffordshire countryside. The clock wasn't there to mark the time of day. It was counting down to Qatar 2022 and the England football team's desired appointment with World Cup glory.

This was Greg Dyke's idea. Dyke had arrived as chairman of the FA in 2013, at one of those periodic low points for the organisation. At the most recent World Cup, in South Africa in 2010, England, under the management of Fabio Capello, had failed to progress beyond the round of sixteen, losing 4–1 to our old foes Germany. In this outcome, England were felt to have fallen woefully short of expectation, though convincing data in support of that argument was actually in short supply: England hadn't been further than the quarter-finals of *any* tournament since 1996. Indeed, in the forty-four years since the 1966 World Cup, England had won only six tournament knockout games in total. As at many points in the nation's footballing history, there was a reasonable contention to be made that the fundamental problem wasn't with the underperformance of the team so much as with the scale of people's expectations.

Nevertheless, the calls had gone out, as they so often did, for root and branch investigations and for sweeping change, and in came Greg Dyke at the top of the organisation. A former director-general of the BBC, and veteran chairman of Brentford FC, Dyke immediately set out his vision for a new England – an England that would first reach the semi-finals of the European Championship in 2020, and then spring onwards from there to match the heroes of 1966 and win the World Cup in 2022. And up went the clock, alongside two others counting down to two closer launch times: the next senior men's tournament, and the next senior women's tournament.

I was working at the FA at the time, as manager of the under-21s and head of international junior teams, and given where we were at that point as a national team, Greg's bold aspirations certainly raised some eyebrows in the building. Some of my colleagues wondered whether the chairman would still be around when the clock reached zero hour. As it happens, he wasn't. Dyke decided not to seek re-election and stepped down in June 2016.

But shortly after that, when I moved up to become manager of the senior team, the clock was still on the wall. And it was still ticking.

Perfect visions

The 'big, hairy, audacious goal' (BHAG) is a glorious term coined by Jim Collins and Jerry Porras in their 1994 book, *Built to Last: Successful Habits of Visionary Companies*. It's a colourful way to describe a commanding vision that is designed to be both ambitious and inspirational. Famous BHAGs include JFK's audacious plan, in his rousing 1961 speech to Congress, for America to put a man on the Moon 'by the end of the decade', and Bill Gates's ambition for Microsoft in 1981 to put 'a computer on every desk and in every home'.

In isolation, these visionary declarations of intent can appear to be simple bits of corporate grandstanding, made almost entirely from hot air and issued in the blithe absence of concrete details about how they're going to be achieved. But, of course, America *did* put a man on the Moon before that decade was out, and Bill Gates *did* put computers in, if not every, then an incredible percentage of the world's homes. I'll admit that, from my position inside the FA, I thought the chairman's call for England to win the 2022 World Cup was just a rhetorical flourish. But in some ways (and credit to

Dyke) it was a classic BHAG: bold enough to make everyone sit up, without being so completely unrealistic as to trash everyone's morale.

Meanwhile, behind the new chairman's call to arms, and much more solidly, a consensus had emerged that the key to future success in English football was the establishment of a 'performance pathway'. The focus was on establishing a pipeline for players from grass-roots to the elite level. I was heavily involved in that work and, accordingly, in the vanguard of a revolution for talent development in England.

Two years earlier, after my departure from Middlesbrough and following a brief spell as a football pundit for ITV, I had received a phone call from Sir Trevor Brooking that had set me on a whole new career path. As the FA's director of football development, Trevor asked me if I would be interested in joining the FA to help structure and implement some plans designed to revolutionise the development of young players in England.

One of the proposals was to change the formats of junior football, putting kids on smaller pitches, in smaller teams – 4 v. 4 at first, followed by 7 v. 7, then 9 v. 9 – before eventually taking them up to the full-scale eleven-a-side. Among many clear advantages, this simple change would mean that young goalkeepers would no longer find themselves dwarfed by enormous full-size goals – a comical situation, when you think about it, though one that had existed in school and junior football for a long time. And it would mean that kids could get more touches of the ball during matches, so potentially had a greater chance of improving their skills. I completely saw the value of these ideas, and my colleague Nick Levett and I devised a series of workshops, and then went all over the country to deliver them to county FAs and win people round to the logic of the changes and make clear the increased enjoyment kids would get out of them. We were essentially working to get the votes at FA Council level that would see these alterations ratified, and I think it surprised both of us how much of a struggle this was in some places. There were people seriously saying, 'But we won a World Cup in 1966 with kids playing eleven v. eleven! Why do we need to change now?' We got it through eventually, but not before I'd learned that the very best ideas will come to nothing if you don't have the ability and the will to sell them to people and get them supported.

During this period, I also represented the FA in the Premier League's discussions on overhauling the professional academy system to produce better home-grown talent. Ged Roddy was the PL's director of football development and his ideas for an Elite Player Performance Plan (EPPP) received some strong pushback. I tried to be an ally to him in those debates, again discovering a lot about the hard yards you need to put in politically in order to secure votes and budget for even the sanest-seeming strategies. Eventually, though, the EPPP was introduced and would prove to be another trans-formational step forward for English football, supporting the development of players from the ages of nine up to twenty-three with extra investment, a stronger games programme, more tournaments, better coaching and improved performance-tracking. We would eventually see it start to deliver in the form of unprecedented success in Junior World Cups and European Championships. It was a tremendously exciting period all in all, and with the construction in all its glory of St George's Park, which was completed in 2012, there seemed to be a genuine and substantial desire in the air to transform the national game.

Then, as mentioned previously, in August 2013 Stuart Pearce stepped down as England Under-21 head coach and the golden opportunity arose for me to replace him, becoming head of international junior teams at the same time and overseeing the entire England junior development programme. I began working with young players like John Stones, Eric Dier, Raheem Sterling, Luke Shaw and Harry Kane, who would go on to play such a vital part in England's story in the following years. It was an enormously illuminating and enjoyable period for me. I was at the heart of the FA, helping young talents unlock their potential, and I was receiving a priceless education in the business and politics of football into the bargain.

On a mission to bring on our young hopefuls, we looked at how successful nations at European and World Cup levels, such as Germany and Portugal, handled their youth categories. Strikingly, we realised that their players were accumulating far more caps and tournament experience than ours. In some cases those players were accruing twenty or thirty more appearances than our players.

The reason was obvious. They had more teams than us. Those other countries were fielding under-18 and under-20 sides – two age categories we didn't have. Their players had the opportunity for an unbroken progression, year to year, whereas we were literally watching talented boys drop through the gaps between our under-17, under-19 and under-21 teams.

The advantage of filling those gaps, then, was blindingly clear. The practicalities of doing so, though, were painfully knotty. In order to establish those additional age groups, we needed funding and also a willingness from the professional clubs to release their players for more international fixtures and competitions, a tricky negotiation always. There was resistance, but we argued our position and we prevailed.

By the time I became manager of the senior team in 2016, I had already been involved in radical changes to English junior football that were specifically designed to enable the next generation to thrive. Now, thrillingly, in what was for me the ultimate outcome, I would get to shape a squad from some of those players and lead them into competition.

First impressions

It was Monday night in late September when the Sam Allardyce *Daily Telegraph* story broke. I was staying in a hotel near St George's Park when I heard about it. By Wednesday it seemed clear that I would be in charge for the next two matches and by Thursday I had been confirmed as caretaker for the next four, to buy everyone some time. The squad announcement was that Sunday and the players arrived the day after, ahead of two World Cup qualifiers – against Malta at Wembley the following weekend, and away to Slovenia three days after that.

Quite the gear shift, then. My feet didn't touch the ground in those first days. To save time, I decided to continue working out of my under-21 manager's office rather than move across into Sam's, which might have looked presumptuous in any case. Frankly, I've never been fussy about offices anyway, and I'm slightly surprised when other leaders seem to have strong opinions in this area. When I was eventually confirmed full-time, I proposed sharing the space with Aidy Boothroyd, my successor with the under-21s, so that we could connect our thoughts across the two teams. Later, in an office redesign after Covid, I left the bigger space to Sue Campbell and Sarina Wiegman from the women's team and took a small office in the corner of the England team's floor, which suited me fine, not least because I had to walk past everyone else every day to get to it – good for connections. There were plenty of other rooms around the place where I could hold larger meetings when I needed to. I know there's a certain kind of business leader who goes in for statement desks and personally curated artworks, but that wasn't me.

Something I needed to confront right away was that Sammy Lee, Sam Allardyce's assistant, was still in post. I knew that I wanted to bring in my own man – Steve Holland, my number two with the under-21 team. For an incoming leader, absolute clarity is the only way through a situation like that, so I sat down with Sammy at the earliest opportunity and had a grown-up conversation, explaining my intentions. Whatever Sammy might have felt about that, he appreciated the clarity and was

73

extremely helpful to me during that handover period — a real ally. It was a lesson to me about these potentially awkward personnel situations: the faster you deal with them and the clearer you are, the better they work out all round.

Steve Holland at that point was embedded with Chelsea as Antonio Conte's assistant and only with us for the camps. That meant, after this first camp, I had to travel to wherever Steve was to hold our planning sessions — a situation that continued until the end of the 2016–17 season, when Steve left Chelsea and came into the England operation full-time. It was a less than ideal arrangement but a mark of how much I wanted us to work together. I'll talk about my working relationship with Steve in a later chapter.

That first Monday morning when the players arrived was less than calm. Just five days earlier, I'd been prepping for an under-21 camp, and now here I was, hovering in the area where the senior players checked in, greeting them informally, finding out how they were after their games at the weekend. I would make sure I had a longer, one-to-one chat with each of them over the course of the week, asking them what was going on in their lives and at their clubs, so this was just a quick 'hello'. I was also meeting some staff for the first time. But mostly I was fielding a constant stream of medical updates, during which it emerged that we were going to be two players down. That's not a particularly unusual occurrence at the start of a camp. What was more unusual was that, after consultations, calls went out to two replacements — and both of them declined to join us. Also, they asked us not to make it publicly known that they had declined to join us.

That was quite an eye-opener at this early stage; also a logistical challenge. But we eventually had a full quota and not long after that, the players gathered in the meeting room and I walked to the front and addressed them as their manager for the first time.

There are always going to be anxieties, addressing a new group, not least one like this, which contained some highly experienced internationals. Looking around I could see the faces of Joe Hart, Jordan Henderson, Gary Cahill and Wayne Rooney looking back at me – all several years into their England careers at this stage. Also present were Dave Reddin, the head of strategy and performance, and Dan Ashworth, the director of elite development, causing me to feel an additional element of being 'marked from the back of the room' as I tried to find my feet.

I appreciated that this was an unusual and potentially destabilising situation for nearly all these players. Many of them were standing in front of their third England manager in almost as many months and, not to put too fine a point on it, there would have been ample reason for them to wonder just what the hell was going on around here. The leadership challenge at that point was steadying a recently rocked boat. I did it by fixing all eyes on the nearest target and giving them a clear message: that I was simply here to keep them on course towards qualifying for Russia 2018 by earning the requisite points in these next two games, and that I would do everything I could to navigate them through the next few days smoothly. The players seemed to respond, and I was impressed by how seriously they trained that week.

Travelling into Wembley on that Saturday for the Malta game was obviously momentous, but at the same time, there is so much to occupy your mind on a match day – selection issues, staff consultations, final team briefings, media duties – that there was no time to step back and think about it in terms of where I was and how far I had come. At that point, the most important thing was the result: a 2–0 win, on the back of a performance that, though not scintillating, at least demonstrated that the wheels hadn't completely spun off in the recent turmoil.

For the game against Slovenia the following Tuesday, I took the first big decision of my England managerial reign: I left out the captain, Wayne Rooney. It wasn't a choice I made lightly. I had played Wayne against Malta, but the fact was he wasn't getting selected for Manchester United in this period, so he had inevitably fallen off his best form. I wanted to give Dele Alli the start at number 10 and create a more solid midfield in behind, with Eric Dier in a holding role. I gave Jordan Henderson the captaincy.

It was a horrible conversation to have with Wayne – someone I had played alongside. But he was absolute class.

'Gareth, I'm not in my club team,' he said, 'so I don't just *expect* to play here.'

He then asked me if he could do the pre-match press conference alongside me so that it was clear that there was no suggestion of a falling-out between us. This was not the last time I would have cause to be impressed by, and grateful for, the humility of Wayne Rooney.

He was equally professional when, struggling to assert

ourselves against Slovenia, I brought him off the bench with eighteen minutes to go. But he couldn't make a difference and we drew my second game in charge, 0–0.

Those dropped points meant I was under a little pressure when we got back together a month later to prepare for a qualifier against Scotland at Wembley. But we had an excellent camp and won the match comfortably, 3–0, and the pressure came off again. My last game as caretaker, and the end of my review period, would be a friendly at home to Spain.

Before that could happen, though, I suddenly found myself crisis-managing a major PR issue. The Scotland game was on the Friday night, and after training on Saturday morning I gave the players the day off, unaware that a 'day off' was interpreted as an invitation for a night out on the town, albeit with a 9 p.m. curfew. Some of the players duly took themselves into central London for . . . ahem . . . a couple of pints. Not ideal, to say the least. But one player who didn't was Wayne Rooney, who chose instead to spend the evening in the hotel where we were staying. The hotel was also hosting a wedding reception and, having been spotted milling around with some of the FA staff, Wayne was invited to join the wedding guests for drinks (apparently in his England training kit – you can write the headlines already). Wayne joined in the celebrations, good-naturedly posed for photographs; and, predictably, some of those pictures found their way to the papers alongside words like 'drunk' and 'gate-crashed'. The media obviously failed to mention that Wayne was injured and was not going to play any part in Tuesday's game against Spain. A small detail like that would never get in the way of an old-fashioned 'England Players Party on Duty' scandal erupting in the tabloids.

I can safely say 'Wedding-gate' was exactly what I didn't need at such an early juncture in my new role. José Mourinho, who was Wayne's manager at Manchester United, gave the story additional legs by predictably blaming the England set-up for failing to look after Wayne, adding a small homily to his statement just to rub salt in the wound: 'I learned when I was a kid, if someone lends me something I have to take care of it even better than if it was mine.'

That was an extra few days of headlines then, with investigations, statements and recriminations. But annoyed as I was with José, I knew he had a point. The incident shone a light on standards and behaviours, particularly among FA staff who, instead of protecting Wayne, joined him at the bar for drinks. Suffice to say, that never happened again with our staff. I was much tighter from that camp onwards about where we stayed, when we were allowed a few beers, and how much control we exercised over players' free time. I wasn't trying to turn the team into choirboys, and nor would I pretend that's what happened. But I did think some adjustments needed to be made to the expectations around 'days off'.

'Wedding-gate' also crystallised what I'd felt across those four caretaker games: the set-up wasn't sharp enough. The spirit was fine; the standards weren't. I didn't sense England was the be-all and end-all for players or staff. When a team hasn't delivered for a while – and England obviously hadn't for a very long time – there's a tendency for sacrifice to give way to self-preservation. You go into a camp hoping to get through it, rather than to make the most of it. And when you finish, you head back to your club, and England drops to the back of your mind until the next call-up. In effect, it becomes tomorrow's problem. If I was appointed full-time, that had to change. My job would be to absolutely make England matter again – throughout the organisation and stretching out to a public understandably tired of underperformance. With no weddings in between.

The incident also exposed a structural issue: we needed more full-time staff. We were borrowing medical and fitness personnel from clubs and, aside from potential conflicts of interest, that arrangement diluted commitment to the cause, offering an easy way out if results turned. I had to remove that life raft. We needed to professionalise the operation. Dedicated people, proper resourcing, and the right blend of expertise. Oh, and very few 'days off'.

We drew with Spain in the friendly that Tuesday, in slightly disappointing circumstances, conceding two very late goals against an admittedly under-strength Spanish side. Had the match ended after eighty-nine minutes, it would have been the perfect conclusion to my caretaker period. But it wasn't disastrous. Two weeks later, the FA told me I had passed the audition and made me England manager on a three-year contract.

Which was irrelevant, of course. There was an initial twelve-month clause, and I knew I would have to qualify the team for the 2018 World Cup and then do well in the tournament or I would be out on my ear anyway. Nevertheless, I was in – and proud and thrilled about it.

Did I sense that my appointment was met by a gale of public approval and with scenes up and down the country of dancing in the streets by tearfully grateful England fans? Well, it would have been nice – but probably not. If anything, I think the mood was 'Well, they've tried foreign, and they've tried the most credible and available English candidates, and neither of those things have worked, so maybe it's time to give the continuity-from-the-juniors option a go.'

But I could live with that. And it might even prove useful from an expectation-management point of view. The important thing was, I had seen enough in the preceding couple of months to know that I could do the job. But I had also seen enough to know that I would have to change things. A lot of things.

England culture: 'How we do things around here'

What kind of culture did we need to build? That was the question I asked myself when I took the England job full-time – and, truthfully, I had been asking it for the whole of my time at the FA. If we were going to shift out of the gear we were seemingly stuck in, and forge a world-beating football team who could compete with the best, we had to be deliberate about the culture we created.

In his book *The Culture Code*, author Daniel Coyle defines culture as a set of living relationships working towards a common goal. Rather than being a collection of qualities or principles that a team inherently *has*, culture is made up of the many actions that a team of individuals together *do*. Coyle argues that strong cultures are built through the consistent application of three key skills: building safety, sharing vulnerability and establishing purpose. These skills, when practised enough, can create a supportive environment in which team members can thrive and achieve success as a group.

For me, culture can be defined very simply as 'the way we do things around here'. At England, it was how we trained, how we travelled, how we fronted up to difficult moments and how we treated each other when things went wrong. It included practical everyday things like punctuality, preparation, respect in meetings, honest specific feedback, and an insistence on professionalism in small moments, such as turning your dirty kit the right way round before handing it back to the kit man. It was what staff and players said about the manager when he was not in the room. It was how much the manager believed in his staff and the players. The markers of culture are intangible and yet very tangible. They are living and breathing. An amalgamation of everything.

Culture mattered so much because of the unique constraints of international football. World-class coaching is critically important, of course, but how much face-time do national team managers get with players? Yes, you've guessed it, not very much. But if, around that coaching, I could deliberately and strategically change the way we did things, and introduce a new identity and purpose to the team, I knew it could be utterly transformative. The culture would end up being a multiplying force.

I knew all this started with me. As the manager I had to live up to the highest standards of behaviour every minute of my time with England. It helped to think back to what representing England as a player had meant to me. Honour was a huge part of it. I'd wanted to play for England, and I knew the players did too. I also felt an overwhelming pride and a strong sense of service and loyalty. I recognised how those feelings had shaped my performances on the pitch and my conduct off it. The idea of 'representing England' hadn't felt abstract to me; it had felt very real. There were times in some of those international games when it had seemed like the entire country was behind us, willing us on, and that sense of togetherness was a powerful source of strength out there on the pitch. And yet, I also knew that representing England was an enormous responsibility that could become intimidating if you let it. So, as a manager, I knew my job was to harness that energy, and turn it into something positive.

I had seen from my time in the game how teams thrived in an atmosphere of trust and goodwill – the opposite of a culture of fear, an approach to football management that has had its proponents over the years. But that wasn't my character, and it wasn't my way. And in any case, wasn't the 'iron fist' style of management now as outmoded in football as it was elsewhere? It was certainly hard to imagine it working in international football, where players were essentially on loan from their clubs and unlikely to respond well to a temporary tyranny descending on them, assuming I had any desire to impose one, which I didn't. And I knew by demonstrating a desire to know, protect and nurture the players – the people behind the shirts – trust, goodwill and ultimately culture would blossom.

Moreover, I wanted players to look forward to coming to St George's Park, to really enjoy their time with the national side and be disappointed when it was over. When people enjoy coming to work, when they trust the environment, they are more willing to push themselves and each other. Enjoyment may seem like a low-bar aim within England when it comes to an aspiring culture, but you have to remember how much negativity had attached itself to the England set-up at this point in history. I was coming in on the back of years of perceived English failure, which, as I said before, could arguably be better defined as years of unreasonable expectation. But either way, the result was the same: an edgy, volatile atmosphere around the England set-up where self-protection had crept in and players had become wary in advance. Put another way, the weight of the shirt was heavy and it somehow prevented players from giving their best. So I felt if I could rekindle this joy in representing the national team, it would release some of the pressure that came with the shirt.

Was all this down to media scrutiny? Top players are used to that, of course, though the attention paid to England was potentially on another level in this regard. England were on the back pages, front pages, showbiz pages. Families got doorstepped, former schoolteachers were tracked down. And the post-mortems were brutal. But it wasn't just the press. The country was watching, and watching very closely, and on the flip side of our nation's bright and fervent passion for its international football team lay, I knew, something potentially darker. David Beckham had been sent off against Argentina in the 1998 World Cup for a momentary flash of anger, and had been ruthlessly pilloried in public for months afterwards. Stuart Pearce and myself knew a lot about the abrasive aftermath of missing critical penalties in England tournament games. Mess up in some way and it was perceived in some highly vocal quarters that you had 'let your country down'.

However you looked at it, there were clearly unique risks attached to exposure at this level, and in 2016 those risks loomed unhelpfully large in people's memories and – for me as manager – would need some negotiating.

Another consideration was that this was going to be a process over a sustained period of time, rather than a fad or a one-off moment. England were not going to become contenders overnight. Even by Greg Dyke's bold, wall-mounted assessment, a World Cup win was still six years off. And since football management is a volatile and impatient business with a famously high churn rate, I knew many of us might not see the end of the journey. But that truth didn't weaken the case for culture; rather, it strengthened it. If anything was going to endure beyond individuals, it would be the way we did things. And if the way we did things now would, over time, improve the standing of English football, then I was all in. Even if I might never see the project through to fruition.

This work changing the culture took place against the backdrop of a massively popular and successful Premier League, where the big clubs held ever-increasing amounts of sway. Negotiations over the release of players, which had been tricky enough during my years with the junior sides, clearly weren't about to get any easier in my new role. I should be clear at this point that I met a vanishingly small number of players for whom an England call-up wasn't regarded as the ultimate honour and a career pinnacle. But some of their clubs weren't shy about implying that international football was a distraction from the real business of the day, and players could hardly avoid noticing that and being at least subliminally affected by it.

Club indifference towards the national project (or in some cases, even, antagonism towards it) didn't help the mood music generally. I noticed in 2016 that friendly internationals were frequently referred to in the wider culture as 'meaningless'. In fact, so often was the word 'meaningless' attached to the word 'friendly' in this context, that 'meaningless friendly' had practically become the official term.

They weren't going to be meaningless for *us*, of course; quite the opposite, those matches were going to be utterly crucial research and development spaces, and vital staging posts. But there was definitely a battle for hearts and minds to be won here, as in so many areas of the transformation I was now in charge of leading.

Credit belongs to the players for buying into this positive culture change. They could have easily believed the weight of expectation was too great to bear. They could easily have been more influenced by their club, and perhaps less committed to the cause. But change they did, living the high standards we set every day. And watching them do so was a privilege.

Finding an identity

In the course of thinking about all this, I found myself considering the whole topic of national identity. What does it mean, in England, to represent your country? That seemed to me to be an absolutely crucial question to be asking during this initial process. How would we define Englishness in the second decade of the twenty-first century? What were the things that would unite our players as a national team, and ensure the togetherness we would need to power us forward and head with renewed confidence into World Cups and European Championships?

Historically, if conversation ever turned to the ideal characteristics of the English international footballer, it wouldn't be long before someone mentioned 'bulldog spirit'. Images from the eighties and nineties of fantastic international servants like Terry Butcher and Paul Ince, bravely battling on with bloody bandages wrapped around their heads, had fixed themselves firmly in the England mythos. That war-bred, fight-to-the-death attitude was still prevalent in my day as a player, when some of my team-mates, in a bid to pump themselves up before matches, would try to knock the changing-room doors off their hinges.

Well, whatever works, I guess. But hadn't players moved on a bit in this regard? Would a modern England team feel inspired to unite around the concept of 'bulldog spirit'?

In a bid to get to the bottom of being English, and

representing your country, we brought in performance coach Owen Eastwood to consult with us on some of these questions of identity as they relate to national team building. Owen specialised in the area of 'belonging', and we commissioned him to write a report for us on this topic. His conversations with our younger players confirmed my suspicions: 'bulldog spirit' wasn't by any means at the top of their lists of attributes they felt an English player needed to possess. This was obviously, at the very least, good news going forward for changing-room doors. Not that strength and tenacity weren't still recognised as important virtues. But the players didn't think of those qualities as the *prime* asset in this context, and certainly not to the exclusion of things like skill and creativity, attributes that would perhaps have figured lower on the lists of absolute essentials written by England players in the past.

All of this was useful to know. It solidly backed up my impression that the national project had begun to labour under some outmoded ideas around English identity – ideas that made it difficult for players to experience a full sense of belonging and which thereby inhibited their performance. And it emboldened me to think that we could put a culture in place to address that. I wanted us to write a new story together, one that embodied the spirit of this young and excitingly talented group – one that still recognised our rich history and culture, but one that was free from the baggage of the recent past and the sense that we somehow *deserved* to be winners, a misconception that had underpinned so much of our disappointment since 1966. And maybe, if I could get that right, it would take the weight out of the shirt.

The end in sight

Another question I was asking myself, going in: how should we frame the ultimate purpose of this work? What, ultimately, were we all trying to achieve in this England project? 'We're trying to win the World Cup' would have been an obvious answer. 'But we'll take a Euros in the meantime, if you've got one,' would have been an obvious follow-on.

And yes, that would have been a most acceptable outcome for all of us right there and then, and we could dream. But, with all respect to Greg Dyke, how helpful would it have been, actually, at this germinal moment for England under my tenure, in a period of unprecedented instability following the unexpected departure of Sam Allardyce, to hang that momentous goal out in front of our organisation as the be-all and end-all? A World Cup win was what we all wanted, without question. But simply wanting to win the World Cup was not, on its own, going to help us win the World Cup. It might even burn us all out before we'd started. I thought we needed to channel that desire through a broader mission. It seemed to me it would be more productive to insist that, over and above our burning quest for tournament silverware, our ultimate purpose was to make ourselves and our nation proud. That felt to me like a worthy and proportionate ambition, and a potentially cogent and inspiring mission.

Related to this, I understood from my own life and career the power and importance of role models and how, for a young player, knowing that they could be in a position to inspire a future generation could itself be inspiring. It was a virtuous circle and I thought there was a power there that we could definitely tap into. It would also cement some ideas I had about the importance of behaviour.

Previous England squads had attracted some unhelpful coverage around going out and drinking during tournaments. Overblown or otherwise, those stories were never less than a distraction when they happened. I wasn't going to be afraid to set high standards here, because I firmly believed that the way we did things, both on and off the pitch, should be a fundamental part of how we framed success. I knew that teams would always be judged from the outside on how they performed – on results. But when it came to judging ourselves, I thought the first question we should be asking was not 'Did we win?' but 'How did we go about our business?' How did we do things? Did we do them the right way, as we saw it? Did we do them in accordance with our culture?

Because outcome was never going to be entirely within our control. Not in sport. Random things happen. The ball doesn't always run true. But the way we did things – that *was* within our control. That was *entirely* within our control. Results couldn't touch that. And it seemed to me that taking

OUTCOMES

1 GREAT JOURNEYS FOR PLAYERS AND STAFF

2 ENDURING STRONG CULTURE

3 CHANGED PERCEPTION OF THE ENGLAND PLAYER

4 TOURNAMENT SUCCESS ON WORLD STAGE

5 A WINNING TEAM IDENTITY

PHILOSOPHY

NO REGRETS.
WE'D DO IT ALL AGAIN.
WE LOVED THE EXPERIENCE.

CORE BELIEFS

- Externally, we'll be judged by HOW WE PLAY. Internally, we should also judge HOW WE GO ABOUT IT
- Our job is to allow players to have freedom to express themselves within a strong framework (ON & OFF THE PITCH)
- If we guide and inspire our players, they will in turn role-model to a generation
- England can teach life-lessons as much as football
- Not everything can be standardised. Expect ambiguity until we get the right outcome
- Wherever possible, we should help out players with tough club dynamics

PURPOSE

- To set standards in sport that make players and the nation PROUD

VALUES

- Person behind the shirt
- Trust & trustworthiness
- Positivity, goodwill
- Adventurous spirit
- Conviction about our purpose & potential
- Rich life experiences

GUIDING PRINCIPLES

- 80% rigour is brilliant if it allows 20% more psychological space
- Start from the assumption we're dealing with good people
- Our wins will not be achieved at all costs or by compromising our values
- Respect & protect our players – whole season without compromising our programme
- Only select risk-tolerant players who can play the way we want
- Don't bend standards under pressure

pride in the way we went about things could be the force that bonded our team together. More than that, it could be the force that bonded our team to the country; a shared pride in a team that did things right, whatever the outcome. It could be the key ingredient, on and off the pitch.

I talked through all the ideas I'd had about the kind of culture we needed in a conversation with Dr Pippa Grange, the FA's head of people and team development at the time, and asked her to produce a one-page summary for me. The idea was to set out with absolute clarity my proposed philosophy for the team, our core beliefs, our shared sense of purpose, our values and our guiding principles – in other words, to sketch out the framework for a new England culture.

I didn't want this plan to exist merely in my head. I wanted it put down where I could see it. You can have a plan in your mind as a football manager, but the game is complex and emotional and the scope for snap judgements and erratic decisions can be immense. Here, at least, I had my philosophy on paper. At the same time, I wasn't looking to set anything in stone. A culture, like a strategy, always needs to be open to evolution. I wasn't even intending to share the document with staff – not at this point. It was just for me, my personal reference point – something I could quietly take out and look at when I needed to, to remind myself of the path.

The diagram reproduced here was the result, with those core beliefs, values and guiding principles feeding our purpose and combining to yield the five main outcomes I wanted us to be aiming at: specifically, ensuring that everyone involved with us felt they were on a life-enhancing journey; building a strong and enduring culture at England that would survive us; changing the public perception of who and what an England player is; experiencing tournament success; and forging a durable winning identity for the national team.

It was only a sheet of paper but I remember reading over it for the first time and feeling really emboldened. The vision looked real. Of course, it was still just words at this point. We hadn't yet built the culture. That would take time and trust and the willingness of everyone in the broader team. But I could now at least have a strong visual sense of the way we were going to be doing things around here, and I now had the means to articulate it to players and staff in the hope of bringing them along with me.

SUMMARY
Changing the Script
On transforming England's culture

- A bold vision can inspire your team and shift their thinking, but alone it is not enough to transform an organisation. Lasting change requires both strategy and culture to make your vision a reality.

- Leaders must win hearts *and* minds to deliver change. You will need to take time to 'bring' people with you. Sell the vision. Explain the logic. Explain the 'why'. Your team will most often think 'How will this affect *me?*'. This is why active listening delivers as it helps to identify, and then solve, the individual's problems in your team.

- You must balance short-term results with a long-term vision. 'Quick wins' breed confidence in a plan and buy the critical factor of time in order to implement change. But over-invest in the short term and you mortgage the future.

- Culture comes from the top, but it is shaped by every team member. It is 'how we do things around here' – a collective effort, built every minute of every day.

- Creating a culture takes time, and the wrong appointment can undermine months or years of progress. When recruiting, select carefully and act decisively if you realise the culture is not right for a team member, or if it's 'not the way *they* do things around here'.

- Teams thrive when a team's identity is clear. A strong sense of 'who we are' and 'what we stand for' accelerates belonging, trust and cohesion.

CHAPTER 4

Drawing up the Blueprint

On shaping a winning strategy

When the chips are down

In 2017 I attended a meeting at the FA that was both highly unconventional and extremely revealing. Others around the table included my assistant coach, Steve Holland, and Dan Ashworth, the director of elite development. And in front of us was a pile of poker chips.

There were no cards, and none were about to be dealt, and yet the stakes seemed strangely high. Indeed, as time went on, each of us was contemplating our next move as if we were in deep and with no option to fold.

Each chip represented a unit of value. Our task was to consider the different components of the national football team that ultimately contributed to performance, each of them given its own box on the huge chart in front of us, and then decide how many of our chips, or how much value, we were prepared to stake on each of them.

There was a World Cup on the horizon – Russia 2018. But there was only so much money in the pot, and only so much time to get ready. So where were you placing your chips? Attacking play? Defensive work? Nutrition? Medical provision? Communications? Penalty taking? It was all up for grabs.

Overseeing proceedings was our head of strategy and performance, Dave Reddin. Dave and Dan both knew that I wanted to be across strategic planning in all departments, and not simply the tactical and technical areas to which previous England managers tended to restrict themselves. Hence my presence at the table and my acute interest in where this game of card-free poker was going to end up.

Inevitably, as the session unfolded and we each gambled our 'chips', it was clear that we were loading up the areas of the board that related to our personal areas of interest. We weren't quite putting everything on red or black, but we weren't spreading the chips around much either. This visual representation soon provoked a discussion. We could all see for ourselves the imbalance forming around the board.

While, at that point, we didn't agree on the best allocation of resources, we all knew that if we didn't find a compromise, the chances were, just like on a real roulette table, we would be taking a huge gamble on a small number of outcomes.

However, unlike a real roulette table, we could predict, or at least project, the likely outcome if we moved our chips around our improvised performance board. Cue an intense game of risk and reward, with plenty of debate as we simulated England's chances of success in Russia. I've never been much of a gambler but, at times, it felt like we were betting our lives on this game.

Clearly, some strategic areas mattered more than others, and we really homed in on those. For example, we all agreed that set-plays were likely to be game-defining. The data on this was incontrovertible: around a third of all goals were scored from set-plays (i.e. from passages of play beginning with a free-kick, a corner or a throw-in, and for which there is therefore an opportunity to prepare). Moreover, the data showed that in a high percentage of tournament games, a set-play yielded the decisive goal. We knew we had to meticulously prepare to defend and attack these dead-ball situations at key moments in the game. We would do everything – minus the shirt-pulling, of course.

So we gathered our chips and invested in a specialist set-play coach, something that was commonplace in sports such as rugby and American football at the time, but which was ground-breaking in football. Allan Russell was appointed into a senior role to execute the plan, while some frantic divvying up took place to figure out how to pay for his salary.

This focus on set-plays proved to be an excellent gamble, delivering clear and immediate results later in Russia. You may remember the 'love train' set-up combining movement, decoys and blocks, which led to the winning goal from Harry Kane in the dying minutes of our opening match against Tunisia. Both goals in that first game, in fact, were from corners that we had plotted and rehearsed. The danger we were causing from set-plays continued throughout the tournament, forcing our opponents to panic and concede penalties in their efforts to stop us, something that happened in our games against Panama and Colombia. Against Sweden in the quarter-final, a corner led to our first goal, and in the semi-final against Croatia, Kieran Trippier scored with a glorious direct free-kick, which, for the record, was a perfect replica of the one he had scored in training on the morning of the game. It was no surprise to us all when international and domestic teams began employing set-piece coaches as a matter of course after they saw the success we experienced in Russia.

Back to that table, and after a marathon session, all the chips finally came to rest. We now had a consensus on the best allocation of our time and resources at the training camps, and in between, up until the World Cup in Russia in 2018. You can see where they fell from the pie chart created to lock in the decisions we agreed.

Don't be misled at first glance by the seemingly greater allocation given to planning over training. Clearly football was always going to be the crucial element of what we did, and a lot of that 30 per cent of planning allocation is accounted for by the fact that we would be spending three times as many days working off-camp without the players as on-camp with them. Plus, planning also takes in such aspects as analysing players for selection, preparing tactical plans and other football-related research projects.

You will notice that in aiming to be the most physically dominant and resilient team, we divided our time and efforts for 'physical preparation' into three categories: recovery and nutrition, optimising capability, and minimising vulnerability.

TO BE RECOGNISED AS THE NUMBER 1 TEAM IN THE WORLD

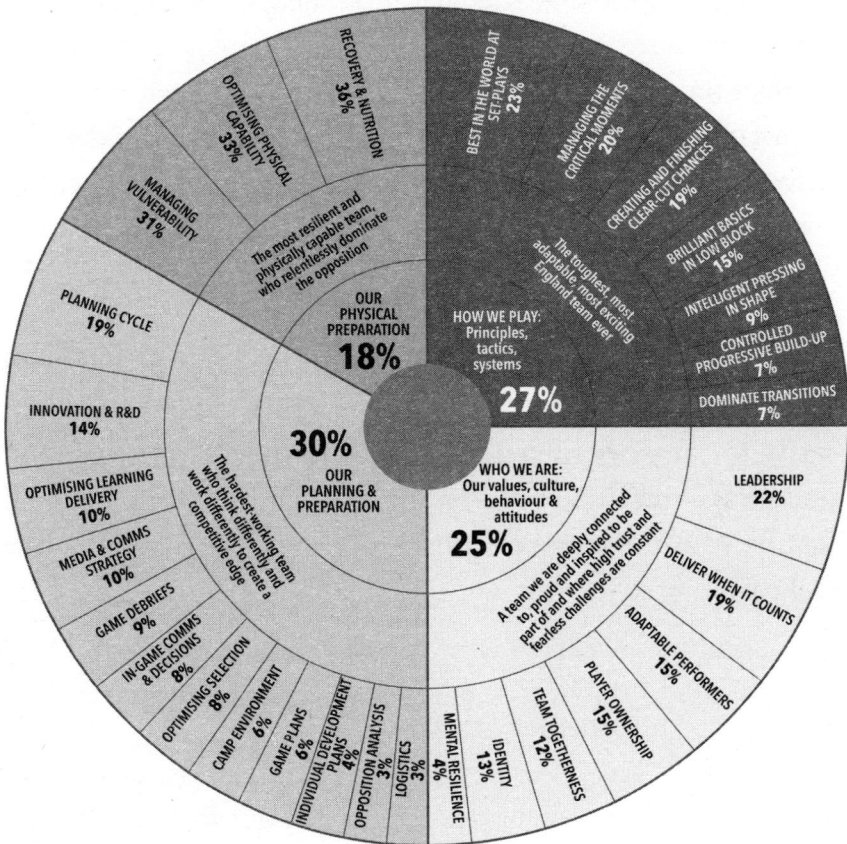

OUR PHYSICAL PREPARATION 18%
- RECOVERY & NUTRITION 36%
- OPTIMISING PHYSICAL CAPABILITY 33%
- MANAGING VULNERABILITY 31%

The most resilient and physically capable team, who relentlessly dominate the opposition

HOW WE PLAY: Principles, tactics, systems 27%
- BEST IN THE WORLD AT SET-PLAYS 23%
- MANAGING THE CRITICAL MOMENTS 20%
- CREATING AND FINISHING CLEAR-CUT CHANCES 19%
- BRILLIANT BASICS IN LOW BLOCK 15%
- INTELLIGENT PRESSING IN SHAPE 9%
- CONTROLLED PROGRESSIVE BUILD-UP 7%
- DOMINATE TRANSITIONS 7%

The toughest, most adaptable, most exciting England team ever

OUR PLANNING & PREPARATION 30%
- PLANNING CYCLE 19%
- INNOVATION & R&D 14%
- OPTIMISING LEARNING DELIVERY 10%
- MEDIA & COMMS STRATEGY 10%
- GAME DEBRIEFS 9%
- IN-GAME COMMS & DECISIONS 8%
- OPTIMISING SELECTION 8%
- CAMP ENVIRONMENT 6%
- GAME PLANS 6%
- INDIVIDUAL DEVELOPMENT PLANS 4%
- OPPOSITION ANALYSIS 3%
- LOGISTICS 3%

The hardest-working team who think differently and work differently to create a competitive edge

WHO WE ARE: Our values, culture, behaviour & attitudes 25%
- LEADERSHIP 22%
- DELIVER WHEN IT COUNTS 19%
- ADAPTABLE PERFORMERS 15%
- PLAYER OWNERSHIP 15%
- TEAM TOGETHERNESS 12%
- IDENTITY 13%
- MENTAL RESILIENCE 4%

A team we are deeply connected to, proud and inspired to be part of and where high trust and fearless challenges are constant

What it takes to win – a chart of priorities

We knew that players could turn up to camp in different states of fitness, and this spread was a reflection of our desire to manage risk and maximise upside on the physical side of the game.

And, of course, 'how we play' was a big focus — our principles, tactics and systems received just over one-quarter of our allocated time and effort. With a clear goal to adapt and excite, we broke the components into areas such as set-plays, managing key moments, controlling the game (and therefore managing more risk), brilliant basics and finishing clear-cut chances (cue Harry Kane) among other areas.

All of this was underpinned by our values, culture and attitudes, to create a detailed illustration of what, in our view, was a world-class strategy for a tournament. For me, the session with the poker chips had been quite literally 'game-changing' in terms of getting a whole-picture view of our organisation and understanding its interdependencies. I highly recommend a few hours spent playing this game, which could be adapted easily for any organisation looking to marshal its time and resources as efficiently as possible towards its next major goal. Just beware if anyone proposes a few practice sessions in a real casino first.

In pursuit of excellence

With a clear tournament strategy in hand, I was now able to drill down into every one of our performance areas — whether that be coaching and tactics, recovery and nutrition, match analysis, game planning, logistics and more. This was about having the determination to improve, the desire to explore and the discipline to execute our plan.

The process led to numerous performance interventions all over the chart – in effect, our version of 'marginal gains'. These small improvements were in our control. They were not gimmicks, but granular, methodical steps we were taking, well away from the limelight. And while I knew there wasn't as clear a correlation between these increments and the outcome as there was in other sports – due to football being a team-based, opposition-focused game, rich in skills and inherently unpredictable in nature – I knew these gains would give us an advantage.

As Sir David Brailsford, the architect of this approach with the British Cycling team and Team Sky, said to me over many meetings, 'marginal gains' is about doing the *important* things better, and assimilating the cumulative effects of these small improvements to find your competitive edge. In other words, do the basics brilliantly.

One of the 'gains' we focused on was around recovery after training and matches. Specifically, sleep quality leapt out as a promising area for development. It was something that had been taken for granted before – 'the players are wiped out, they're bound to sleep well' – but, as we found out, there was much more to it than we thought, and there was much need for it. Not to mention the fact that improving sleep was comparatively low-cost versus other recovery options such as cryotherapy – an added bonus.

We now challenged our medical team to examine a list

of optimal practices around – for want of a better phrase – getting a good night's kip. And they didn't disappoint. There were precedents in and out of sport. Sir David Brailsford, as you would expect, was across the subject. His team had themselves been inspired by the Royal Ballet, who had given a lot of thought to their dancers' sleeping arrangements when they were out on physically demanding tours. So we took these learnings, conducted our own research, and minutely examined such contributing factors as bedding, lighting, temperature, noise, natural supplements and preparation strategies. Crucially, for me, we embedded these learnings in a practical and frictionless way, into a tournament environment, away from the creature comfort of the players' homes.

We took mattress toppers and a range of differently filled pillows, we monitored food and drink intake, we gave out magnesium and cherry juice supplements, and we issued an information leaflet on sleep hygiene, among many other protocols. We did, however, draw the line at physically tucking in the players and turning off the lights.

I think some of this attention to detail initially surprised them. In fact, there was so much to take in it probably kept them up at night! But they soon bought into the process, and I'm sure one or two even took their pillows back home to guarantee a better kip while playing for their clubs.

All this said, at this point in the England journey, I wasn't always just looking for 'marginal gains'; I was often looking for enormous ones. But, quite frankly, they were nowhere to be seen.

By sea, by land (by coach)

To refer back again to our strategic priority diagram, exactly 25 per cent of the pie chart was devoted to the segment that read 'WHO WE ARE: Our values, culture, behaviours and attitudes'. Sub-sections within this area included 'mental resilience', 'team togetherness', 'adaptable performers' and 'leadership'. In the centre of the segment was an aspirational statement we had workshopped: 'A team we are deeply connected to, proud and inspired to be part of and where high trust and fearless challenges are constant'. I'll admit that I hadn't intended the 'fearless challenges are constant' part to begin imminently. But such is the life of an England manager that in the summer of 2017, I found myself taking the squad of players on an unannounced two-day Commando training course in Dorset.

Dave Reddin was partly to blame. He had been with the England rugby union team, who, on their way to winning the 2003 World Cup, had been taken on a Marines-run military boot camp, featuring cross-country yomping and Commando assault courses. Dave swore by it. But then Dave wasn't going to have the managers of the country's biggest Premier League football clubs coming after him if one of our players got stuck somewhere halfway round an assault course and couldn't come home. I, on the other hand, would be catching many shades of hell if anyone picked up a serious injury doing something as off-piste as this. But it was an end-of-season camp, when the clubs switch off a little – and the only time we could possibly make it happen.

In true Commando style (of sorts), I headed down to Devon for a recce and to meet the officers who would be looking after us. It didn't take long before I was entirely convinced of the value of reporting for duty at Commando Training Centre Royal Marines in Lympstone at this particular point in our England journey. It would take us completely out of our bubble. It would be a bonding experience for the squad and staff. And it would send a message, internally to the players (but hopefully not to their club managers), and externally to the world. The Marines call it 'dislocated expectation'. I just hoped and prayed that 'dislocation' didn't involve a player's joint.

The theory goes that you are plunged, quite literally at times, into something so far out of your comfort zone that you can't even imagine it, and now you've got to adapt and cope. You find out a lot about yourself at such moments, and, at this early stage in my England managership, I thought it would be a brilliant lesson in building resilience for the entire team.

The trip would also be communicating my ambitions for our project and a simple message to every player present – 'These are people whose work has consequences far beyond anything we face. They're an elite unit serving the country. Match their standards, and we'll become an elite England team too.'

The players weren't to know anything about this plan in advance. On their schedule for that day at St George's Park was a presentation – of Owen Eastwood's work on identity, in fact, that I mentioned earlier. And at the end, entirely out of the blue, some uniformed Marines were going to burst in and tell everyone we were leaving. The players would be given a couple of minutes to call their families and inform them that they were going to be out of reach for the next forty-eight hours, and then they would hand in their phones. (This was a stipulation for the course, but also extremely handy from my point of view if their clubs should try to reach them during all this.) Then we'd all be flown by helicopters down to Lympstone and two days of intensive physical and mental challenges would begin. Although nothing as hard as an England press conference, of course.

That morning when the Marines showed up, the players were, I think it's fair to say, stunned. But they all made their last calls and handed in their phones, a detail I suspect might have required just as much inner resolve as the thought of being barked at by a drill sergeant. I don't know what Harry Kane must have thought. This was his first camp with us since I'd been full-time manager (he'd been injured for the previous ones) and just a couple of hours in, I was ordering him to join the Army.

Unfortunately the weather that morning had closed in, so the helicopter flight had to be scrapped at the last minute. Instead, everyone was now facing a five-hour coach journey – and without phones. That said, it wasn't yet a 'dislocated expectation', given how much time footballers spend on coaches.

Once we were there, though, the dislocation properly began, and the players took to it brilliantly. We were issued with our uniforms and sent off to camp out on Woodbury Common. To my surprise, some of the players had never slept in a tent before. The next day our Green Beret instructors took us on several long yomps, led us on a mock raid of a building, and took us through an assault course which included the notorious 'sheep dip', where we were plunged and dragged through a tunnel of filthy water. All of the staff, including me, joined in on all of these exercises, which I think earned us some extra respect from the players, especially those of us (no names here) who obviously struggled but persisted anyway. By the end of the day everyone was plastered in mud and happy for the showers and the comforts of the Marines' barracks – which, it goes without saying, were a good deal more spartan than we were used to on England trips.

Bonds were formed and, on the final night, I looked around at the players and soldiers, sitting, chatting and drinking beers together, and found myself reflecting on the moment. While their paths had taken them in such different directions, they'd all come from basically the same kinds of backgrounds, and they were all connected by a similar desire: to be the best they could be and represent their country.

It goes without saying that this was a totally different experience from going to a warm-weather camp in La Manga, Spain, or somewhere similar. Not that I hadn't enjoyed La Manga camps as an England player. Lovely golf course, no sheep dips . . . But this was just so radically different from anything we usually did on international duty – an absolute removal from our comfort zone. Very much a 'dislocated expectation'. And let's face it, this helped us redefine the 'fearless challenges' we were about to face on our field of play.

As news of the trip filtered out in the media, it redressed

some of the public disconnection between the players and the country from previous years. People could relate to the message the trip sent. They could see these were normal lads who wanted to do their best for their country. Inwardly for the players, the trip had told them that here, in this England team, they were going to be pushed, and pushed extremely hard. But that didn't mean they weren't going to enjoy the experience and grow from it. Even in a short space of time, I believe we instilled in the team a different kind of resilience.

To this day, if you asked Kieran Trippier, I am sure he would say that the trip to Devon was one of the best things he ever did with England. And I don't think he'd be the only one.

Incidentally, whatever Harry Kane thought about it all initially, he passed with flying colours. I had asked the Marines to identify, over the course of the two days as we went through the various challenges, the players in whom they saw leadership qualities. The officers highlighted a few main candidates, but the one they were unanimous on was Harry Kane. I made a note.

Media and performance

When we weren't playing soldiers, we were scrutinising every other part of our performance strategy, asking ourselves the same question: how can we optimise operations here in a way that, however indirectly, will enhance our chance of success on the pitch?

We knew media and communications was a major 24/7 operation at England, especially since we were the only football show in town when the games were on. And we also knew that England media relations had been a source of tension, conflict and frustration for decades. At best, a kind of uneasy truce existed; at worse, there was outright hostility, with the wrong kind of press coverage at the wrong time distracting the team and distorting the mood in the camp. Our fantastic media team would don their tin hats and prepare for battle at every camp.

There was a famous case, early in the World Cup in Mexico in 1986, where England's campaign had got off to a faltering start and a picture abruptly appeared in the papers of the manager, Sir Bobby Robson, leaning on a hotel balcony with his head in his hands and a faraway expression on his face. It was used by the papers to imply an England camp already in despair and longing to come home – when the reality was they had everything to play for. (In fact, you may remember this was the tournament where England made it to the quarter-finals, and were knocked out by Diego Maradona's Argentina in the now legendary 'Hand of God' match.)

Never mind the fact that Sir Bobby's hands were pressing the headphones of a Walkman to his ears, rather than holding his despairing head, and that he was intently listening to a recording of himself on Radio 4's *Desert Island Discs*. Of course, the damage was done by the time the real story came out.

But could media relations really be an area of performance gain if we approached it in a different way? Rather than 'fulfilling our obligations', was there a less grudging, more positive way to think about it?

Our communications team decided to write a strategy paper to examine the impact of media relations on performance. A new way of looking at an age-old problem. As part of scoping that project, in early 2018, a small delegation of us visited the Super Bowl in Minnesota, contested that year between the New England Patriots and the Philadelphia Eagles. A few days before the game itself, we attended the NFL's extraordinary Super Bowl media day. It was an amazing event – a press conference with added razzmatazz. Or rather, razzmatazz with an added press conference. In an enormous hall, in two separate hour-long shifts, the players and coaching staff of both sides sat at individual booths where people were free to approach and chat. It was extremely relaxed and clearly open to correspondents of all kinds. In fact, a woman in a wedding dress, complete with veil and train, seemed to be going around offering the players proposals of marriage at one point.

During the trip, I overheard the Patriots' coach, Bill Belichick, who was notorious for being less than enthusiastic about the media, say, 'It's our opportunity to speak to our fans,' when a journalist provokingly asked if he was enjoying himself. That reply stuck with me. It seemed to be exactly the right attitude to me – a long step from 'fulfilling our obligations'. If I too could imagine that I was talking directly to our fans during an interview, rather than a journalist seeking an undermining headline, it would keep me in a much better headspace. I spread this thought among the players. If we could all reframe our thinking in this way, then maybe our relationship with the media would start to feel more productive. And let's face it, if Bill Belichick could do it, anyone could.

Back at home, with the NFL as our model (give or take the industrial hall and the wedding correspondent), we introduced an all-squad, pre-game press event at St George's Park before the team travelled to Russia in 2018, conducted in a welcoming, informal atmosphere – a first step towards defusing the typically confrontational relationship between press and team at tournament time.

In a bid to extend this new approach to greater openness and visibility, we decided to embed an official team photographer at our Russian base, a completely new idea (and to some extent fraught with danger). We would grant access behind the scenes in a controlled way, whilst preserving the space and privacy that the players needed to rest and recover at key times between matches.

And then, once we were out in Russia, our physical performance coaches ended up pulling a masterstroke. They had constantly been encouraging players to use the swimming pool after training because water was a really efficient way to ease tired muscles. However, at the end of a tough session, many of the players just weren't that thrilled at the prospect.

But the coaches had cunningly thought to pack a secret weapon: inflatable unicorns. Big ones. Ones you could plausibly ride on. The team walked in one day to find the pool positively bobbing with them.

Now we were talking. The swimming pool suddenly

became the go-to destination after training. With inflatables in the mix, post-session rehab had clearly never been such a lark. Meanwhile, the team's photographer quietly documented proceedings from the water's edge and the images from those sessions – not least the one of Harry Maguire piloting a unicorn through exceptionally choppy waters – ended up going viral around the world.

The dissemination of those images wasn't an accident either. Freshly energised from the NFL Super Bowl trip, our communications team had fleshed out their media relations performance plan to embrace social media for the first time. Rather than relying on traditional written and broadcast channels to reach our fans, as we had done in the past, we now recognised there was a new generation of supporters online we could engage with directly. Thanks, in part, to the unicorns, our social media content 'blew up' (almost as quickly as the inflatables, you might say). Fans in their droves were liking and commenting on our more relaxed behind-the-scenes footage. The strategy helped to give, I think, a more genuine insight into the players' personalities and the often playful bonds between them. All the while, our communications staff could reclaim a degree of narrative control.

Revitalised recovery sessions and top-quality comms: it was two positive outcomes for the price of one, and unsurprisingly we deployed the power of the inflatable unicorn again at the 2020 Euros. At about £20 each, and very easy to source online, those unicorns probably represent the best value for money of any budget item in my entire reign as England manager. I was less enthusiastic about the fact that the players hatched a plan to wear budgie-smugglers for one of those sessions, but you can't have everything.

In the pages ahead, I'll continue to describe the optimised performance, in areas such as penalty-taking, opponent analysis, in-game communication and base-camp environments, and their effects in 2018 and beyond. Expanding the team to drive this performance in those areas where we felt we would get the greatest return meant we travelled to Russia with a support staff for the players of eighty-five people, everyone in their separate departments working in lockstep in accordance with an intricate schedule that was planned down to the last hour of every day.

It was a far cry from an under-resourced operation supplemented with part-time staff and most of the chips stacked up in one area of performance when I started with England. And an even further cry from my earliest playing days at Crystal Palace, when I'd climbed on board the coach and headed off to away games with a manager, an assistant, a physio and a kit man.

Now, in 2018, I had oversight of an England World Cup campaign that had acquired the attention to detail and rigour of a military operation – albeit one with a frontline role for inflatable unicorns.

Real-world testing

The tournament in Russia was our first proper opportunity to assess our progress under my management – the first full-scale stress test for the organisation we had put in place. We had gathered plenty of insight from the training camps, friendly matches and qualifiers that had taken us there. I had begun to instil our culture and we had done our work on strategy and performance optimisation. But only now would we discover how our developing team would acquit itself in a tournament setting at the highest level, under pressure, with the world watching.

I was acutely aware at this stage of setting us up for failure by encouraging unrealistic expectations, whether it was inside or outside the camp. One unguarded remark from me about going all the way and winning this thing could, at a stroke, have undone all our good work on dialling down the hype around the players. So instead we set ourselves a minimum performance marker: we had to qualify from the group stages and win a knockout match. In other words, we had to reach the competition's quarter-finals. Hit that and we could regard ourselves as having met our targets for Russia 2018.

When this proposal was first put to the players, in a meeting at St George's Park, there was an audible rumble of disappointment. Many clearly felt this was unambitious. Footballers are ultra-competitive people, after all. Everyone agreed that going around the place shouting about how football was coming home obviously wasn't a clever idea at this point in history, but . . . only the quarter-finals? Shouldn't we be setting our sights higher?

It was then pointed out to the players that England hadn't won a knockout game in ten years. Winning the quarter-finals would make us the most successful England tournament side in a decade. We all wanted to go as far as we could, of course, and nobody was suggesting that we should pull up short if we found ourselves on a run. But there was a weight of history here that made a quarter-final place a realistic peg to aim at. After a bit more rumbling, the players saw the wisdom.

At the same time we recognised that, in terms of holding the team hostage to fortune, going public with this minimum performance marker would be almost as ruinous as boasting that the trophy was already England-bound. Instead, in line with our culture and our mission statement, we talked publicly about wanting to come home having made our supporters and ourselves proud, and said no more. We all knew that winning matches would be fundamental to that, but we consciously targeted an outcome that focused on how we played and carried ourselves, rather than one that was recklessly index-linked to dramatically deep progress in the tournament.

In the end, to my enormous delight, we glided past that performance marker in Russia, winning not one but two knockout matches (one of them on penalties, of all things; we'll talk about that history-reversing outcome later). In other words, we reached the semi-finals and at that point we hit what had been Greg Dyke's original target for Euro 20, still two years away.

This was brilliant for everyone's faith in the process. Our performance provided evidence that we were on track, or even ahead of schedule by some people's metrics, and that could only breed belief. England teams in the past had trudged home after tournaments feeling disconsolate and punishing themselves because they had fallen short of the hype. We had changed the record in that regard. We had brought good vibes back to the team and the country – enabled England fans to believe again. It may have helped that there was a heatwave back home. It was a summer of endless barbecues and football on big screens. But best of all, England fans seemed to be happy about pulling on the shirt again to support and watch us. We had rediscovered a pride in England. As a team, we could return home with confidence and a sense of purpose, knowing that our culture and our strategy were beginning to deliver for us. And we could set our sights optimistically on the future.

SUMMARY
Drawing up the Blueprint
On shaping a winning strategy

• Strategy works best when it is built together. Involving multiple team functions in strategy conversations not only creates buy-in, but strengthens shared ownership, creates better understanding of the overall plan, and builds an acknowledgement of each other's challenges.

• Data should inform strategy – do not solely rely on intuition or tradition – but you must prioritise only the data that will support your goals, to allow ruthless focus on budgets and time.

• Instead of just tweaking existing ways of working, re-imagine them. A 'blank sheet of paper' approach can lead to ground-breaking ideas and big performance gains.

• Innovation sometimes feels uncomfortable. But leaders occasionally need to back unconventional ideas, provided there is strong evidence behind them.

- 'Marginal gains' aren't gimmicks – they are incremental improvements in the fundamentals which develop into 'major gains'. Think about how you can adapt the concept to your own business, or your life; and, with limited time and resource, identify where the gains will be greatest.

- Talk less about 'outcome goals' and more about process. There is little to be gained by discussing your objectives publicly. You can't control results, but you can control preparation and execution.

- A strategy is never set in stone. Just like each England tournament strategy, constantly review what is on track, what needs adapting and what should be scrapped. Some things won't work, but everyone will learn from the process of trying new methods.

CHAPTER 5

Choosing Your Eleven

On the art and complexity of recruitment

Talent pool rules

Shortly after I was named permanent manager of England, I gave a press conference in which I openly stated one of my fundamental policies on team selection. I would, I firmly declared, 'Never pick a player on reputation. Form has to come into it.'

What I was making clear here, in a moment of early leadership assertion, was that nobody would be getting into any England team of mine on their past glories alone; everybody would need to be bringing some game.

As statements of intention go, it was perfectly honest . . . but also slightly bold.

Six years later, I found myself sitting in the same seat, in front of many of the same journalists, explaining that it's 'impossible to pick England players on form alone'. Journalists seem to have longer memories than elephants and I was duly put through the media shredder for changing my tune.

So what had happened? Well, reality set in. The plain facts of English football had caught up with me: despite how much I wanted to, it simply wasn't possible to pick an entire squad of England players on the basis of how they were playing at the time.

In many respects, the challenges involved in selecting an England squad are, I'm sure, the same as the challenges of recruitment in any other organisation. Every business has its own metrics and markers of what excellence looks like, its sense of the desired balances within its team, and its determination to go out and secure the very best. In this context, weighing a job candidate's form (read: most recent track record) against their reputation (their wider past experience) is probably a calculation every leader has to make at some point, whether they're hiring a new sales lead or looking for a reliable left-back.

Moreover, every organisation understands that recruiting poorly in terms of capability and, in particular, character can really set a project back, and cost time and money to rectify. So, everyone in that position will know how much pressure there is to get the right people on board directly, even if, in your business, the ultimate decision might not automatically result in a flabbergasted article in the following morning's *Daily Mail*.

At the same time, there's an aspect of recruitment that makes the England manager's job unique, if not in the entire world of business, then certainly in English football. And that's the talent pool.

For me, unlike for club managers, there was unfortunately

no January transfer window in which to go shopping internationally for the next Lionel Messi. There was no 'summer war chest', courtesy of the owner, to bring in 'new blood', no tantalisingly available out-of-contract star to come in on a major deal and solve our historic 'left-side problem'. The talent pool the national coach has at their disposal is, by definition, confined to our shores. It grows as grass-roots systems develop new players but, due to injuries, form, player availability and the make-up of our national leagues, it can also shrink. And this is where, as manager, you end up getting caught between a rock and a hard place and making your most controversial selection decisions.

It's a plain fact that during the eight years I was in charge of England the talent pool shrank. When I took charge in 2016, around 38 per cent of starting players in the Premier League were eligible for national selection. By the end of my tenure, it had dropped to more like 32 per cent. Some weekends during Premier League matches it would fall to 28 per cent. The quality of our domestic top flight has clearly been improved massively over the last few decades by the influx of international players. As with globalisation more broadly, and as companies in all industries will attest, an injection of international talent can turbocharge innovation and growth. And the Premier League has grown into one of the world's very best.

But it also means that nowadays fewer English players regularly represent the top teams in our country. And if you're the national coach, that's a headache. It certainly makes competing to win on a global stage more complicated.

My granddad (*second row, centre, surrounded by family*) was a veteran of the Second World War and carried himself with quiet dignity.

My mum and dad showed me love and support, and a competitive streak.

Alan Smith, my coach at Crystal Palace when I was an apprentice player, challenged me to develop an inner steel.

During my playing career I was proud to be captain at Crystal Palace (*left*), Aston Villa (*top-right*) and Middlesbrough (*bottom-right*). I still can't figure out if it was just because I was the sensible one!

Playing my last game for Middlesbrough in the Europa League final against Sevilla in 2006, after which I went straight in as manager.

Playing for England for the best part of a decade was one of the greatest honours of my life. Missing the penalty in the semi-finals of Euro 96 (*below*) was one of the worst moments of my life.

Learning from one of the best. Terry Venables had an all-round assuredness that was particularly impressive in high-pressure situations.

Learning lessons the hard way. When I stepped into my first manager's role at Middlesbrough in 2006, it was a case of 'too much too soon'.

As head coach of the Under-21 team, working with young players like John Stones, Eric Dier (*second from right*) and Harry Kane (*far-right*). These players would go on to play a vital part in England's story.

With assistant coach Steve Holland. A loyal, trustworthy and challenging 'number two' is a priceless asset to any leader.

Above: Being unveiled as the new England manager at Wembley on 1 December 2016.
Below: My first press conference (of many!).

During the 2018 World Cup, we encouraged players to use the swimming pool after training to ease tired muscles. Our secret weapon? Inflatable unicorns.

One of my regular informal catch-ups with vice-captain Jordan Henderson. The more you know what is going on with your team, the more you can help them.

Being put through our paces at Commando Training Centre Royal Marines in Lympstone (*top and middle*). The trip instilled a sense of belonging, unity and resilience which propelled us to the 2018 World Cup.

In the dugout at the 2018 World Cup in Russia. Never underestimate the importance of high-quality, committed staff: Steve Holland (*centre-left*), Martyn Margetson (*centre-right*), and Allan Russell (*far-right*)

It's a similar story in the Uefa Champions League. The top European club competition is, you could say, a kind of finishing school for elite footballers. And at the moment we're a long way behind other countries in packing off our students to be finished there. In terms of Champions League minutes played during the 2022–23 and 2023–24 competitions, English players were sixth, behind players from Spain, Germany, Brazil, the Netherlands and Portugal. Meanwhile, in the most recent figures for the Europa League, Europe's second-tier competition, England was only the tenth-best represented country by player. This is despite the fact that two English teams, Manchester United and Tottenham Hotspur, reached the 2025 final.

To crunch those domestic numbers, in 2023 we often had sixty-six players starting each week in the Premier League that I could consider for England selection. This might sound like a lot, but if you break it down that's six players for each position on the pitch, assuming an even spread. Again, not bad – except . . . there's never an even spread. Goalkeepers, midfield pivots, left-footed left-backs – these players tend to be in much shorter supply than the rest. During my time with England, we had very few players to choose from in those positions who were playing regularly at a high level.

I'm not saying the Premier League should change its rules on foreign players, I'm not arguing for quotas – I'm not actually arguing anything at all here. I'm simply setting down in cold terms what an England manager in this current era faces. For me as head of talent recruitment, and trying to do the form v. reputation calculation, this limited and slowly diminishing talent pool would throw out some selection challenges that were interesting, to say the least.

Take your pick

If we were to list the ideal criteria for selection for the national team, we would start by looking at players who were playing in big matches in the latter stages of the Champions League, or pushing to win the league with their club, or ideally both. Why? Because the burden of playing against the best players in the world, under intense pressure, correlates closely with playing for England in a major tournament. The parallel isn't perfect but it gives a lot of solid data to work with.

As we start to assess a player excelling for a side in the mid to lower areas of the table, things get more complicated. Here, there is less evidence of performance in the biggest games under the biggest pressure, and some of the top-line numbers on form can be a little deceptive. So, for instance, there's a player at a mid-table club who has been banging in the goals recently. But have they been banging them in against the top teams or simply mopping up against weaker opponents? Do they score decisive goals at 1–1, or most frequently when their team is already 3–0 up and the opposition just wants to go home? How do they cope defending against the very best players? Are they athletic enough to cope against quicker, stronger midfielders?

Let's take an imaginary player – a fan favourite who is undoubtedly playing well for his club but who, to our eye, is not quite at the level to contribute to a winning England team. Now let's compare him with an established player, proven at international level, but currently on the bench at his club because a world-class overseas player is ahead of him in his position. Who should we pick? Generally, we went with the latter because his record showed that he could hit the required level. But he wasn't in a rhythm of playing, so this was – bang to rights – a judgement made on reputation rather than form.

Essentially, I couldn't avoid being accused of double standards. On the wing or at right-back we had a plethora of high-level options. So, on a tight call we looked more at form and the nature of the opposition. In positions where we had less strength in depth, we inevitably had to view the decision differently. We might play a proven player out of his pre-ferred position, because we knew the alternative was certain to fall short of what was required.

For me, all things considered, announcing the squad was the bit of the England job that I least looked forward to. First, I had the horrible task of informing players that they weren't going to be selected. (I'll talk more about these calls later in the book.) Then, with that unpleasantness out of the way, I had to sit in the media dock and be ripped to pieces on the decisions I've articulated above.

My hands were tied, really. I could hardly say to journal-ists, 'Yes, we left out player X because, between you, me and the rest of the country, we don't think he's good enough,' and so I'd just have to soak up the flak. At the same time, I quickly learned that the questions asked at a squad announcement – and the headlines that followed – were practically always about the players I had left out. The press seemed to take a 'glass half empty' approach in this area. Or certainly a 'squad half empty' approach. Fans of the players I had so brutally overlooked would always back their men, of course, and so would their managers, so there was always a healthy supply of juicy quotes for story-building in that area – and less juice, I suppose, in 'Manager Thinks Good Player Is Good'. There was nothing I could do, really, except roll with it and then try to avoid the papers for a couple of days. Oh, and also wear a hat, pulled down low, on my way into certain Premier League grounds after weeks in which my squad announcements had ignited particularly hot debates.

There is one thing I'd like to take this opportunity to set straight, though: every now and again, I'd get accused of 'having my favourites'. Quite right too. I did. My favourites were good players, who could handle the pressure of playing for England, gave everything for the team, fitted well into the group and helped us to win big matches. So, yes, I had my favourites. Guilty as charged. And if you had been the leader, I strongly suspect they'd have been your favourites too.

The knowledge in the room

However, in the midst of the storminess and controversy inevitably generated by this aspect of England leadership, the thing I could be absolutely confident of at all times was that our recruitment process was fantastically thorough. I cannot stress this highly enough. It was the thought that securely bolstered me whenever the flak was flying. Given our list in any week of sixty-five or so eligible players to assess, plus a handful who were with clubs abroad, we were usually able to establish pretty quickly that maybe a third were not up to international level. That would leave a longlist of around forty-five whom we would then be monitoring intensely, using a combination of live scouting, televised games, clips downloaded from the FA database and internal reports from clubs.

On Monday and Tuesday mornings, I would meet with our coaches, analysts and technical directors. Here, I would talk through every one of the forty-five players on the longlist, get the medical reports on those who were injured, and perhaps request information from a club as to why a player might, in our view, be underperforming. Meanwhile, from the picture we were assembling, I was constantly consider-ing options: how blends of creativity, speed and dependability would balance each other, how various players might work together in different systems, and how various players might complement, or not, our team's intended overall approach to the fixtures ahead.

I should stress that what we were trying to do at this point was build a squad, and squad selection is a different art from team selection. Generally, the best teams have what we call a strong spine, which is to say robust representatives in the roles of goalkeeper, centre-back, centre-midfielder and centre-forward. If you're strong through those areas, you've got half a chance. Moreover, I found that, by the time you got to the stage of picking your best in-form team, there were rarely more than a couple of close calls to be made. It would have become largely apparent during training what the bulk of the names on your team-sheet were going to be, and those remaining one or two decisions would normally be swung by very precise considerations about the nature of the opponents you were about to face.

Picking the squad, however, there would normally be far more close calls to make, with form and fitness tending to be the deciding factors. Also, you were obliged to be thinking about those players who were very unlikely to play many minutes and might possibly get none – the 'squad players'. You'd have to make a smart call there, because obviously nobody is likely to be ecstatic about sitting around and not playing.

I speak from experience here; that was my role at the World Cup in Japan in 2002. I didn't get a minute in that tournament and there were definitely days when I found my duties irksome. It was quite a nice trip for my parents, who got to do a lot of sightseeing. But less so for me, not least on the days after matches, when the non-starters had a full training session on their own, often to a soundtrack of 'encourage-ment', shall we say, from the starters, lightly jogging and stretching nearby. But I recognised that my role was to train well, challenge the first team, support them positively and be ready for my moment, if and when I was called upon. In tour-naments under my management, I loved the fact that, the day after a game, so many of the first-team players would come out to watch the back-up players do their session. It spoke to a real camaraderie and sense among them of the whole group's importance. And as manager, I felt those day-after sessions were the most important ones of the week to be fully present at and supportive of, knowing as well as I did how hard it is to push yourself the day after you have missed out on the adrenaline rush of playing.

I know that it takes a certain kind of character to play that supporting part in a squad, and often it's a role with a short shelf-life. Players might be happy to do it for a period of time, but even the strongest and most selfless characters can find it hard to endure the travelling and the being away from home if they don't feel they're going to get at least a crack at playing. It was something else that we monitored very closely.

Did our monitoring include data? Of course. Data is everywhere in football now and across industry, of course. I've been privileged to have had many meetings with the legendary Billy Beane, the man who effectively revolutionised the deployment of statistical performance analysis in sport, and the figure at the centre of Michael Lewis's famous book *Moneyball*. Like so many, I'm in awe of Billy's game-changing work around the numerically identifiable aspects of performance that are most likely to affect results, and keen to be shown anything potentially advantageous in this area.

At the same time, I would make one broader observation on data's use in relation to talent identification and recruitment. When we were close-tracking those forty-five players or so, I noticed that it was an extremely rare day when the data flagged up something we hadn't already observed and noted about them. Our staff, collectively, had whole decades between us of watching players develop, and there was a craft knowledge in the room when we discussed our selections that was shown over time – by the data itself, indeed – to be highly reliable. We knew our talent pool. We knew each other. We knew how to separate sound information (the evidence of our own or other trusted eyes) from unsound information (executives at clubs you visited recommending players as England prospects because a call-up would instantly increase their value. This happens). We saw ourselves as making 'data-informed' decisions, rather than 'data-driven' ones.

It enabled me to have enormous faith in my eventual recruitment decisions. I was happy to back myself in those post-squad-announcement moments when louder voices were doubting me, because I knew that we were watching the whole group in more detail than anyone else in the world. Our practice at England seems to me to offer a decent model for business here: if you really analyse the talent pool in which you are operating, using craft knowledge and data, but with the emphasis on craft knowledge; and if you constantly recruit based on that knowledge, replacing the talent that leaves in the meantime, you end up in a pretty good place.

Youth and experience

A major consideration around both squad and team selection was the numerical balance of young and older players. It was a constant question: what, right now, is the optimum distribution through the squad of youth and experience? It spoke to a universal truth about recruitment in a group context. It can never ultimately be about the individual in isolation. There is always a bigger picture.

My twenty-three-man squad for the 2018 World Cup in Russia had an average age of just over twenty-six, which made it the third-youngest squad ever selected by England for a tournament. There were risks, clearly, in tipping the balance towards youth. But it was entirely in keeping with what I saw as the mission: backing these young players that our new development pipeline had been bringing through, and using them to build a new England.

The advantage of these players' youthfulness was most evident in their energy and pace, and in their freedom from inhibition. They were hungry, and with a point to prove. They were all fiercely ambitious. Everything was ahead of them at that point. That brought a sense of drive and competition right across the squad. All of this was unequivocally great. At the same time, that fearlessness in the young is often there because they have yet to experience failure, and that can lead to naivety, so there's potentially a trade-off to consider.

In addition, I had a specific concern about whether these younger players were mature enough to pull and push at each other – to have those honest conversations about each other's performances that are so vital for raising the standard and getting the best out of everyone, both in training and on the pitch. This matters in any team environment. Colleagues have to be brave enough to be open and unafraid of upsetting each other – raw but respectful. That's a delicate balance, but it's an utterly crucial factor in a winning team: when you're comfortable enough to challenge each other and not have it held against you — when you can move on quickly from disagreement. And sometimes that only comes with time together. It seemed to me, at the point of selecting the 2018 squad, that there was still work to do in that area for these young players.

But I had at least seen many of them forge friendships while progressing through the national junior sides, and I sensed those bonds would be strong enough for them, with encouragement, to engage openly with each other eventually. And I was pleased to see this happen. As we spent more time together, their growing belief in our team culture and the value of what we were doing gave them a platform on which they could feel comfortable about opening up. And their increasing willingness to challenge each other was a big part of the fire that took us all the way to the semi-finals in Russia.

From young players, I could get energy, fresh ideas and a sense of daring. Senior players could bring insight and perspective and the certainties that come from having been tested before. But the blend of the two was where the real chemistry took place. Right at the start of a camp, I always asked our senior players to ensure they had lunch or dinner with anyone new to the set-up. They could help the young arrivals settle, while also quietly letting them know what was going to be expected of them while they were with England.

It was here that I thought Jordan Henderson really showed his class. Later in 2020, when a young Jude Bellingham turned up in the squad, Jordan suddenly had another direct rival for his position in the team. Yet it was Jordan who took Jude under his wing, helped him find his place in the group and effectively served as his mentor. In turn, the presence of Jude fired Jordan to up his game. Both players ended up making vital contributions on the pitch in the four years after that.

As new players emerged, particularly over the last six years of my reign, we often faced a decision between an older player who was more experienced but might not ultimately take us where we wanted to go, and a younger player of manifest potential who wasn't quite oven-ready. In the short term you can suffer for these kinds of calls. As the younger player learns and improves they can also make costly mistakes. Those mistakes can then lose you matches, and suddenly, because football has never been an environment that encourages patience, the pressure is on you, as manager. Nevertheless, in that situation, I can confidently state that ninety-nine times out of a hundred we looked to the horizon, in accordance with our mission, and backed youth, making decisions that would ultimately benefit England in the longer term, and developing players like Bellingham, Declan Rice and Bukayo Saka.

Arsène Wenger once said something to me that affected me profoundly. 'We should manage as if we are going to be here for ever,' he said, 'in the realisation that we could be gone tomorrow.' That really resonated and it clearly applies way beyond football. Constant short-term decisions for the sake of expedience ultimately prevent organisations from evolving. Long-term decisions might not always suit a manager on a short contract, but if they are demonstrably in the interests of the organisation, then they're the right decisions every time. As leaders, we should be prepared to accept the possible short-term negative for the greater good, even if it looks like we'll be gone before that greater good occurs.

Captaincy material

In football, a manager's choice of captain sends an important message in so many ways. It's the moment the leader identifies his leader, and it sends a message to the team, to the fans and to the opposition even. It becomes a huge part of how a manager defines himself and gets defined.

Going into Russia 2018, I felt I needed to pin my colours to the mast in this respect. I had been rotating the captaincy across my first camps, partly in response to injuries and partly in response to senior players, the most obvious captaincy candidates, coming to the end of their time and drifting out of the first XI. (Wayne Rooney, who was captain when I took over, was one such. Gary Cahill was another.) I had given Jordan Henderson the armband during that rotation period too. His experience, selflessness and willingness to call out others made him, for me, the most 'natural leader' in the group. But Jordan was missing quite a lot of football with injury and fitness issues at that time. So one month out from the World Cup, in a meeting at St George's Park, I announced to the players that our captain would be Harry Kane.

Harry was twenty-three, going on twenty-four – young for the role; in the modern era only Michael Owen and (by a handful of days) Sol Campbell and Steven Gerrard had been younger. He hadn't captained England at under-21 level and he wasn't the captain at his club. He was a prolific and talismanic goalscorer, but forwards aren't frequently given the job; it tends to go to players who are more centrally placed on the pitch. But I thought he had outstanding personal qualities, I knew he would definitely play, and I thought he could grow into the role.

He was a meticulous professional and I believed he could set the standard every day. He had high expectations and a strong sense of belief. And he had shown that it was possible to be one of the best in the world over a consistent period of time, which I felt was a great message for a young skipper to be imparting to a young team. In our camps over the previous eighteen months, he had demonstrated not only his own elite drive, but that he recognised the importance of bringing others with him. I knew that you don't become a top international side just by having a good captain with strong values. Excellence has got to spread right through the group, and I thought Harry could potentially make that happen.

I also thought that being captain might gain an extra per cent or two out of Harry. And I think that proved to be the case. Captaincy breeds ownership, and in the subsequent six or seven years he barely missed a game, never mind a camp. Perhaps his commitment would have remained full-throttle in any case, led by his personal pursuit of the England goalscoring record. But the captaincy certainly didn't hinder his desire in this regard.

It was good to watch him expand into the role. His voice gradually began to carry more weight in the team meetings

and he was eventually prepared to stand up and give alternative views to mine. We didn't always agree, but where I
differed from him I always spent time with him to explain,
so he in turn could filter the message through to the group.
He was, and continues to be, an outstanding ambassador for
the team and the country, and to have simultaneously found
time to obliterate the scoring records of Charlton, Rooney
and Lineker is quite something.

However, appointing Harry wasn't the end of my thinking
on leadership within the team. I wanted to take a non-
traditional route (certainly in football) and share the load
more broadly. With Harry leading from the front (quite literally) I wanted to develop a support team of other senior
players, so we were drawing on a deeper well of experience,
ownership and responsibility.

We often talk in football about the desirability of having
'leaders on the pitch' and I decided to follow that to the letter:
leaders, plural. Only five members of our 2018 group had prior
World Cup experience. Jordan Henderson was one of that
number, which also included Raheem Sterling, Phil Jones,
Danny Welbeck and Gary Cahill. These more experienced
players were among a senior cohort – also including Fabian
Delph, Ashley Young and Eric Dier – who could share some
of the burden that might normally fall on the captain alone.
Together with Harry, they were respected and admired by the
younger players, had a dedicated work ethic and a willingness
to help others. Their combination was a huge assistance to me
as a leader, and I am sure to Harry, as captain, too.

Eight years later, on the eve of Euro 24, I developed the

concept a little further by naming a leadership group that blended two senior players – Harry and Kyle Walker – with two junior ones, Declan Rice and Jude Bellingham. My reasoning was, the squad size for that tournament had increased to twenty-six, and there were a lot of younger players in the group whose voices I wanted to be heard and represented. Sometimes, younger players can be a little bit more reluctant to approach the head coach and talk about what they're thinking and feeling. So having a small group of player 'leaders' of different ages meant I could get a broader sense of what the mood was on the ground. I didn't want to miss anything, after all; it's always important to know what the players are thinking. And it shouldn't just be for the old to lead. Sometimes the young actually have a great deal of experience behind them, which in this case was abundantly clear when I considered some of the big games our younger team members had played in.

I could have put more players into that leadership group, but I felt four was enough. It allowed me to meet them collectively as well as individually during that tournament. Generally, we'd discuss training requirements ahead of the next match, or share feedback about everything that was going on in the camp and during games. On reflection, I could have given even more responsibility to these leadership groups, and asked for more accountability. Perhaps I could have used them to develop individuals even more too, although there are huge time constraints on that process in international football. I would argue that a spread captaincy yielded tangible dividends for the coherence and focus under pressure of our team, on and off the pitch, and would potentially do so for any team, football or otherwise.

The team behind 'the team'

For nine and a half months each year, the England team consists of everyone *but* the players. They're with their clubs, and I think a lot of people assumed we were just drumming our fingers in those periods, staring mournfully out of the windows of St George's Park and waiting for them to join us. Far from it. Even when the players were absent, I was working full-time and flat out with the wider team to prepare for the camps and the tournaments and to ensure that, every time the players were released to us, we were in the best possible position to capitalise on the time we would have with them.

As I mentioned in the previous chapter, by the time we went to Russia for the 2018 World Cup, the players were merely the highly visible tip of our operation's massive iceberg. At the 2024 Euros in Germany, the England team comprised a twenty-six-strong squad of players and more than fifty supporting personnel. Pitch-side, this ranged from coaches, medics and physios to our analysts, communications, commercial, transport, logistical and security staff.

Meanwhile, back at St George's Park, in a kind of Mission Control scenario, we had two teams at work to support us during tournaments. One was the analysis team, which featured coaches from the national junior teams. They were tasked with watching every game taking place and logging the tactics and personnel of every opponent so that, as the draws for the later rounds became clear, we had all our intel ready to go. Each coach would have a group of opposing teams to cover and when our next opponents were known, the relevant coach would fly out to deliver a presentation to us on the ground, covering tactical approaches in every phase of the game, their preferred set-ups and how we could best exploit them. Key video clips would already have been forwarded to our analysts at the tournament so that the meeting content could be fast-tracked. In the tournament's knockout stages you might only have thirty-six hours to turn this stuff around, so speed was of the essence. Our experience across four tournaments enabled us to get ever-more efficient at this.

The second group in Mission Control was what we thought of as our crisis management team, including the CEO, the CFO and the technical director and also some of the on-the-ground staff who would call in online. The term 'crisis' here was used to mean 'needs doing now' – tasks like ticket allocations and travel arrangements for broader FA staff, as well as – annoyingly from my point of view – open-top bus tour planning. Obviously, I was pleased that we got far enough in at least three of those four tournaments, including the 2024 Euros, to make this an item on the agenda, but I hated having to think about it because it seemed presumptuous and arrogant, not to mention fate-tempting. However, by-laws are by-laws and, unfortunately, trophy-waving arrangements need to be put in place with police and councils several days before they are needed – assuming they are needed, which (no spoiler alert necessary) they weren't.

Anyway, you get a sense, I hope, of the width and depth of our wider team. And I recognised, from the moment I stepped up as manager, that the task of assembling that team was going to be as critical as the task of calling up the players. Accordingly, even though this broader brief wasn't technically in the job description, as leader I felt I needed to be right across it.

When vacant or newly created posts were going to be filled, I wanted to meet all recommended candidates. I was involved in the appointment of our sports psychologists, our fitness coaches and our medical team. I don't believe England managers had historically got involved in these things, but it was the way I saw the job. Indeed, it was this aspect of managing the wider team that led me to fight against the job title 'head coach'. That wasn't what I was; I was the manager. The reality was, I had to bring these people together, I was the one they were looking to for leadership, and I was the one who had to create harmony and focus within that team. I couldn't see anyone else in the organisation being in a position to do that, given that the CEO can't be in the dressing room or across everything at the training ground. It had to be me.

So, where I could, I attended job interviews. Beyond the matter of their experience and credentials, which were pretty much a given by the time they got to the interview stage, I needed to feel assured that any incomer would be a good fit with the England project as a whole, that they were bringing the right character and personality. There's no science there, unfortunately. But the analogy I would use for international camps was that they were rather like a family holiday: everyone gets along at first but as the week wears on, there's the potential for a feeling of claustrophobia to build. Suddenly one or two members of the group start to get a bit twitchy and it can quite easily go from happy campers to 'I'm a footballer (or staff member), get me out of here'. Camps were a sealed environment and you wanted to be in there with people you knew you could get along with. You needed team players, in other words – and not just on the pitch.

Every member of our unit was going to be making a difference to the team's performance, however indirectly, and every one of them needed to know that that was the case, and to feel motivated by it. People in any organisation want to feel they're contributing and they want to be valued and recognised for the work that's being delivered. And that's a leadership task also. When we travelled, I felt responsible for everyone that came with us – felt the need to check in with them all, whether it was eating with them, chatting with them, joining the staff quiz or getting a sense from them about issues that might be developing. I wanted to have my finger on the pulse of all of that, and it takes time and energy, which are in short supply as you work through a tournament. But it needed to be done.

Back at St George's Park, there were obviously far greater numbers of people involved in our work, but I tried to get to know everyone, from the executives to the cleaners. And I know from the letters I received when I left that this mattered to people – mattered more, in fact, than I was aware of at the time. It was simply important to people that they felt appreciated, and I know that the vast majority of our staff did. I don't think that's exceptional leadership. Frankly, I think that's

Gareth Southgate (Manager)

Head Coach
— Attacking Set Play Coach
— Goalkeeping Coach / Defending Set Play Coach
— Assistant Coach

Performance Analyst
— 2nd Performance Analyst
— 3rd Performance Analyst

Sports Psychologist

Doctor
— 2nd Doctor

Physio
— 2nd Physio
— Soft Tissue Therapist
— 2nd Soft Tissue Therapist
— Osteopath Job Share
— Movement Therapist

Physical Performance
— 2nd Physical Performance
— Nutritionist
— 1st Chef
— 2nd Chef

Lead Team Manager
— Team Manager
— Security Manager plus x 3 Security
— Team Travel Manager + Air Charter
— Kit Manager
— 2nd Kit Manager

Head of England Communications
— Senior Comms Manager

Senior Player Liaison

Senior Video Producer
— Video Production

Senior Media Manager
— Photographer

England 'org chart', 2021

normal good manners. But I can see that today perhaps what I consider normal good manners aren't the norm.

People talk about 'job hierarchies' and about some roles being more significant than others, but how, actually, do you rank the 'significance' of jobs across the wider team? Maybe I should talk here about our kit men, Pat and Neil. It would be easy to view the task of laundering the kit as an essential but ultimately low-impact contributor to a team's performance. That's by no means how I saw it.

The logistical complications alone of Pat and Neil's work were vast – transporting hundreds of items of individually tailored kit around the world, preparing for all weathers, making sure every tiny bit was in the right place in the right order at the right time, for training and matches. Now imagine if, getting ready for the biggest game of his life, a player discovers the wrong-sized shirt on his peg, or realises that his boots haven't been packed. Pat and Neil's job was a classic example of one of those roles where a million things done well pass unnoticed, but one tiny mistake creates a potentially campaign-scuppering drama. You need exactly the right people in such roles, and Pat and Neil were exactly the right people. And that's before we even consider their elite-level work as quiz compilers for the team's competition nights.

High-performance teams need high-performance staff. Indeed, you can't aspire to be the former without installing the latter. And that's in every department, without exception. Ultimately, at England, the character of the wider support team helped to shape our culture as much as the players on the pitch did.

Trust in feedback

In order to make our wider team cohere, we held weekly multi-disciplinary planning meetings. Here, I could join all the heads of department, from communications to coaching and from operations to psychology. During planning for camps, we would gain an insight into every department's objectives for the week and understand the pressures each department was under – for example, what our commercial team needed to deliver in order to fulfil contractual obligations with sponsors. And then, in the camps, we would all meet every night to review what had happened that day, discuss any broader observations and check the plan and timings for the following day.

The common theme in all these meetings was that I decided not to chair them, and, with any item on the agenda, I tried not to be the first person to pipe up. This might have seemed counter-intuitive, given that I was the head of this group, but the whole point of these gatherings for me was that I wanted to know what the rest of the team thought. I had learned – from personal experience as well as from watching others – that once the leader gives an opinion it can often deter others from proposing an alternative. Indeed, I quickly realised that people nodding when I addressed a meeting didn't necessarily mean they agreed with me. They were nodding because . . . well, I was the leader and they felt they ought to.

If you speak too soon as a leader you risk not hearing what people genuinely think and you potentially miss out on a better solution to a problem. So in those meetings, I would try to hold back for a while and listen, which is perhaps leadership's most vital skill, though much underrated. It's important to be aware that it takes a lot of trust and confidence in their own position for people to challenge the opinion or proposal of the person in charge. But such challenges are critical for team success and, by extension, they're a lifeline for leadership.

This was where I was blessed, at England, in my number two. Steve Holland first came into my orbit in 2013 when I took charge of the England Under-21 team. He had earned an impressive reputation as an assistant coach at Chelsea, where under various top managers – Mourinho, Ancelotti, Hiddink, Benítez, Conte – he had been part of teams that had won the Champions League, Europa League, Premier League, FA Cup and League Cup . . . the full house, basically. As well as working at a high level with the senior team, Steve also had an excellent grounding in youth development.

I met him to talk about the possibility of joining me in coaching the under-21s. His passion for the national team was clear to me straight away. He also recognised, as I did, that the generation of young English players about to emerge had the potential to develop into a properly formidable force – that this was a very good time to be doing this kind of work. There was only a part-time role on offer, but I was delighted when he accepted.

At that point, we didn't really know each other. People move around in football, of course, so I had got plenty of insight by asking those who had worked with Steve, and I imagine he had done the same with me. But all Steve and I really knew for sure about each other was that we shared a fervent desire to help make English football better. And that was a very solid place to start.

From the beginning, we got along. What became apparent to me very quickly was Steve's integrity. Where he dissented from me, he would challenge my views, but it was always with the best interests of the under-21s at heart. That led to a) discussions founded on mutual respect; and b) constructive outcomes. In other words, it was the kind of dissent that is the best way forward.

We complemented each other in many areas. Steve had more than twenty-five years of experience of coaching on the grass, while my experience leaned towards playing in and leading teams. It was natural, then, that, with the under-21s, I would focus on tactically briefing the players and Steve would lead the training sessions. Despite the common view that the head coach should be the one with the whistle, we found it was more productive for me to observe, listen and comment. Steve delivered each session exactly as I wanted, allowing us both to play to our strengths.

When we moved up to the senior team, Steve's experiences with Chelsea meant the step was a smooth one for him. Dealing with high-achieving players presents a different challenge to working further down the leagues, and working in the air-fryer environment of the England team is a world away from youth football. But Steve and I were both well versed in the complicated dynamics of handling club managers, superstar players and the global media. There wasn't much here that was likely to surprise us — or not for long, at any rate.

What was obvious to me about Steve was that he so clearly loved the work. He loved being an assistant manager. He recognised that the role is itself a singular art and he had made himself widely schooled in it and utterly expert at it.

Richard Hytner has written about this in his book *Consiglieri: Leading from the Shadows*. It goes back through history, focusing on the under-sung but utterly invaluable work of a particular kind of character (rock-like, self-sacrificing, all about the outcome) who excels at being a number two: Thomas Cromwell with Henry VIII, for instance, William Seward with Abraham Lincoln, and, more recently, Charlie Munger with Warren Buffett. Hytner doesn't get up as far as Steve and me, which is a pity. Maybe he's planning that for a later edition. In all seriousness, though, the book is an extremely illuminating demonstration of something I came to understand very fully while working with Steve: that assistant leadership is its own specialism.

Steve remained at my side as my assistant coach throughout my time as manager of England. As part of the process for selecting players, we would watch a minimum of eight live games a week between us, often two a day at weekends, and on the way home we would call each other and talk about individual players and points of interest, tactically, from the matches we had just seen. He was the guy to whom I quickly articulated my intentions on the touchline, just to be sure I wasn't missing anything. We shared an office for eight years, oversaw 102 international matches, and talked football for an incalculable number of hours.

We didn't see eye to eye on every call I made, but that's

actually a healthy thing in any working relationship. In fact, I would suggest that the time when you and your assistant seem to be agreeing on every single detail is the time to worry about whether the dynamic between you is right. Even when he ultimately disagreed with me, Steve always acknowledged my reasoning and backed me in front of the players. I always knew when I had delivered an effective talk to the team, because Steve would offer me a quiet nod of approval from the other side of the table. It was a small gesture, in keeping with his character, but it meant a great deal. To my mind, there was nothing he hadn't achieved as a number two.

In the search for trusted confidants, which all leaders need, it's so tempting, as a first resort, to look to people who closely match us – share our backgrounds and attitudes. We imagine, I guess, that we'll feel most comfortable there, with the easy fit. But one should never underestimate the value of thinking more outwardly about it and looking further than that, to the people who are going to bring things that we can't. My working relationship with Steve entirely revealed that to me. We need alongside us individuals who are strong in areas we don't specialise in, who see the world differently from us and, above all, who are prepared to tell us the things we might not want to hear.

SUMMARY
Choosing Your Eleven
On the art and complexity of recruitment

- Clear recruitment principles, when set out beforehand, will give you an important reference point when deciding on candidates. Given that it is rare to find the 'complete package', be clear what are you prepared to compromise on and what are the non-negotiables. Take your time to get things right — recruit in haste and you will repent at leisure.

- The 'character' of candidates is the foundation of smart recruitment. Just like in football, data plays a key role in forming a credible shortlist, but your intuition on whether the candidate will fit your culture is the ultimate measure of whether a candidate is right.

- Investing in youth may have risks in the short term, but harnessing the energy and daring nature of young people can unleash transformative results in the medium to long term. Balance fresh talent with experienced team members so that standards are maintained and mentoring flourishes.

CONTINUED OVER

- Your choice of captain or deputy sends a powerful message about your values and the culture you are trying to build.

- A team full of superstars won't work, and every team needs a supporting cast of dependable, energy-giving team players who bind everything together. Make sure 'mavericks' are given the space to perform, but never allow anyone to sabotage the culture, no matter how exceptional they may be.

- People are employed by companies but go into battle for leaders and those around them. Relationships are crucial and are built on time invested in getting to know your people.

- A loyal, trustworthy and challenging 'number two', who has a skillset which balances yours, is a priceless asset to any leader.

CHAPTER 6

How the Team Talks

*On the language and tactics
of driving performance*

Sharing hard truths

When a tough conversation needs to be had, most of us, I'm sure, will feel an instinct to put it off. That's rarely a good idea.

In my second season as Middlesbrough manager, I faced a situation with my captain, George Boateng. During the busy Christmas period, we had gone to Portsmouth, turned in a good performance and won 1–0. George had been suspended, so he hadn't played that day. With our next game just three days later, at home to Everton, I decided not to mess with a winning formula and to keep the same starting XI, without George, even though he was now eligible.

Leaving aside the wrongs and rights of this call in itself, my next move was definitely a mistake. I asked my staff whether they thought I needed to speak to George before training and explain my decision to him personally.

From this distance, I can see my own psychology here very clearly: this was an awkward conversation I would have preferred not to have, and I was hoping my staff would give me a reason not to have it. Which they duly did. The consensus was that informing George he wouldn't be in the team wasn't essential, coming off the back of that win – that the move was self-explanatory.

So we went out onto the training ground, with me already feeling, deep down, uneasy about the call we had just made, and, after the players had done their warm-up, I announced the team for the Everton game and broke the squad into groups for training.

I sensed George starting to bubble at his exclusion, but he dutifully took his position in the non-starters group and training began. Literally thirty seconds later, George's replacement in the team, Mohamed Shawky, the Egyptian international, limped off the pitch with a hamstring injury. I then called George over into the team. At which point George understandably became upset with the lack of communication.

Now, I'm happy to say that George and I are friends today, and now that he is himself coaching I know he would accept that he could have responded better to what happened that day, because we ended up with a situation that affected the team – and for a couple of years our own close friendship – which thankfully is behind us now.

And all because of a conversation I didn't have.

Twenty years on, I'm wiser. For one thing, I wouldn't

have made a final decision on team selection so early; I would have allowed the players to train, rotated people in and out so that everyone knew their jobs but not the starting XI, and waited until I had clarity on all the medical updates. Often in football, these 'selection headaches' resolve themselves because of unforeseen issues such as player injuries, or a personal issue that forces your hand. In this instance, the whole problem with George would have been avoided if I had bought myself a little more time. Delaying decisions isn't always good practice, but if there's a good chance the delay will give you more information, and therefore a better outcome, it's worth holding out.

Aside from the nuances of juggling selection decisions for a weekend game, the bigger learning for me here was that, by trying to avoid having a difficult conversation, I had created an even bigger issue. George had understandably felt a lack of respect, and that was my fault. It was an exceptionally painful learning for me, not least because the pair of us had been team-mates. But I had to accept that my handling of the situation had given it the opportunity to escalate.

And this is the thing about difficult conversations: often there is unlikely to be a positive outcome for the recipient (and sometimes the messenger) in the short term. At least one person is going to be at best disappointed, and more likely disgruntled and angry. You may, as I did with George, want to delay that tough exchange. But the reality is, it's coming at some point. And in my experience, the longer you put it off, the more of a surprise the difficult conversation is likely to be to the other person, and the tougher the exchange is going to become.

I can say now, though, that this incident shaped my thinking and my conduct in this area forever. It inspired me going forward to ensure that my communication with players was regular, respectful and thought-through. What do I want and need to say? How is this likely to land? How do I want the other person to feel at the end of the discussion or meeting? What might I need to avoid saying that might cause a bigger issue or cause me a problem further down the line because I've set a precedent or given an explanation that could be used against me in the future?

Every conversation needed a plan of some sort. Was I delivering bad news? Was I trying to explain a decision? Was I trying to make a coaching point to challenge the player? Was I trying to make sure a player not in the starting team was motivated and ready to play his part from the bench? All of this needed to be carefully considered and strategised in advance. I quickly learned that if I turned up for difficult conversations underprepared and without absolute clarity on the conversation's desired outcome, then I risked coming across as complacent and detached, and was practically bound to make an already bad situation worse.

It was so important to me to get it right that I even went as far as writing down the desired flow of the conversation in advance, and mentally rehearsing it in my head, before delivering it to the recipient.

As England manager, many of the most difficult conversations involved telling players when they hadn't made it into the squad. In an ideal world, I would always want to do this face-to-face as it shows more respect, empathy and care. It also means you can use body language to spot reactions and adapt more easily in the moment. In effect, it improves your chances of delivering bad news well.

But for a national manager whose players were stationed all over the country, that was frequently impossible, and in many cases I had no choice but to pick up the phone. It was never satisfactory, but it was unavoidable.

However, I could at least adopt for those calls the same approach that I would have taken had the player and I been directly opposite each other, in accordance with the learnings above. I could plan the conversation thoroughly in advance. I could ensure to the best of my ability that the person was hearing this news from me before they heard it from anyone else. I could explain the reasons behind my decision and do so with respect. I could prepare in advance for any kind of reaction that they might have. And, if appropriate, I could remind the player of my belief in them and make them aware they had every opportunity to earn their place back in the future. Even if that caused another set of difficult conversations with someone else they might be replacing.

I was keenly aware of the emotional stakes here. At international level, not getting selected carries implications even more devastating for a player than not being picked for that weekend's game. And when you're telling people that they haven't made it into the squad for a major tournament, that only intensifies. For some of these players, going to a World Cup with England was a lifetime dream. And I had to be the person who told them this wouldn't be happening. Failure to get a much-desired promotion is going to be deflating in any job. But maybe you would at least have the option to take a view, switch roles – switch countries, even. That wasn't the case here: this was all or nothing. And it wasn't just the player's dreams you were dashing in that conversation; it was the dreams of their partners and families and the people who had supported them through their careers and had yearned for this moment too. So I never underestimated the responsibility and impact of these conversations.

Because of this human dimension, I gave a lot of thought to how we finalised a squad, as we approached a tournament, under my leadership. I'd seen this done in a variety of ways as an England player – not all of them perfect. Mostly the policy had been, at the last camp prior to a World Cup or European Championships, to invite along more players than were eventually going to be needed. This made a certain amount of sense because there were always warm-up matches to negotiate at that stage which could cause injuries and necessitate last-minute replacements. But it was incredibly harsh on the players who ended up getting cut. One minute you're on the verge of representing your country in a European Championship or a World Cup; the next you're going home to face your family and friends and tell them that you didn't make it.

In 1998, I was part of Glenn Hoddle's England squad that travelled to La Manga in Spain for a final camp ahead of the World Cup in France. Our group was five players over the twenty-three-man squad quota because, I imagine, with two warm-up games to get through in that period, Glenn wouldn't have wanted to risk travelling any lighter. However, this then meant that a last-minute cull had to take place.

Glenn, to his credit, wanted to do this humanely – by talking to every player individually in a hotel room set aside for that very purpose. Practically, though, this involved a board going up with twenty-eight separate appointment times on it – in hindsight quite clearly front-weighted with the lads who were about to be chopped. Meanwhile the whole camp was in a state of high anxiety, something which ran right through the entire squad. I was a regular starter for England at that time, but, until I'd had my meeting, I was still on edge, and so, seemingly, was everyone else.

As the meetings began, most of us gathered round the pool from where, quite by chance, we could see the balcony of the room belonging to John Gorman, Glenn's assistant. Some players were clearly going to John to try and get advance notice of their fate – including, as it happened, Paul Gascoigne. We watched as John emerged from the room with Gazza, visibly trying to calm him down, Gazza having, however indirectly, picked up wind that he was about to be sent home. That, of course, sent another ripple through the group. 'He's not going!' 'He's not taking Gazza!' It was a shock and, of course, a huge story. Gazza, famously, did not take the news well and left the camp immediately and without his luggage.

On that occasion, selection had inadvertently become a spectacle involving the entire squad, which ideally, as a leader, one would want to avoid. In 2002, I saw Sven-Göran Eriksson take a different approach by picking a World Cup squad with a handful of pre-designated stand-by players. Everyone knew their role and it was much calmer, and it remained in my mind as a reference point when I was later thinking about how best to manage a 'clean' and drama-free selection process ahead of Russia 2018.

I also benefited at that time from an enormously honest and valuable session with Stuart Lancaster, who went through all of the learning he took as coach from the 2015 Rugby World Cup, where England had not managed to qualify from the group stages. Stuart warned us that taking too many players with us pre-tournament could give the feel of a 'selection camp' when ideally we wanted a 'performance camp' honing the team. That chimed with me. In my own playing experiences, it was only after the squad was finally confirmed that a level of anxiety left us and everyone bonded and focused in on the tournament ahead.

So, for Russia I named a squad plus an additional group, including Adam Lallana and Tom Heaton, who were only with us for the preparation unless injuries occurred. And I was able to repeat that method successfully ahead of the 2020 Euros, too. Again, it's about the benefits the whole organisation reaps when you give people clarity about their roles.

At the Qatar World Cup in 2022, the issue didn't arise. The tournament took place in the middle of our league season, so there was only a week of build-up, which enabled me to take the squad and no extras. It was only ahead of the 2024 Euros that I had to revert to the old-school way of doing things. We found ourselves facing numerous doubts over fitness and needing to assess key players in the warm-ups, and that meant taking additional players to whom it was impossible, in the circumstances, to offer clarity. I found that enormously frustrating. In the months leading up to any tournament I would be having constant conversations with the players to let them know where they stood in the batting order, as it were, so that at any point everyone would have the clearest picture possible of their likelihood for selection. That was a key part of keeping the squad on track and maintaining motivation among the subs, and it's obviously a key practice for leadership: communicate constantly to let people know where they stand. A continuous loop of discussion and feedback will make these challenging conversations easier when they come, too. But in football, injuries throw the best-laid plans out of the window and that was painfully the case ahead of Euro 24.

There were young players in the group for that tournament (Curtis Jones, Jarrad Branthwaite, Jarell Quansah) who probably knew they were unlikely to make it. And then there were Jack Grealish and James Maddison, whose hopes were higher. The day I told those two they wouldn't be coming, I also had to leave Harry Maguire behind, on injury grounds. So that was three big characters lost at once, which had a tangible impact on the group. You sometimes see 'survivor syndrome' in those circumstances, with players asking themselves 'Why me, not them?', not to mention people simply being upset on behalf of their friends. There were no dramas: indeed, unlike what can sometimes happen in football teams, none of the left-behind players created a public issue, reflecting, I like to think, both their maturity in accepting the calls and also their feeling that they had been dealt with as respectfully as possible. Whatever their feelings towards me, we avoided an issue for the team. But there was certainly heartache and sadness and I was forcibly reminded why I had tried so hard to avoid this particular selection scenario for so long.

If non-selection had its stresses, then de-selection had its own particular emotional issues, too. Sometimes along the way, as my time in the role lengthened, I found myself eventually having to leave out players with whom I had lived through some incredible England experiences and forged a deep emotional bond – players with whom I had history, in the best sense. This is the journey: you set off with these players and advance together for a period, but the brutal meritocracy of football and the need to progress inevitably leads to churn. You get extremely close to these people, know them thoroughly, consider them your own. But form, fitness, psychology, tactics, competition for places, considerations of how best to prepare for the future – all these things could be competing at various times to force you to make decisions about these players and their futures, leaving sentiment entirely out of the equation. It calls for ice-cold objectivity and the tightest possible focus on the future performance of the team.

A case in point was when I had to tell Jordan Henderson that he wouldn't be in the prep squad for the 2024 Euros – this despite the immense shifts he had put in on behalf of the England project over the years, and the benefit I had personally reaped from his consummate professionalism, not least with the younger players, which I talked about earlier. But the harsh reality was, at the point that I picked the squad, Jordan was about to turn thirty-four and hadn't been getting enough minutes of top-quality football to justify his inclusion ahead of other candidates. It was a horrible decision, but I had to be tough and make it.

I remember hearing Sir Alex Ferguson talk about dropping Jim Leighton, Manchester United's first-choice goalkeeper, for the replay of the FA Cup final against Crystal Palace in 1990 (back in the days when replays were a thing), after the first tie had ended 3–3. Thirty years later, they still hadn't spoken. I sincerely hope that won't be the case with players I left out of squads, but I also have to understand and accept the enormous disappointment they would have experienced as a consequence of my decisions. That's the landscape as manager: I had to make those hard calls, the calls I felt would get the best team on the pitch at that particular time. My own emotions simply couldn't come into it.

And then, when people react to the decisions you've made as leader, whether predictably or unpredictably, you've simply got to soak those reactions up and not be hard on yourself about them. In the same way that you hope the players aren't going to be taking it personally, you have to refuse to take it personally also. My old coach Steve Harrison once said to me, about a manager's relationship with his players: 'They might fall out with you, but you should never fall out with them.' That's a valuable piece of advice to try to hold onto very firmly in leadership, wherever you are doing it.

You see it differently as a player – you are on the receiving end of, at best, disappointing news and, at worst, something devastating. You can understand, in some cases, why that may lead to anger, bitterness, and even resentment. But I am sure every player would prefer an objective decision, explained carefully and delivered compassionately, rather than delaying the inevitable or an ambiguous explanation when it arrives. Here, again, I could call on my own experience. I was frustrated, near the end of my international career, when Sven-Göran Eriksson took the decision not to put me in his starting England teams. He didn't really give me an answer when I asked him what I needed to improve upon to get back in. I was extremely fond of Sven, and he was probably just being kind (notwithstanding the fact it would've taken him a while to explain everything I needed to improve on). But, frankly, if he'd said, 'Look, I've got Sol Campbell and Rio Ferdinand, and they're bigger, stronger, quicker and generally better than you,' I probably would have shrugged my shoulders, said, 'Fair enough,' and gone back to training with the reserves.

Clarity is always important at moments like that. If there's a way back, a person deserves to know. And if there really *isn't* a way back, a person deserves to know that, too. It was a rule I always tried as best I could to apply.

Sometimes, I wasn't just leaving a player out of a camp by not selecting them; I was, in effect, bringing down the curtain on their days as an international, ending a whole phase of their lives. It was a truly dreadful position to be in. But it wasn't something I was going to back off from. I felt I had to give new players their chance – and the opportunity, sometimes, to grow without being overshadowed by big players behind them on the bench. And those big players were owed the respect of my honesty when that was the case.

Wayne Rooney was a case in point, when, you may remember, I left him out of the squad in May 2017. Wayne had missed the previous camp too, in March, but that was through injury. He was still not getting game-time at Manchester United under José Mourinho – the reason I had put him back on the bench for the World Cup qualifier against Slovenia the previous year. He was thirty-one and short of matches, and so many other players in that area of the pitch had come into form around him: Harry Kane, Jermain Defoe, Marcus Rashford, Jamie Vardy, Adam Lallana, Dele Alli . . . And with such a rich source of talent coming through, deep down I thought this could be the end of the road for Wayne.

I really had no idea how this decision was likely to play with Wayne but I had made the decision a week in advance, which meant I had time to travel to see him and could at least be face-to-face with him when I said my piece. I needn't have been so anxious. Wayne listened and then surprised me by practically taking the burden of the moment out of my hands. He acknowledged that this was a transition period for him, that he was closing in on retirement, and that the time was clearly coming for him to stop playing international football altogether. The humility and dignity Wayne showed me in that moment has really stayed with me. The kicker here was that Wayne then left Manchester United for Everton, began making regular appearances and started scoring goals again. That August, three months after I had de-selected him, I found myself asking Wayne to re-join the squad for our games against Malta and Slovakia. Wayne very graciously declined and elected instead to retire from international football formally. It illustrated how vital it was to make those non-selection exchanges go as well as possible, as you never knew when you might be calling someone back. But it also showed me how impactful it was for a recipient to receive difficult news in a dignified way. If a hard truth is delivered fairly, and the recipient responds well, it will leave a lasting and positive impression on the person sharing the news.

Telling players they were no longer part of my plans was an aspect of management that I never relished, but it was one I moved towards, as best I could, with purpose and courage. In my experience, there is no way of making this aspect of leadership easy. But there is preparation we can do, which at least means we perform in these regrettable moments as well as we can, which is to say with maximum consideration for the recipient.

In my business, the team was always going to come first, of course, and performance ultimately had to come before feelings. But as leaders we should never lose sight of the key fact: the primary component of the machine we are seeking to optimise is human. Sadly, I've seen that crucial truth overlooked in redundancy processes, both at businesses I've worked at and elsewhere. I'm sure that people justifying this would be quick to invoke legal reasons, but I've been involved in a number of restructures which have been, to my mind, completely inhumane, with people in management positions given scripts to read from and instructions not to engage in further dialogue. This has felt anything but compassionate and transparent and it has always resulted in massive disgruntlement, with even 'survivors' who retain their roles ending up feeling real resentment for the organisation because of the process. Perhaps HR experts will shake their heads and accuse me of naivety for advocating 'honest conversations' at such junctures, but I can only point to the impact I've felt in a management position and observed on the shop floor.

Managing expectations

There's something else I've noticed about difficult conversations. They can often become far less difficult if you give continuous and honest feedback prior to them.

It's my opinion that most teams and organisations never reach their full potential because they avoid these regular, sometimes micro-, moments of candid appraisal around performance. Conversations that challenge positively are sincere and truthful in nature, and delivered as soon as you have the opportunity to have them. And I'm not just talking down the chain of command, but feedback up it too.

At England, I tried as hard as possible to continually feed back to players on the areas where I thought they were performing well and the areas where I thought they had room for improvement.

Notwithstanding the obvious benefit in terms of their development, I also wanted to be as transparent as possible about where players sat in the pecking order of selection, so that there would be minimal surprises when a team was announced and a rival for an individual's position was named ahead of them. Generally, this approach saved tougher conversations further down the line, and had the extra benefit that players could prepare themselves for the likelihood of starting or being on the bench, ready to contribute.

Managing underperformance

Of course, giving positive feedback was often quick and easy; players love to hear good news – don't we all. More critical assessments of their performance needed to be delivered more sensitively.

It helped that I had a reference point from my own playing days, when coaches would think nothing of pulling me to the side to deliver an unfiltered, pointed and, sometimes, brutally honest assessment of my shortcomings. Commonly known in football as a b******ing. I would instinctively take it personally and the whole interaction would feel negative and deflating. Worse still if it was done in public, or in front of my team-mates. Rather than being inspired to improve, I would resent the message, and the messenger too.

Even so, once the criticism had sunk in, I would eventually register that the coach had a point: there was an area that needed my attention. And then I'd want to know how to set about improving.

Over time I eventually realised that the coach who pulled

me up sharply and told me something I didn't want to hear wasn't just trying to 'shred' me; he was ultimately trying to help me become better. But if I had known that when the criticism was delivered, it would have made the process a lot quicker and more comfortable.

Now that it was me in that position, addressing performance issues with players, I wondered if there was another way to go about it. What I realised was that criticism from a leader is going to be easier to hear, and easier to act upon, if it's obvious there is a shared desire for a positive outcome. If you can create a sense of shared ownership, of a mutual goal, then you can potentially ensure that criticism lands constructively every time. And that was what I wanted to cultivate as a manager.

It also helped, I think, that I understood the England players' world. I could relate to playing for England, how good it could be, how tough it could be. It helped, too, I'm sure, that I was happy to show vulnerability, certainly with regard to my own playing career, and also sometimes as a manager, when I thought I could have made better decisions around a game. I would be prepared to put a hand up and admit my own mistakes when I made them.

Consequently, when underperforming players were challenged by me, I don't believe that they felt unfairly 'dug out'. On the contrary, they were able to feel that I was working with them to make things better. It didn't mean that I was going to back off on individual criticism, but it did mean that I was going to frame that criticism as a challenge to improve, a challenge in which both of us – leader and team member – had an equal, vested interest.

The debrief – formal and informal feedback

As well as managing expectations and managing under-performance, one of the great advantages of giving regular, direct feedback is that it helps a leader to develop individuals, which in turn has the benefit of improving the whole team. Sport provides a natural cadence for such feedback to be shared in the aftermath of games and performances.

At England, as a group of coaches we would debrief after every match and training session, and then we would decide how we were going to deliver the key messages back to the players. This feedback would usually take the form of meetings with the whole group, but sometimes in smaller units, such as the defenders, for example, or one-to-one sessions with individuals.

Again, as we have discussed previously, all of these meetings were planned and thought-through. Who was going to deliver the meeting? What information did we want to get across? What outcomes were we hoping for?

I led all of the team 'debriefs' with players. Within these, there were times when I wanted opinions from the floor and other times where I wanted to get very clear points across, with no discussion. The beauty of having multiple camera angles these days for matches is that there can no longer be confusion about what happened in a game. A lot of time was spent with our analysts preparing for these meetings, ensuring the weight of evidence was incontrovertible. I am sure that, with the wealth of data available to most businesses these days, such analysis of performance is also likely to be readily available, whatever your line of work.

The other balance I always had to find in delivering feedback was how critical to be and what tone to adopt, particularly in front of the whole group of players. Of course, individual criticism is better delivered one-to-one. This protects ego and saves embarrassment for the individual. There is also more opportunity to couch one criticism in several compliments, which can help to avoid too big a blow to the person's confidence.

However, sometimes points needed to be made and the whole group needed to witness them – particularly if a senior player had shown a lack of effort or made a poor decision. The group would know what had happened, and they would be waiting to see whether I was going to have the courage to call out the 'big name' players, or brush over them and only criticise the 'easier targets'. I never went looking for confrontation in these moments, but I certainly knew I needed to be consistent in challenging everybody.

What the coaching team and I learned over the years was that when we wanted more interaction and input from players, our meetings with smaller units or one-to-ones with individuals were far more productive. People tended to be more reluctant to speak up in bigger groups. As our groups became smaller, our discussions became more open, and we all learned more.

Counter-intuitively, our debriefs were often more critical after we'd won, because we wanted to double down on standards and avoid complacency. And frankly, we'd sometimes win without playing well. So the emphasis was always on the performance, not the result. That also meant that when we lost, we often focused more on things we had done well. We never avoided the details that might have cost us the game, but unless we'd been awful and performed below standard, there were normally lots of good things to analyse. This helped keep the confidence of the group high and demonstrate that we were on the right track. We just needed to address the small details.

When it came to individual performance debriefs with players, it was impossible for me to have eleven or more detailed sessions, with all the footage that goes with them, after every match we played. So I tended to delegate and trust these to my coaches with a clear brief from myself, but I always made sure to speak with my coaches afterwards to check how things had gone and what had been discussed. This meant I was up to speed with everything.

I saved my individual meetings with players for broader performance discussions, or general 'catch-ups' on what was going on in their lives. I often preferred to keep these informal – we'd have them perhaps over a cup of coffee, or walking off the training pitch. Some players were still awkward talking to 'the boss' and there was also a thirty-year age gap at times, so I wanted the players to feel as comfortable as possible in 'opening up'. The more I knew what was going on with them, the more I could help them.

That said, I wasn't looking to make every conversation comfortable. To improve, there has to be some critical feedback or at least a 'challenge' thrown down for the individual to respond to.

These discussions often started with me asking questions and listening a lot. I wanted a sense of whether the player and I viewed his form similarly, or whether behaviours and any external factors (a problem at home perhaps) might have been affecting his form. At least if the player was conscious about underperforming or some specific issues, I felt I was pushing at an open door and was able to move quickly towards creating a plan to help them to improve. If there was less self-awareness then the performance review could naturally become a little more awkward.

Some players I have managed (and I would have included my younger self in this category) could be overly critical of themselves. In their performance reviews I would take a different tack, trying to help them to keep their individual mistakes in perspective, and to encourage them to recognise the areas where they were doing well.

As a young coach, I found this whole process more uncomfortable. Now my view is simple: I'm going to try and help you become a better player or a better individual in your role and so even though this might be a difficult truth for you to hear, it's coming from a good place. I obviously still think about my language and how I frame these messages, but ultimately I've learned that it's up to the recipient to be open to feedback and, even more importantly, to be prepared to take the advice on board.

If I was at a football club, or if I was in a more conventional business that didn't limit my access to the team, I would have had more opportunity to address performance issues and influence them with day-to-day conversations. But nonetheless, areas for improvement were regularly discussed at international level. And they also applied to me.

Feedback on me

The longer I was in the role at England, the more concerned I became that people would avoid challenging me. I'd seen some organisations where the boss was an object of too much respect or too much fear. Either way, it meant that the boss wasn't challenged enough. People would avoid passing on feedback that could help the whole organisation, or they might soften it so much that the boss would regard it as unimportant.

I have encountered some leaders whose 'door is always open' but who don't really take well to being challenged. The best people I have met within football and in business have wanted to know everything that might make them better. In fact, they would hate the thought that people had ideas or feedback they didn't pass on, or were disgruntled and didn't share the real issues that they saw or felt.

I remember a few times at the FA we carried out '360 degree' feedback, a method of performance analysis that I know is widely used across organisations in a variety of industries. It was an opportunity for people who worked with you, and for you, to provide honest, anonymous feedback without fear of recrimination. And I was all for it. It was a way for me to ask my staff 'what do you think I could do better?' without putting them on the spot.

The feedback I received? Well, the biggest learning for me was that people worried I would get dragged away from the most important business because the demands on my time were so great and so varied. Added to the fact that my natural instinct was always to give people time, it meant I had to be extra vigilant when it came to all the things you would like to do versus all the things only you can do. My wonderful PA Josie – unlike the equally wonderful Catherine from Middlesbrough, who I failed to delegate enough to – became an expert in saying 'no' ever so politely to requests that would drag me away from all the things I was ultimately responsible and accountable for. That's a lot of video messages, appearances and auction prizes I probably owe.

Talking to your team

There are times as a leader, in any field, when the continuous beat of managing and sharing feedback makes way for the moment of truth. Whether it's the final briefing for a boardroom pitch, rallying soldiers before they go into battle, or, in my case, readying players for a knockout game, this is the final huddle before it's time to perform.

At England I was constantly reflecting on how, when and where to deliver these team talks to maximise the impact on the players' and the team's performance. You would think that right before kick-off is the optimum moment to deliver such an address, just when a final download of information can stay fresh in the players' minds. But in my experience this is the worst time to do it.

My final team talk usually happened a couple of hours before kick-off, in a quiet meeting room just before we boarded the bus. The timing and place mattered: controlled, free from the noise and distractions of the stadium, close enough to game time to sharpen focus, but far enough away to avoid overload.

All the scenario planning, the briefing on roles and positioning, and the purposeful practice as groups and individuals — all this was already done. Every communication with the team up to that point, from my welcome at the beginning of each camp to the continuous messages we layered in throughout training, had been psychologically preparing them for the game.

So this final talk was consolidation, and no more.

The very worst time to teach or coach someone is, in my experience, on the threshold of performance, when tension is rising and the working memory narrows; big downloads go in one ear and out the other.

In this last pre-match address, I would always keep it clear and uncomplicated, looking for the balance between emotion — rousing players for the game — and reinforcing the game-plan. Finding that sweet spot between anxiety at one end of the spectrum and complacency at the other.

It's easier to convey these things as a leader if your team

can 'see' them in you first. Players would 'read' my body language well before they heard my words. I wanted my team to be fired up and excited about the challenge ahead, but also steadily confident in their ability to deliver. I did my best to project these emotions as much in my demeanour as I did in the message of the team talk itself.

Once my final address was done, I would tend to say very little, formally, in the remainder of the build-up to the match. And I believed that in saying very little, it actually said a lot: 'I trust you, I support you, I believe in you.' I wanted the players to feel like they 'owned' the game – not to be hearing my voice, or the voices of the other coaching staff at that point, but to be focusing on themselves and their own preparation.

As a player myself in these situations, I'd often felt ready just before a game, only for a manager to 'talk over' my own readiness; I wasn't going to do the same. My job in these final minutes was to read the room, offer a quiet word where it was needed – a small reminder or reassurance one-to-one – and then get out of the way, so that experienced athletes could follow their routines and arrive at kick-off in the right headspace.

I thought it would be good if, as an extension of that 'owning the game' process, the last person the players heard from collectively before they went out onto the pitch was one of their own. So, a few minutes before kick-off, I would ask the captain to address the team. In my time, that was usually Harry Kane. I think most of us, when we imagine a piece of oratory that's designed to energise a team just before it goes into battle, instinctively think of the rabble-rousing, 'Once more unto the breach'/'band of brothers'/'dogs of war' type stuff as the basic model, accompanied by a lot of pounding on the badge – the full Shakespeare breakfast. When it came to rhetoric, that brand of eye-bulging, warrior-like emoting wasn't Harry's style, nor was it ever likely to be.

But there are plenty of other ways to convey belief, to instil confidence, to express the meaning of an occasion and to bring people with you. If Harry and the others weren't up to Shakespeare's standard, and if they were out of their comfort zone in that moment, it was fine by me – I wanted them to get comfortable with being uncomfortable. And the real point was that I was handing the game over to them – after all, I wasn't going to be with them on the pitch. They were going to be the ones handling it.

At those matches where Harry wasn't available, I would delegate the pre-match talk to whomever I had given the armband in his place. Over time, we must have seen eight or nine different players stand up to do it, and I found it fascinating to see the different ways they handled the challenge and the different tones they struck. None were identical in style. Some talked with great ease, and seemed to know just what to say in that moment. Others initially got in a bit of a pickle. It wasn't down to a lack of ability; it was purely the newness of the experience. And, as briefly uncomfortable as it might have been, they all got through.

Feeding back under pressure

What effect can a manager really have in the short moments available to him in a half-time interval? What can you say to a team of tired, possibly emotional players, in the briefest of windows, when there are forty-five minutes still to play, the stakes are high, the energy levels are low, when some need a bandage, some need an orange and some need the toilet, when some are requiring reassurance and others require a prod?

Very little, really. But your 'very little' can still have an enormous impact.

I learned this the hard way as a young manager at Middlesbrough. In one match, returning to the dressing room after a disappointingly under-powered first half, I decided I was going to try and shake the team awake by showing them a side of me that they hadn't seen. Venting had never been my style, but on this occasion, I was going to vent.

To a stunned reception, I went in loud and hard. I went firmly at one of the players in particular – telling him that his challenging for the ball had been feeble for forty-five minutes and that I wanted far more assertion from him. I may have used other words than 'feeble' and 'assertion'.

It certainly fired the player up. In response to this confusingly out-of-character dressing-down from his manager, he went out for the second half, launched himself almost immediately into an over-aggressive tackle and received a straight red card.

Now, it could be said that on the pitch the player is responsible for his own actions. But in this case, with the player trudging back down the tunnel to the dressing room, I had to acknowledge my part in the offence. My approach had not been helpful. And, quite apart from the fact that we didn't end up winning that game, the episode brought another lesson home to me.

That incident starkly demonstrated that people will respond to criticism differently, depending on their own characters, and that I needed to be far more flexible around that than I was being at the time. If I wanted to get the best performance from my team then it was on me to tune in, ensure that I knew the characters of my players thoroughly, and tailor my communications to them accordingly. In these circumstances, it is typically assumed that the best tools in a leader's box are shouting, heckling and reading the riot act. But in this case, as so often, the best tool was emotional intelligence.

There are famous clips on YouTube of apoplectic managers mercilessly tearing lumps out of their players at half-time, while those players tremble and stare at the ground in silence and mortification. The scenes look like ancient history now, and that's because they are. I can't think of a single elite manager operating in the game at present who works that way. Certainly nobody's buying that approach in an international dressing room, and I don't see why anybody should be buying it in any modern workplace.

With England, the half-time interval was carefully choreographed. We valued consistency here as much as we valued it anywhere else in the operation. While the players took time to gather themselves, relax and take on nutrition and fluids, I would be consulting with the coaching staff – a summary, effectively, of the conversations we'd been having on the bench through the first half – to finalise the key points we needed to make. We'd also receive a medical update so that we could take a view on players who were struggling with something and might need replacing, now or later.

Then I would address the players. Tone-wise, it was always about judging the moment and the psychological state of the team. Had their performance been anxious and did they need reassurance and composed tactical advice? Were they dominating the opponent and did we need as a team to guard against complacency? Or had the players already been complacent and did they need a more challenging approach to shake them out of their state? Sometimes as a leader you need to offer the team the right kind of energy and use that brief period of time you have to try and alter their collective mental state.

The risks of destructive overload at that point were as high as they were just before the match, and perhaps even more so given that the players now had forty-five minutes of football in their limbs. The watchwords were: concision, consolidation, clarity.

Choosing the moment to have your say

In health management – and also in some specialist areas of the military – they talk about two types of performance review: the 'hot debrief' and the 'delayed debrief'. The hot debrief is a review conducted as close as possible to the relevant event, evaluating responses and performances while what happened is still vivid in everyone's minds. The delayed debrief, by contrast, is a more considered, structured review taking place with the benefit of some distance.

Football's version of the hot debrief would be the conversation in the dressing room directly after the game. Its version of the delayed debrief would be the review of the game the following day, back on the training ground. Instinctively, my preference was for the latter. The time to gather and reflect always seemed valuable to me, along with the opportunity to watch the game back in full and discuss things with players who had, by then, at least had a chance to get their breath back.

However, one idiosyncrasy about international football is that, when the second match in the international week is at home, the players get changed afterwards and head off into the night. They would go back to their clubs and that would potentially be the last I would see of them for a month. On those occasions, I found myself conducting a hot debrief whether I liked it or not. Players would be tired, emotions would potentially still be running high, and I literally had about five minutes to sum up the prior ten days of camp, before I would get swept off for my media duties.

It was far from ideal. In that circumstance, I certainly didn't avoid saying when I thought we had underperformed. At the same time, I knew it was counterproductive to be really critical, with no opportunity to pick up with the group the following morning when emotions had settled. My critical message would have been the last thing the players heard from me – the impression they left the camp with. Mindful of that, my model at those moments was the one used by Terry Venables, who had always preferred to watch the game back again before passing judgement.

Thankfully, we hardly lost a qualifier across my eight years and so it was rare we left those camps on a low. I did confront that situation after some Nations League games, though – the worst being in June 2022 when we got hammered 4–0 by Hungary at Molineux. This was the last of four matches that summer – a ridiculously busy schedule in a non-tournament year – and the players were going to be leaving for their summer breaks straight afterwards. Some of the media suggested one or two had already left. I had rotated the team, which certainly ended up giving us the opportunity to find out a few things about a few players, but not the things I would necessarily have chosen to find out at that point. We were soundly beaten and everyone was shellshocked. When I spoke, I tried to frame what we needed to learn from the experience, but I knew deep down that I was the one who would be living with this result for weeks, while the players headed off to the beach and, likely, switched off. I must say, though, I couldn't blame them for that after the demands of the football calendar.

A hot debrief can certainly be a learning opportunity – and having studied, visited and spoken to the Red Arrows air display team, I know that they are big believers in them. For our purposes, however, I felt the delayed debrief, with time for emotions to cool, allowed for calmer, more objective reflection and potentially more durable feedback. We would have data on hand to support deep analysis. We would have been able to watch the matches again – and I lost count of the times I had looked at tapes and found myself thinking, 'Actually, we weren't as good as I thought,' or conversely, 'Actually, there were more positives there than I had realised.' And it enabled us to cover key performance areas systematically, and gave an opportunity for constructive discussion.

It also – and this was almost certainly its chief advantage – gave greater scope than a post-match scramble for giving proper weight to the things we had done well. Those should never be entirely out of the frame in any performance review. There can be a tendency to regard the chief business of performance monitoring as 'catching somebody doing something wrong'. On the contrary, we were taught on youth development courses the benefit of 'catching somebody doing something right' – praising and reinforcing the positive behaviours rather than constantly pulling people up. I took that policy into senior management and I think it could usefully sit at the heart of all performance reviewing, not just in football.

Managing elite performers

Even in teams packed with talent, you sometimes find individuals who are truly world-class. They come in all shapes and sizes (quite literally, when you think of Messi and Ronaldo), they can be prodigies or legends, introverts or extroverts, a talisman or a showman. In football, these individuals win games, they are often unplayable and, like it or not, they tend to attract a media circus.

These people are vital to a team – but can bring challenges of their own. And as a leader, I would always ask myself if they needed extra attention, or a different style of management, to maximise their potential, get them to gel with the team, and minimise the external noise and distraction. Even before I was a manager, I witnessed how complex but crucial these individuals could be.

As a player, Paul Gascoigne was extraordinary. Instinctive and improvisational in the way he played the game, he could change the course of a match with a single moment of brilliance – and frequently did so. Our England careers crossed from 1995 to 1998, and it was a privilege to play alongside him during those years. He was the most talented footballer I ever played with.

But if he was a handful for the opposition, he was also a handful for the manager. Gazza stories are, of course, legion. All of his team-mates can tell you a horde of them. I have a memory of watching Terry Venables, then the England manager, give a live interview to the BBC from our hotel during a tournament. Behind his back, Gazza appears, clad only in a white dressing gown, and begins dancing and larking for the camera. It was the only time I saw Venables completely lose his rag.

Only after I became a manager myself did I come to appreciate the full extent of the challenge Terry must have faced in leading that team. By his own admission, Gazza tested the boundaries of professional conduct. It was just the way he was wired. Self-discipline, in the way that most other players understood it, simply wasn't on his agenda. But he also delivered when it mattered most. He was an outlier, a match-winner, and in football – or any high-performance setting under pressure – we need these match-winners.

Whether it's the speculative trader dealing in risk, the software developer finding solutions to complex coding problems or the maverick striker who scores you a hat-trick, unique specialists often don't sit naturally in a team environment.

As an aside, I have observed non-conformists in my teams – both staff and players – who haven't been the equivalent of world-class match-winners, but whose strong contributions have still been well worth the extra effort required in managing them. Some individuals have been quieter or more introverted, and might not always mix well with others in some social environments, but they might still be very prepared to strongly challenge others in a positive way for the team due to their own significant talent. It is worth embracing these idiosyncrasies for high-performance. As a player, I witnessed the careers of a number of elite footballers who were very strong-willed and, at times, bold enough not to go with the crowd in terms of feeling the need to fit in socially. These characters were 'different' yet hugely valuable to their teams.

But whether you are managing match-winners or more outspoken team members, how do you accommodate these personalities without it being perceived by the rest of the group as special treatment? I know from conversations with business leaders that this is as much an issue in the wider world of work as it was for me at England. How do we maintain unity in the face of an individual's potential challenge to it?

During my eight years in charge, we were never handling what you might describe as a Gazza scenario – i.e. a situation in which our best player by a mile was also our most high-maintenance player by an equal distance. But we certainly did have 'high-maintenance players', those individuals that consistently managed to get themselves into situations that required the possibility of disciplinary action, or at least a discussion as to whether they needed reining in. They became the most regular individuals discussed in staff meetings. They were the players I ended up having the most one-to-one meetings with.

It's hard to know if they sought out this attention (I expect in some instances they did) or whether they were just rebels who lived life to the full, and had a different view of risk and 'normal behaviour' to most people. I wondered whether these types of individuals had an unusually developed sense of their own worth and value to teams, and had been aware of this value from a very young age. Consequently, they had perhaps been indulged throughout their careers. I suspect they occasionally wanted to remind leaders 'you need me, don't forget it!' Whatever the reason, and there is likely a kernel of truth in myriad interpretations, the same traits that make these individuals tricky to manage often also make them creative or special.

Without a doubt we had important players who were

high-maintenance – pushing boundaries on time-keeping, wanting to report later than the rest of the squad, missing a camp, and so forth. At times there were personal issues in the public domain – usually incidents on club duty – that forced us to ask: *Can we really pick them with that hanging over them?* For England, the bar is higher in terms of public scrutiny and what is deemed acceptable. What might pass at club level could quickly become a complex and even, at times, national debate.

Fortunately, by the very nature of the environment, mis-behaving players were less of an issue for the national team. You have far less time together – which means less opportunity for trouble (though not impossible, I should say) – and there are no binding contractual issues. So if a player wasn't meeting our expectations in terms of behaviour, we could just decide to de-select them and then see if they were prepared to change their ways. Some did, some didn't.

The key principle for me was unity. When someone crossed a line, I would always highlight the impact of their actions, comments, body language – or whatever it was – on the broader team. Often I would ask, 'Do you see the issue this causes me? Do you understand how your team-mates might view it?' Framing the issue in terms of the group was usually the most powerful lever. And when disciplinary measures had to be enforced, consistency mattered more than anything. It's one thing to drop a young player when they push the bound-aries of, say, time-keeping. But when you drop a senior player for doing so – which I had to do on a couple of occasions – it sends a powerful message about the firmness of the lines that you have drawn. It says, very straightforwardly: 'I stand by these rules, and so should you.'

But there was another side to this. If the 'difficult' players consume too much of your energy, the quieter, more reliable members of the squad risk being overlooked, which can cause the quiet creep of disharmony. To keep the balance, I made a point of checking in with the lower-maintenance players – who always had issues, like everyone else, but who were more likely in temperament to dutifully get on with things without making a fuss. I loved talking to them and would often say, 'Look, you're a dream to work with and sometimes I forget to tell you that. Thank you.' Yes, a simple 'thank you' can go a long way in elite sport. Or, if I thought they were going through a difficult period, and if I didn't think they were really as 'fine' as they said they were, I would offer support by saying, 'I trust you to get on with things, but I recognise this is a tough moment. How can I help?' A simple question like this can go a long way too.

Ultimately, it's the culture you've established as a leader that must be preserved, and tolerance of a maverick performer must always be seen to serve the greater good of the team. Work hard to keep them in line so they can unleash their brilliance, and work equally hard to sell this pact to the group itself, who will only tolerate a high-maintenance talent as long as the performance is there.

But nobody, however gifted, can be allowed to tip the group into disruption or division and derail the mission. That was my absolute red line and, I have to admit, at times it was a fine line to tread.

My assistant coach, Steve Holland, had a neat way of putting it: 'We love low-maintenance, high-performance. We'll accept high-maintenance, high-performance. But high-maintenance and low-performance? That's for no one.' That, in the end, is the consideration that decides everything.

SUMMARY
How the Team Talks
On the language and tactics of driving performance

- Difficult conversations can, by their nature, be difficult to deliver. Recognise that by putting them off you can risk misalignment with your team, and even resentment from the individual when they do eventually take place. Have the discussions early.

- When delivering bad news, prepare well and be clear about the outcomes. Respect comes through clarity and communication, even if the best achievable outcome from a conversation is to minimise the fallout.

- Tough calls may hurt, disappoint or frustrate your team members, so give each message with empathy and respect. Don't take negative reactions to your feedback and decisions personally. Remember, even if someone falls out with you, never fall out with them.

- Make time for regular developmental feedback. Improving every individual improves the team. Catching underperformance early can avoid much tougher conversations further down the line. Equally, remind yourself that it's good to 'catch people doing things well'.

CONTINUED OVER

- Your people are the heartbeat of your organisation. Be open in your deeds, not just in your words. This means actively listening to your team's challenges, considering their ideas for improvement, and practising being non-judgemental. This will make you more approachable.

- Find the balance between loyalty and fairness. Loyalty to team members is important but cannot be justified if it prevents up-and-coming performers from developing. Ultimately, whatever decision you take, it must always be in the best interests of the team.

- Elite performers can be complicated to manage. High-performance/high-maintenance individuals might be worth the effort if the team outcome is improved, and if the team will accept a compromise along the way to achieving their goal. But never undermine your 'non-negotiable' values for anyone.

CHAPTER 7

One Badge, One Team

On the power of unity

Taking a stand

In the final seconds of time added on in a European Championship qualifier against Montenegro in Podgorica in March 2019, I watched with bafflement as Danny Rose, our left-back, launched himself into an aggressive challenge. It was a late tackle in every sense. Danny was booked and, almost immediately afterwards, the referee blew to end the match.

I didn't get it. We were 5–1 up, the game was won, and Danny's challenge seemed entirely unnecessary. Why would he do that? From my position on the other side of the pitch it looked like an act of pure frustration, as if emotion had got the better of him, and I wasn't impressed. We spoke about this kind of thing all the time in the camps. Back in the dressing room, I made it clear to Danny that I expected far more discipline from my players, from the first whistle right through to the last.

Danny simply let me express my annoyance and didn't respond.

A few minutes later, on my way to face the media, a member of our communications team took me aside. They had been stationed near the home end during the match, and they wanted to let me know what had been going on. Throughout the game, Danny and some of our other black players, including Callum Hudson-Odoi and Raheem Sterling, had been getting appalling racial abuse thrown at them by a section of the Montenegrin fans. On the bench we had heard nothing, but a few of the commentators had picked up on it.

My heart sank. I had just called Danny out over an incident I hadn't properly understood, and disciplined him in circumstances where I should have been offering him support. Worse than that, it appeared to me that Danny felt unable to speak to his own manager about what he had just faced. He hadn't said anything about the abuse at half-time, and nor did he raise it in his defence when I criticised him afterwards.

I knew that Danny had experienced racism in an England shirt previously, while representing our under-21s. That was in Serbia in 2012, when Danny had to play through monstrous abuse from the crowd, including monkey noises, and when he was also, while taking a throw-in, struck by stones. Danny had said afterwards that his concentration on the game had got him through the first hour of this nightmare, and then deserted him. He was sent off after the final whistle for kicking the ball away in frustration and was racially abused by members of the crowd all the way to the tunnel. There was widespread outcry about this afterwards, including from the British government. Yet, after two months of deliberation, Uefa issued the Serbian FA a fine of £65,000 and the instruction to play one game behind closed doors – a paltry punishment.

The saddest part for me in Montenegro was that Danny seemed to believe there was now no point even complaining. Where would it get you, when naked racism, filmed and broadcast, was met with merely dilatory and token action by the authorities? Why would a person in that situation have any faith that the system would protect them? I found myself thinking about Danny's life and wondering how much of this stuff he had had to put up with over time. Playing Sunday football as a kid in Yorkshire? Walking to school? Just being out on the street? How much had he ever been able to feel that society truly had his back against racism? And now, in an England dressing room, I had accidentally weighed in on Danny, too.

On the flight home, I stood up and addressed everyone. I began with a personal apology to Danny for the disgusting abuse he had been the victim of in the match. And I apologised for my lack of understanding in the dressing room. As sincerely as I spoke, I knew that 'apologise and move on' simply wasn't going to cut it. Racism wasn't a new problem in football, of course; it had been a persistent and abhorrent scourge for years. And it had always sickened me. But what happened in Montenegro that night made me see the nature of the situation with stark clarity. And, as the leader, it made me see it from a position of accountability and action. If we were putting our team members in these positions, I had a duty of care. I couldn't just shake my head regretfully and hope this ugly, nasty, 'fringe' stuff would go away. I needed to work out what we, as a team and as an organisation, could do better to protect and support our own people when they faced such depravity. The next time something awful like this happened, I needed us to be ready.

Back at St George's Park, my first step was a full debrief of the events in Montenegro with Martin Glenn, the FA's CEO. He was in complete agreement with me that we needed to be better prepared for these circumstances and gave me his backing to come up with a reactive strategy.

We duly pored over the official Uefa guidance on dealing with racist incidents in stadiums. In 2009, Uefa had drawn up a three-step protocol, 'empowering referees to act against racism'. Essentially, if the referee became aware of racist behaviour from the crowd, the game could be paused and a warning issued over the public address system (step one). If problems persisted, the referee could then halt the game a second time, introduce a suspension 'for a reasonable period of time, for example, five to ten minutes', and then restart the game after a second public warning (step two). If the abuse then continued after the eventual restart, the referee could (step three) decide to abandon the match.

The protocol seemed pretty inadequate to me. It appeared to be giving racism two free strikes. And there were grey areas. The focus was very much on the conduct of the referee. It said nothing about the players' and managers' own agency in all this. It offered no guidance on the exact consequences of a walk-off for a team's continuing participation in any tournament. Under the umbrella of 'zero tolerance', it seemed to be open to highly inconsistent application. And, of course, in Montenegro it hadn't been applied at all. Everything considered, it left a lot up in the air. But these were the rules as we had them.

That autumn we would be coming together for the camp before a Euro 20 qualifier against Bulgaria in Sofia. After Montenegro, this fixture was worrying me. England players, including Ashley Cole, Ashley Young and Theo Walcott, had been subjected to gross racial abuse in Bulgaria during an international in 2011, after which the Bulgarian FA had been fined. Moreover, racist behaviour by some Bulgarian fans in games in June against the Czech Republic and Kosovo had just led to further Uefa sanctions: another £65,000 fine and two games with 'partial stadium closures'. One of those partially closed games would be ours. There were red flags over this fixture, to say the least.

I had a long conversation with Chris Powell from our coaching team. Chris was a former England team-mate, someone I could talk to openly and honestly, and someone with his own dreadful experiences of racism as a black footballer, playing from the late eighties to 2010. I asked Chris what he would have wanted, as a player, going into this Bulgaria game, given what had happened in Montenegro and given the possibility of some kind of flare-up in Sofia. Chris told me that first of all he would have appreciated seeing the issue formally acknowledged within the camp, discussed openly and recognised as a potential problem. This hadn't happened in Chris's experience, and he said it would have led him to feel supported. Beyond that, he would want to know that a clear, universally agreed plan was in place for what the team was going to do if the premonitions proved right and there was a problem on the night.

I was extremely grateful to Chris for his counsel and candour. I made the decision to organise a meeting for the squad, right at the beginning of the camp leading up to the Bulgaria match. Despite the usual pressure to focus straight away on the football due to the time limitations we had with the players, addressing this issue of racist abuse head-on was way more important. My notion was to open the meeting by stating that, in the upcoming game in Bulgaria, we would potentially once again be hearing racist abuse from the crowd, and then I would open it up and encourage people to express themselves on the topic and discuss what we were going to do about it. I talked in advance to Harry Kane and Jordan Henderson and asked them to contribute first. As captain and vice-captain, their status in the team obviously carried weight. But I also felt that it would powerfully establish the theme of support if two white players were the first to express their feelings on the issue.

After much thought, I decided to stage the conversation in our meal room, at the end of dinner. For one thing, it was important that everyone, players and staff alike, should be as comfortable as possible so that they felt able to speak freely, and this informal setting would help with that. We'd be sitting together at tables rather than lined up in ranks and facing the front, as we would have been in the meeting room, and it could more easily become a discussion we were having as a group.

I was sensitive to the fact that sometimes fear of saying the wrong thing, particularly about race, can hold people back. So, when I spoke at the beginning, I tried to make clear that we were talking in a spirit of openness and tolerance. If someone tripped over the wrong phrase or word along the way, I wanted everyone to skip past it in the recognition that we were all targeting the same outcome: the right to play football free from racist abuse and for our team-mates to feel completely supported.

I can't say that it was a comfortable session. I framed the discussion, Harry and Jordan said their pieces. Some of those who had suffered abuse during games, as well as at other times, found the strength to talk about it and spoke particularly powerfully. At the same time, a couple of our black players seemed uncomfortable with the spotlight being shone on this question. Maybe they were embarrassed to be at the centre of a group conversation. Perhaps they had experienced even further abuse on occasions when they had spoken out before. Perhaps they simply had no faith in the system by this point. Or maybe, as they said, they just wanted the focus to be 'on the football'. But it was obvious that we were dealing with complexities here that it would take more than one team discussion to unravel.

Nevertheless, we emerged with an agreed plan of action for the Bulgaria game. We would go along with the Uefa three-step protocol, as flawed as it was, in the interest of abiding by the tournament rules, and we would invoke that protocol ourselves, proactively. If players were abused by the crowd during the game, I wanted them to communicate with Harry, as captain, who would then report it to the referee. I wanted the complaint to go through Harry to avoid it looking as though any abused player was individually leading the protest. After the statutory issuing of the second warning, we would hold a team huddle. If everyone agreed, we would leave the field for a suspension of play. And if the abuse resumed after the restart, we would take the biggest measure open to us: as a team, to a man, we would walk off.

Abandoning the game like that would send out a powerful message, without question. But it would also be complicated. For one thing, despite our going back to Uefa in the intervening weeks for further clarity, there was still some uncertainty about how walking off and forcing the game to end would be interpreted in terms of tournament rules. Would the match be replayed? Would we forfeit the match? Forfeit our place in the tournament? How would the fans in the ground take it? How would the media react? On the night, I knew that all these considerations would still be bubbling. However, as we headed for Bulgaria, and whatever awaited us there, I hoped that the black players at least knew that they weren't going into this potentially hostile scenario alone – that we were all in this with them.

The debate caught fire in the media in the days before the game. Would we walk? Would we not? Framed as a 'racism row', it dominated the advance media conferences. Some voices wondered why we weren't boycotting the match in Bulgaria altogether. I understood why people felt that way,

ONE BADGE, ONE TEAM

but my position was clear: while I had no control over how fans might behave, I could give my team a chance to play while taking steps to protect them. In the middle of all this, the president of the Bulgarian FA complained to Uefa, accusing me of 'unjust branding of the local spectators as people inclined to discriminatory behaviour'. I wasn't by any means branding all Bulgarian fans as racists, let alone Bulgaria as a racist country. That was far from my intention. And nor, incidentally, was I by any means denying that England had problems of its own in this area. Just before this match there had been an incident of racist crowd abuse in a National League game between Hartlepool and Dover that felt as bad to me if not worse than episodes I knew of in other countries. In Sofia, I tried to defuse the situation by making it clear, as diplomatically as I could, that it didn't matter where racism occurred, or when it occurred: my concern, as leader, would always be for the protection and support of my players. But controversy still hung in the air.

All of this meant there was a lot of tension in the air on the night of the game. I'm not sure I've ever walked into an atmosphere at a football match quite like the one at the Vasil Levski stadium that evening – such an odd mix of the febrile and the nervous. Some sections of the stadium were entirely empty, in accordance with those Uefa sanctions. But in the populated areas, the atmosphere was loud and fierce. Nevertheless, our players didn't seem distracted. They got on with their job superbly, and we were 2–0 ahead after twenty minutes. Maybe everything was going to be OK.

That was when the monkey noises started. First Tyrone

Mings was targeted, and then Raheem Sterling, and then Marcus Rashford. This went on for a couple of minutes until the players spoke to Harry, and Harry went to the referee. Play was paused and a public announcement went out, asking that the noises be stopped or else the game would be suspended, and possibly abandoned. The game then resumed and we scored two more goals, to go 4–0 ahead. But the abuse of our players soon picked up again, exactly as before. Once again, Harry went to the referee, and once again play was paused.

The referee now came to the touchline and asked me if I wanted him to suspend the game and take the teams off. At this point, I gathered our players to consult with them – the most extraordinary and depressing on-pitch huddle of my career. I told everyone that if we were going to leave the field at that point, it was going to be a collective decision. As there were only a couple of minutes until half-time, the team view was that we should play on until the whistle and then review things as a squad in the dressing room.

If that on-pitch huddle had been extraordinary and depressing, this half-time interval was even more so. We needed to do all the usual half-time things – rest, hydration, medical assessments, etc. – but was there even going to be a second half? Everything was dwarfed by the bigger debate: were we going back out? In one sense, it was a blessing that we were so far ahead in the game. Had we been behind, and had we then ultimately chosen to abandon the match, it would only have invited accusations that we were playing the system to avoid defeat. That 4–0 lead was clarifying. In this case, our motives were not going to be open to question: it was going to be about the racism. But I felt a lot of pressure as leader in that debate with the players. It was like being on a tightrope – trying to find the balance between supporting the players and doing the right thing with regard to the bigger issue, while knowing deep down that everyone in that dressing room would far rather play the game out and not be the centre of the story if that were possible.

During the break I was given word that the most significant troublemakers had now been ejected from the stadium, and that piece of news probably swayed things at that point. If this was the case, and the racists had been removed, the players felt comfortable agreeing to play on. However, the players were equally in agreement that, at the first sign of any further abuse, there would be no need for further warnings or discussion. Regardless of the consequences, if there were any more incidents, we would be coming off.

So we went back out. Yet, as the second half got under way, I turned to Steve Holland next to me and expressed my doubts that we would be playing for long. The atmosphere was still rancorous. We now found ourselves trying to focus on the game while simultaneously straining to hear any noise or chant from the crowd that might trigger a walk-off. In truth, it was hard, from the technical area, to work out what was abusive chanting and what were other chants – and it was incredibly distracting and enervating to be doing so. I was worried that, if we missed anything, our stance on this whole issue would end up looking hollow. I also knew that if we took the decision to walk off it would be headline news all over the world. The responsibility to get things right weighed more heavily on me that night than in any other match I had served as England manager.

Somehow, somewhere in the middle of all this a football match was happening. I felt for the referee that night. The Uefa protocol placed all the onus on him. He was wearing the obligatory earpiece to communicate with his assistants, and it must have been next to impossible for him to monitor the crowd at the same time as officiating the match. We scored again, and the home crowd, now contemplating a properly crushing defeat, grew more subdued. The noise from the section containing our supporters, who had been magnificently supportive of our players in the face of the abuse they had received, grew more dominant. It eventually began to look as though we might just make it to the final whistle. However, the uncertainty and the tension lingered. When he finally blew for full-time, the relief was so immense, I could feel a weight lifting off my shoulders.

I was so proud of the team. The players' conduct had been exceptional. Tyrone Mings had been making his England debut that night and had suffered repellent abuse – a sad and awful outcome. And yet afterwards he told me that throughout the game he had at least felt supported. In a dark situation, we had pulled together and drawn protectively around our people who had been attacked. We had forced the Bulgarian fans to take responsibility for themselves. As a direct result of our actions, around fifty perpetrators had been forced to leave the stadium, and players in the team who deserved protection had felt empowered. And as a leader, I had seen the

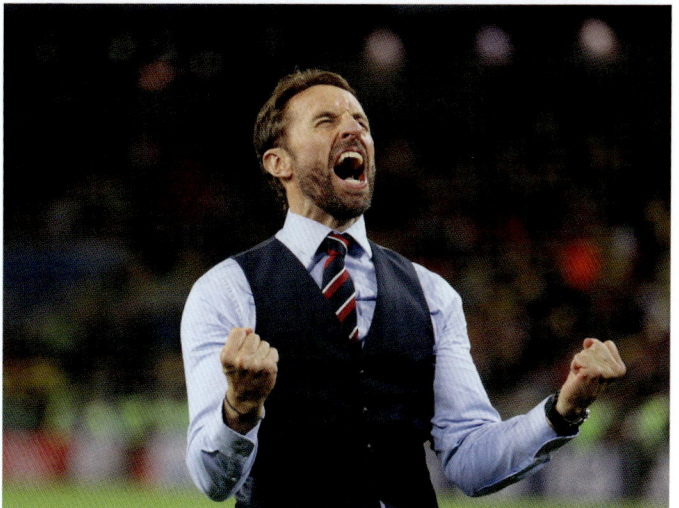

...cstasy. The stadium erupted
...s Eric Dier scored the
...winning penalty against
...Colombia in the round-of-
...xteen in the 2018 World
...Cup. I hugged anyone and
...everyone within reach. We
...ad finally won a shoot-out
...a major tournament.

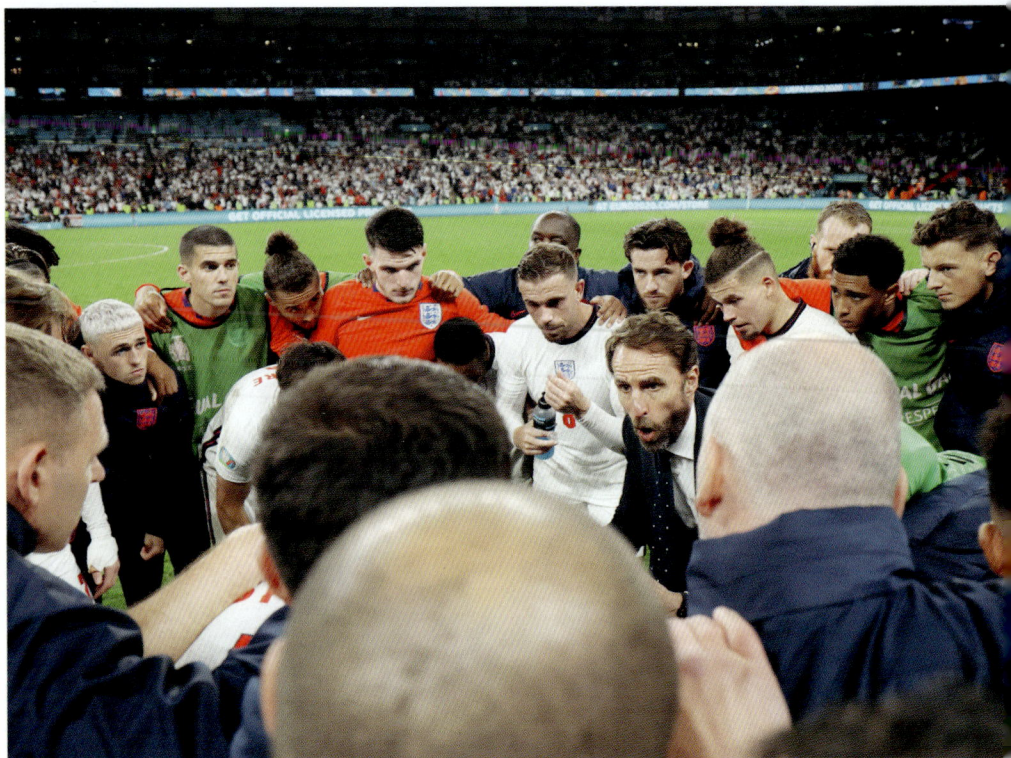

Above: Our huddle at half-time in extra-time during the Uefa Euro 20 final against Italy at Wembley. Below: Consoling Bukayo Saka after we heartbreakingly lost the shoot-out.

Taking the knee during the 2022 Qatar World Cup.

ude Bellingham (*centre*) celebrates with the team after Jordan Henderson (*right*) scores the opener in our 3—0 win against Senegal in the round-of-sixteen. We played some of our best ootball in Qatar.

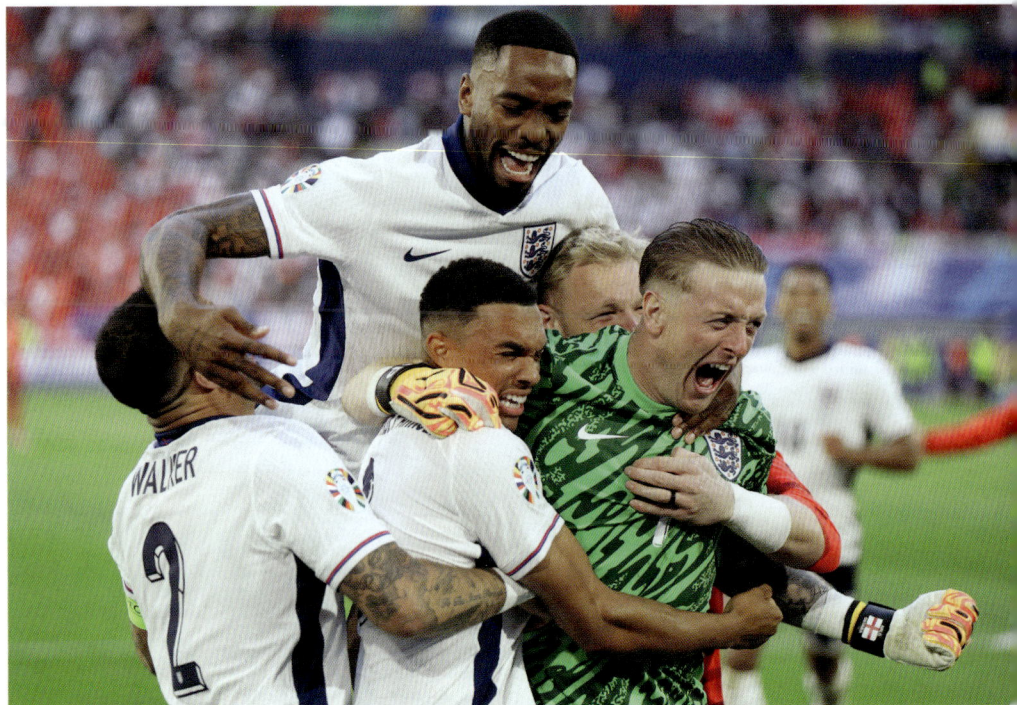

Clockwise from left: Kyle Walker, Ivan Toney, Jordan Pickford and Trent Alexander-Arnold celebrating our penalty shoot-out win against Switzerland in the quarter-final of Euro 24.

Our victory against the Netherlands in the semi-final, courtesy of a goal by Ollie Watkins in the ninetieth minute, was just as sweet.

With kit man Pat Frost. Together we won the all-important England padel tournament back at base camp during Euro 24.

A quiet moment with my family on FaceTime after the penalty shoot-out against Switzerland in Euro 24, before facing the world's media.

Final preparations in my hotel room before the final of Euro 24.

The Euro 24 final. Cole Palmer's excellent goal, scored just 142 seconds after we brought him on as a substitute, levelled the game at 1–1.

After a late Spain goal, our dreams of an equaliser were crushed when Marc Guéhi's point-blank header was headed off the line in the dying minutes, after Declan Rice's powerful header was parried away by Spain goalkeeper Unai Simón Mendibil.

Winning my 100th cap managing England is a milestone I will always treasure.

Celebrating my knighthood with my wife Alison (*pictured*) and parents at Windsor Castle was emotional.

Giving the 2025 BBC Richard Dimbleby Lecture on the importance of leadership today.

Visiting 10 Downing Street to discuss how we can help young people thrive in the UK.

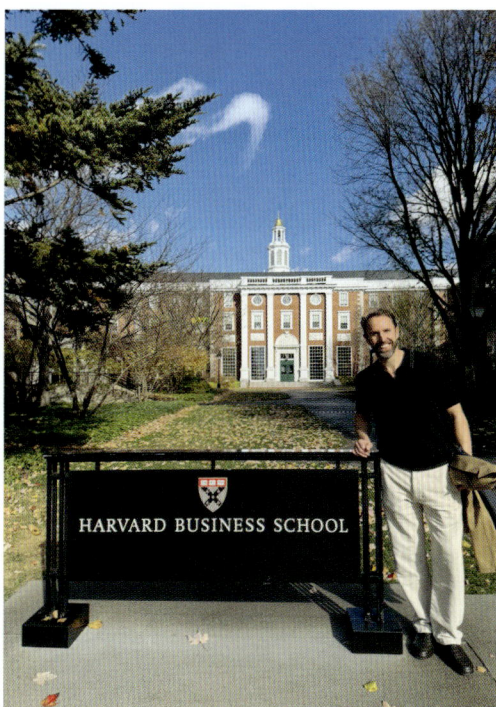

Back to school. A trip to Harvard Business School to present a case study on my England experiences.

The King's Trust do incredible work to help young people achieve their full potential.

The leaders and role models of tomorrow. Left: Visiting 600 young soldiers at the 2025 graduation parade at the British Army Foundation College. Right: Meeting Paralympian medallists Greg Slade (*left*), Louise Fiddes (*centre*) and Andy Lapthorne (*right*).

power of discussion, joint ownership of issues affecting the team, and collaborative decision-making create a solid sense of unity that the team definitely carried forward from there and which fed directly into our performance.

Oh, and we won 6–0.

I find it impossible to look back on that ugly night with any real sense of satisfaction, but all of those outcomes I will take.

We play as one

The following year, in May 2020, the debate around racial injustice flared globally after the murder of George Floyd by a white police officer in Minneapolis. That shocking incident in broad daylight caused worldwide outrage, with uprisings, marches and protests, many of them under the banner of the anti-racism campaign group Black Lives Matter. The killing of Floyd also started an urgent worldwide conversation about institutional racism, not just within US police forces but in organisations everywhere who felt newly challenged to reflect on their practices and assumptions.

This included across the entire FA. A town-hall-style staff conference was hosted to address the pressing subject – a virtual meeting, due to the lockdown restrictions that were in place then. The FA's leadership team went into this conference call with the view that the home of English football could regard itself as broadly progressive in its work around diversity and representation. What nobody at that leadership level anticipated was the degree of anger that was felt in the room about this assessment.

Members of staff from different backgrounds and positions were rightfully upset about what had happened in America, and their feelings were heightened by what they perceived as a sense of complacency from those in authority. While diversity and equality certainly did exist within the organisation, it became less apparent in the senior ranks. It was the first time that I had heard the phrase 'white privilege', and those words stung when I considered my own position. My first thought was slightly defensive: I felt I had worked incredibly hard in my playing and managerial careers to earn the opportunities that I had received, and something in me slightly prickled at the idea that they had been gifted to me in any way. Then I paused to listen harder, and realised how much I needed to learn.

I had always considered myself to be broad-minded, but I had never truly considered in depth the extent to which life was weighted in my favour because of my racial background. Afterwards, it was my daughter who helped me begin to explore the issue. Coming from a generation that is more attuned to the subtleties of racial injustice, she was able to talk to me about the issue in ways I hadn't previously considered. If I wasn't white, I realised, life could have worked out very differently for me. She also recommended to me a book on the subject, *Why I'm No Longer Talking to White People About Race* by Reni Eddo-Lodge. I read it and it was extremely enlightening.

As I educated myself more about the subject, and started to appreciate more fully the work that lay ahead for all of us in promoting unity in the FA, I reflected on what it meant in particular for the England team. More than half of our players came from black or dual heritage backgrounds, with family roots in Africa, the Caribbean, Asia and Europe. Most of our support staff, however, were, like me, white. There was no question about our team's skill and dedication, but, as with the upper echelons of the FA at that time, I felt that more diversity would strengthen the connection with our players who needed to feel as if they belonged.

In my view, the best way to drive change in this area was to make sure people could see what was possible. There had to be visibility. A concerted recruitment effort would be the starting point. But as potential candidates began to see themselves represented within the team, and to realise the door was certainly open to them, I believed over time the change would take on its own momentum. (And as I write now, nearly five years down the line, the FA is far more diverse in its representation, from board level all the way down and in the support team around the seniors.)

In the middle of this period of institutional reflection, the Premier League was the first football organisation to grant an allocated period of time at the beginning of matches for players to show their solidarity against racism by taking the knee. This symbolic gesture of non-confrontational protest – one with hundreds of years of history behind it – had been adopted by Colin Kaepernick, the American football player, in 2016 in objection to police brutality and the ongoing failure to address racial inequality, and had then been taken up widely across many sports.

Should the England team take the knee? This was the discussion we now had. With our experiences in Montenegro and Bulgaria still fresh in our minds, the will to do so among the players was very clearly there. We saw the gesture as potentially one of support for equality and each other – an outward display of our unity on this issue. A young, multiethnic national team, in England shirts, taking the knee on the international stage would certainly be a powerful image and could take the gesture to another level in terms of attracting attention to racial injustice. Accordingly, we decided to adopt the gesture before our games, starting with a Nations League match against Iceland in September 2020. In line with the Covid restrictions that were in place at the time, those first few games in which we made the gesture were staged in closed stadiums and televised to big audiences. When the players took the knee in silence, it was a potent moment.

However, continuing to use the gesture in the rescheduled 2020 Euros – set back to 2021 by the pandemic – was more complicated. Unlike the Premier League, Uefa, the tournament's organisers, didn't mandate taking the knee. If we wanted to continue making a statement we would have to do so, not in a short moment of grace at the referee's behest, but in the immediate countdown before the game started. Not every competing country shared our view that taking the knee should happen, so suddenly we had to consider the slightly farcical possibility that we would be kneeling on the pitch while the opposition were ready to kick off.

Since the events in Montenegro, we had learned that the most effective way for us to establish where we were on an issue as a team was through collective debate. During this process, some of our black and mixed heritage players questioned if it was worth continuing to take the knee at all. There was a suggestion that, nearly a year after the gesture's adoption by the Premier League, people were beginning to question its impact. I was saddened to learn that people felt the gesture wouldn't change anything. I read it as further evidence that they believed racial inequality was now baked into sport, and into society generally, and beyond reconstruction.

But this contention in turn led to other team members making the counter-case – that the sight of England players continuing to make their pledge against racial injustice on an international stage might, at the very least, start conversations among people watching. And maybe those conversations would potentially loosen the hold of those entrenched views and make a difference further down the line. Ultimately, everyone was onside. We agreed that, for Euro 20, we would be bold enough to inform our opponents of our intention in advance and take the knee at every game we played.

Throughout, I aimed to listen and understand while initially holding back my own opinions. Once again I was discovering that in leadership there are moments when it's vital to judge where the group is on an issue, and recognise when a consensus is forming, before imposing yourself on the debate. In this instance, I was in total agreement with the players' consensus and, when I did ultimately speak, I was unreservedly of the opinion that adopting the gesture was the right thing to do.

Ahead of the Euros, we played two warm-up matches, against Austria and Romania, at a ground very familiar to me – Middlesbrough's Riverside Stadium. We won both games but it was the gesture before each match that attracted attention. These were the first times that we had taken the knee with fans present following the Covid shutdown – albeit only 7,000 of them, in accordance with the continuing restrictions. As the players knelt, a clear majority of the people in the sparsely occupied ground supportively applauded the gesture. But, from a smaller section, there was audible jeering and booing too.

It was a confusing and deeply unsettling thing to hear. What worried me was that our black players could assume the booing was being directed specifically at them. The mixed reaction became a talking point in the media. For us, kneeling was quite simply a small symbol of solidarity against discrimination, and a signal of our own unity as a team. As such, the gesture seemed to me to float entirely free of partisan politics. However, some interpreted the move as an endorsement of specific, politically aligned organisations that operated under the general Black Lives Matter banner, and framed our knee-taking as a political stance that they felt the national team had no place taking. We were guilty of 'taking the knee for Marxism', as one extreme banner put it. A politician declared, on these grounds, that he was boycotting all England games from this point (which I have to say I didn't lose any sleep over). Headlines duly followed. I was enormously disappointed to see the gesture getting twisted like that – especially by people who I suspected knew very well that we were simply taking a stand for the principle of human equality, but who had their own agendas to serve.

Still, as a team, we were undeterred. We agreed that we were taking the knee together because we believed in its importance, and we resolved to do so throughout Euro 20. In the week leading up to our opening game, the so-called controversy around the gesture continued – although, from our point of view, there was no controversy. On the contrary, we were doing something that felt absolutely right at that particular moment. Indeed, what grew tiresome was being repeatedly called upon to explain an action that, to my mind, spoke entirely for itself. Meanwhile, the spinning of the moment for political gain continued, but now with the Prime Minister and the Leader of the Opposition, no less, at loggerheads in the House of Commons over who had or hadn't sufficiently condemned the booing of the gesture in Middlesbrough that time.

Finally, we got to the opening game, at Wembley against Croatia. When the players kneeled, a small number of people could briefly be heard booing, but they were rapidly overwhelmed by a vast majority applauding and now even cheering the gesture. I felt vindicated by the reaction, although it wasn't the important thing: we were ready to ride out any kind of reaction at that stage. Crucially, we had ignored considerable external pressure and stood by our beliefs. There had been criticism, but we had not crumbled before it and we had used this simple but effective means to express support for each other, forge unity between ourselves and send a message. And we were undeniably a stronger team as a consequence.

New England

During that politically charged period in the build-up to Euro 20, I was interviewed by Ben Haines from The Players' Tribune, an online platform that publishes conversations with professional athletes. We talked about what the England football team meant to me – I produced the formative memory of running home to watch my hero, Bryan Robson, play, and score, in the 1982 World Cup in Spain – and then about what playing for England had meant. And that in turn led us to discuss the idea of national identity and Englishness, which was something that had certainly grown more complex in my lifetime and which, to my mind, we seemed to be struggling with as a nation.

That conversation led to a proposal from Ben that what I had to say might resonate with people beyond football. Which is how we came to write 'Dear England', which took the form of an open letter to the country, on the eve of Euro 20.

The thrust was pretty simple, I thought. I wanted to articulate what it meant, at a national level, to be united. It seemed like an especially important moment to be thinking about this. It wasn't just that we were going into a football tournament, a considerable portion of which, including the final, England would be hosting. More than that, we were all emerging from the pandemic and an unprecedented period of enforced isolation. We were having to learn again, quite literally, how to come together. But we were doing so in the face of ever-more divisive forces, on social media and in politics – forces that could even turn a gesture as simple as the taking of the knee into something inflammatory. The voices of those who got their pleasure from inspiring disunity seemed to have grown louder than the voices of those who were interested in bringing us together. There were too many binary arguments, not enough nuance.

Yet, in a fractured political landscape that seemed to lack advocates for community, I was the manager of a national team that prided itself on its culture of unity and its social values. The players were from a range of roots and life experiences, and they represented their country, in the broadest sense. They were a young, multi-ethnic team, formed entirely meritocratically, in which everyone earned their place through talent and performance. They therefore belonged explicitly in a space where they would be judged, not by the colour of their skin but by the quality of their football. My hope was that, in our young team, England would see itself reflected, and that, by our efforts on the pitch in the tournament ahead, we could provide the country with something to get behind, and an opportunity to recognise our heritage and our shared values and celebrate what it meant to be English.

When 'Dear England' was published, it resonated to a degree that I hadn't even begun to foresee. The letter went viral on social media and inspired comment pieces in the press. Readers were constantly coming up to me and talking about it; black, Asian, white, male, female, old, young, parents, grandparents, all thanking me for what I had said. I found myself praised for bringing a calm and moderate tone to a topic – national identity – that had grown angry and divisive. The patriotic case for a more inclusive country was clearly one that people were very enthusiastic to see made. People from all sides of the political spectrum seemed to respond to my idea of a kind of progressive patriotism – an England we could all get behind. And they seemed to come away from the letter with a positive attitude to the England football team, and to what the team represented, going into that tournament. In all this, I was hailed for showing 'political courage', though, really, I had just said a few things from the heart, as I felt them, authentically and passionately. Maybe that's what 'political courage' is.

I certainly didn't anticipate that the letter would inspire James Graham to write a play based on it, which would eventually be staged at the National Theatre in London. And even less that the part of me would be played by Joseph Fiennes (that was an extremely generous decision from whoever did the casting). That whole outcome still seems entirely surreal to me. (I didn't see the production but people told me that Fiennes did an excellent job, and even carried off the waistcoat, as unlikely as that may seem.)

But, overwhelmingly, people recognised the connection I was trying to make between the values represented by the England football team and the contemporary national identity beyond football. They recognised it, and they recognised their own place in it. (You'll find the original letter reproduced at the back of this book.)

Of course, 'Dear England' had its dissenters. In standing up for what I believed in about unity, I appeared to alienate a small section of the team's fan base. I felt disappointed about that, naturally. I was trying to bring everyone along – or, if that was unrealistic, as many people as I possibly could. But if you're going to commit to your convictions, you're going to risk alienating a few people, and if leadership means anything it means walking on through this prospect and remaining firm.

The fact was, throughout Euro 20, a team that embraced its multicultural heritage seemed to inspire a new kind of patriotism. The flag of St George was unfurled from bedroom and office windows up and down the land, and flown from cars and vans, with, it felt to me, a new kind of pride attached to it. It seemed to stand for something broader that summer – like more people felt able to be a part of it. It was possible to believe (and this had not been a fashionable view for many years) that the England football team could show us the best of ourselves, and that feeling seemed to have a freshly unifying effect on the nation.

That summer I believe our England team felt not only backed and supported by one another, but by the country. We experienced a wider feeling of unity, and the life-affirming impact of standing up as one team together for something when it is right to do so. And the players channelled this powerful force of togetherness into the tournament, and all the way to the final.

SUMMARY
One Badge, One Team
On the power of unity

- Before judging a moment of uncharacteristic behaviour in an individual, find out the root cause of their conduct. Often a team member acting out of sorts is a signal that something deeper is happening in their life.

- There's power in showing vulnerability. Admitting mistakes, or being transparent when you don't have the answers, is not a weakness but, rather, a strength. These traits demonstrate authenticity and can build trust with your team.

- Diversity in background, life experiences, skills and personalities, from the top to the bottom of your organisation, can make everyone in your team more 'emotionally intelligent'. This will enable you to have a clearer understanding and perspective of your group, and can improve your decision-making as a leader.

- Sharing perspectives in an open forum can lead to mutual understanding. As a leader, you need to frame these discussions carefully to ensure that different views do not become divisive or marked by judgement.

- Every decision has a consequence and it's unlikely that any decision will be universally accepted. Being aware of the repercussions that stem from your choices is key, but so too is sticking to your convictions if you believe them to be right.

CHAPTER 8

When the Whistle Blows

On turning pressure into performance

On the spot

England v. Colombia, Round of 16, 2018 Fifa World Cup, Spartak Stadium, Moscow, 3 July.

Eric Dier has just completed the long, solo walk from the centre circle to the penalty area. The end behind the goal he is facing is a sea of yellow Colombia shirts. At the other end of the ground, in reds and whites, our fans stand with their arms raised anxiously behind their heads. If Eric scores, we go through to the quarter-finals of the World Cup.

Back in England, frozen with tension, millions more watch on televisions in living rooms and sports bars and fan zones. England have never won a World Cup penalty shoot-out. Five tournament ties have gone to penalties in the twenty-two years since my miss in Euro 96. England have lost all of them.

Standing on the touchline, part of the chorus line of support staff and substitutes looking on with linked arms,

I'm sharing in the knife-edge tension that these moments of decisive drama always bring. I am acutely aware of the prize hanging within our grasp at this moment – a place in the last eight. I am acutely aware also that defeat in this match will see our tournament campaign defined as a failure and could also possibly cost me my job.

Yet, for all that, there is one thing, as leader, that I can feel calmly sure of: whatever now transpires, score or miss, Eric Dier is as prepared for this moment as he possibly can be.

Right from the start of my tenure as manager, I wanted to make penalty-taking an integral part of the England team's training programme. Given that almost every tournament-winning team will have to succeed in at least one penalty shoot-out on the way to lifting the trophy, it made clear sense to focus in on this aspect of the game. And it made particular sense for England. As a history of failure at that point in key matches had accrued, a narrative had clearly taken hold: 'Then it goes to penalties, and we lose.' The nation felt it; the players felt it. The penalty shoot-out had become a psychological barrier. We needed somehow to get beyond that barrier – find some way to take control and change the story.

But to what extent was a penalty shoot-out actually controllable? There was a lot of conventional wisdom suggesting it wasn't. First, penalties were 'a lottery'. That was the analogy almost everybody used – managers, players, pundits, journalists, fans . . . It was the analogy I'd heard all through my playing career, and was what I took to the penalty spot with me at Wembley in 1996. The practically universal belief was that, once a game reached that stage, you were in the hands of fate.

Second – and this was said almost as frequently – there was no useful way to practise penalties. It was impossible to 'duplicate the pressure'. Taking a few pens against your own goalkeeper on the training ground before heading in for a shower didn't in any useful way map onto the high-pressure experience of stepping up in a full stadium with hundreds of millions of people watching around the world and your country's destiny in your hands.

'How do we win a penalty shoot-out at a major tournament? How do we get England beyond the penalty hoodoo?' That was the problem we set ourselves in January 2017, eighteen months before we departed for Russia. And it all started with data. Lots of it.

We assigned a team of five game analysts, and general statistical wizards, to study every aspect of the penalty shoot-out process. They didn't hold back, researching more than a hundred penalty shoot-outs, conducting numerous interviews with experts and compiling a rich dataset, covering every possible detail. From the moment the referee blew the whistle to end the game, to the last penalty strike deciding the winner, no stone was left unturned. Whether it was how the taker received the ball, the placing of the ball on the spot, angles of run-up, pause-times, breathing, target areas to aim for, as well as numerous other insights, it was all there. I was enormously impressed at the level of detail they had covered. So much so that I was worried about swamping the players with the quantity and nature of some of these findings – paralysing them by giving them too much to think about, which would, of course, be the opposite of the desired effect. Yet there was clearly fantastic and potentially game-changing stuff in that research. And by applying the right detail, in the right way, at the right time, I was confident no team up to that point would have prepared as carefully for penalties as we did for 2018.

What was clear was that the 'lottery' narrative around penalty shoot-outs encouraged a feeling of helplessness. What we needed to do was change the perception of control, not just of the penalty kick itself, but of the whole shoot-out process, so that the players felt they had agency and ownership – that they were not just being dispatched up to one end of the pitch as hostages to fortune.

To this end, we broke the shoot-out into four phases:

Phase 1: The break after extra-time
Phase 2: The centre circle
Phase 3: The walk
Phase 4: At the penalty spot

Then we set about looking for practical ways in which we could optimise behaviours in each of those phases with a view to eliminating distraction, alleviating pressure and enabling performance.

Those moments after the game ended and before the shoot-out (phase one), for instance, had historically been unstructured to the point of chaotic, with players and staff crowding together on the touchline and coaches rushing around with notebooks looking for volunteers. Could we do things differently there and be better prepared? Could we channel our communications in that phase so that the players had access to a calm environment that encouraged composure and focus before the task that awaited them? Could we find an edge on teams who were less well organised?

And then what about the behaviours of the players waiting their turns in the centre circle (phase two)? Where were they going to stand? Along the halfway line, with arms locked? That had become the standard procedure, but there was nothing in the rules to stop you going closer to the front of the centre circle, maybe making that walk to the penalty area just a little bit shorter, bringing the watching team closer to the kicker and possibly even adopting a dominant position on the pitch relative to the opposition. Was there a competitive advantage to be gained here?

And then, how were the players going to respond to successful penalties and to unsuccessful ones? I'd had interesting discussions with our Olympic hockey people about their preferred policy of reacting evenly, without extreme emotion, to both goals and misses, and the psychological security of that. We also showed our players examples of teams where players left the centre circle to welcome back the returning kicker and enfold them back in the group, in both triumph and despair. None of these were aspects of the event that I wanted us to over-manage, and ultimately we left it up to the players to make their own decisions according to how they felt as a collective. But just by showing them what was possible and investing time and thought into these things, we were revealing to the players ways in which they had agency during this event in the match, and dismantling the 'hands of fate' narrative.

As for the walk phase (phase three), we encouraged our

goalkeeper to seek out the ball and carry it to our incoming taker. We wanted to avoid the opposition goalkeeper handing the ball over to our player and maybe getting into his head and undermining him. And we liked the way that the 'long, lonely walk' aspect could be diminished for the kicker if his team-mate was waiting for him with the ball at the end of it.

And, of course, we worked on penalty-taking itself (phase four). Some of the players were regular penalty-takers with their clubs, and for those we decided not to change things, on the grounds that they already had routines they were comfortable with. But we knew a shoot-out would potentially involve the whole team, so we devoted time to training up those who weren't regular takers and giving them a routine they could depend on. In particular, we wanted them to realise, in the crucial moments when they were shaping up to shoot, that the referee's whistle was not a starting gun: they didn't need to come sprinting in, they could take their time. Our data convincingly showed that England players over the last two decades were more rushed over their penalties than the players of almost any other nation – the accumulating legacy of failure playing a role in that sense of panic, no doubt. Approaching the ball in your own time, having a well-established pre-shot routine, maybe using breathing in order to settle before the run-up – all of these strategies were means to take greater control of the situation, and we put them in front of the players who needed them.

We rethought how we practised penalties as well. It may be true that you can't exactly reproduce the pressure of the competitive moment in front of millions of watching eyes. But, when you think about it, the same was true for *all* the work we did on the training ground, and it didn't stop us rehearsing defensive blocks, transitions, corners, free-kicks . . . So now we rehearsed the penalty shoot-out, too – the whole thing, with a referee, the obligatory solo walk from the circle, one chance to score only, etc., and we did this when the players were tired at the end of training. We did full shoot-out dress rehearsals, both at St George's Park and out in Russia, and having that practised strategy in place, and the maximum role clarity it bestowed, definitely took some uncertainty and some heat out of the situation when we eventually faced penalties in competition.

Now, just to be absolutely clear, we were under no illusions here: none of this would mean our players would definitely score and that we would definitely win every penalty shoot-out we now faced. That's not how this works, and that was never the deal we were offering the players here. Goalkeepers make great saves, goalkeepers make lucky saves, kicks go wrong, things come unravelled. This was still sport, after all, so we were inevitably dealing with the uncontrollable to some degree. But by homing in hard on detail and controlling the things that we could control, we would be giving the players the best possible ownership of a highly pressurised situation, and the best chance to perform and succeed.

We could be confident, then, that our granular and collaborative work over the previous year and a half had put us in the best possible position when that round-of-sixteen game in Russia eventually went to penalties. We had been collecting the data from every player's performance as a penalty-taker with their club and we had logged every penalty that they took with us in training. These numbers gave us a constantly updated 'batting order' for the twenty-three-strong squad, with the players knowing exactly where they stood in the line, in complete contrast to the desperate last-ditch casting around for volunteers that used to take place after the final whistle. And we knew how many of our top penalty-takers were on the pitch as extra-time drew to a close, which meant that we could make tactical substitutions specifically to strengthen the penalty-taking line-up if we thought it was prudent.

In Moscow, with seven minutes of extra-time left in the match against Colombia, that meant bringing on Marcus Rashford. Harry Kane, our captain, was already on the pitch. Both players had penalty conversion rates of over 85 per cent. Statistically, the pair represented our strongest shoot-out candidates. Also on the pitch was Kieran Trippier, who wasn't a regular taker at his club, but our training had provided him with a routine that he was able to trust, which in turn gave us the confidence to assess him as another one of our best options. Those players took our first three penalties, and all of them scored.

Meanwhile, in goal, Jordan Pickford produced a wonderful save from Carlos Bacca, having dived the right way, and came close to stopping two other Colombia strikes, one of which struck the crossbar and came out. Working with our goalkeeping coach, Martyn Margetson, Jordan had studied where the opposition's players liked to place their penalties and written the information on his drinks bottle – not a brand-new tactic but certainly one that England hadn't utilised before. Again, the preparation paid dividends.

The plan did not run faultlessly, and nor could we have expected it to. Jordan Henderson saw his penalty saved. Then there was the fact that Jamie Vardy, another substitute we had brought on during the game with a strong spot-kick record for his club, had flagged up an injury at the end of full-time. Vardy had been down to take our fifth penalty. But we had now at least got ourselves into a position to win the match with a penalty – a scenario that our research told us statistically improved our chances of success to over 90 per cent, which was way above the norm. (When the fifth or 'sudden death' penalty is to equalise and to effectively 'stay alive', success rates drop to around 63 per cent.)

So it was then, with the score level but advantage to us, that Eric Dier found himself stepping forward. Like the rest of the squad, he had developed a process in training that he felt comfortable with executing. In other words, unlike me in 1996, when he walked to the penalty area that night, he did so with role clarity and a plan.

Calm and confident, Dier took a purposeful run-up, struck the ball hard and low to the left-hand corner, too powerfully for the diving keeper to reach it. The stadium erupted, Eric wheeled away in jubilation to be pounced on by his team-mates, and I hugged anyone and everyone within reach. It was a truly cathartic moment – for me, certainly, but more importantly for the team, and for the country.

We lifted no trophy that night in Russia but we did lift a psychological barrier, and I regard that as one of the most transformational nights for the team under my management. The past had been reckoned with. And the fans could, and did, rejoice because England now, finally, had a team that could win a penalty shoot-out.

A sudden death

Now let's come forward – to Wembley in July 2021. Three years on from the World Cup in Russia, we've made it to our first tournament final since 1966 and we find ourselves potentially facing another penalty shoot-out. This time it's against Italy, and this time it will be to decide the European Championship.

As extra-time plays out, and we remain in the hunt for our nation's first trophy in fifty-five years, the tension is almost tangibly ratcheting up around the stadium. With stakes as high as any I have ever experienced, and in an atmosphere of electric intensity, I must stand by the touchline and make careful calculations. With five minutes to play, the score at 1–1 and Italy looking ever dangerous, events in the match have significantly impacted our choice of penalty-takers on the pitch. Only two of our top seven candidates are currently in play. Marcus Rashford and Jadon Sancho are on the list but both are still behind me on the bench.

I have to make a decision at this point. If I bring those two players on now, sacrificing lower-ranked penalty-takers, it will give them a few minutes to settle into the game before the shoot-out, if it comes. But that reshuffle will leave the team hugely over-weighted with attacking players at a time when a goal from Italy will almost certainly sink us. If I wait, on the other hand, and bring on those two subs right at the end of the game, the team will retain its balance for these potentially decisive last few minutes, but Marcus and Jadon will go into the penalty shoot-out 'cold', without game time.

In the heat of this moment, I have to make the decision that I judge most likely to yield success. I recognise the risks inherent in bringing on players right at the last. Equally, our research into games where players came on fresh for a shoot-out has shown it can still make a positive difference. Just a few weeks earlier, in the Europa League final, Manchester United brought on Juan Mata and Alex Telles in time added on as their match against Villarreal headed for penalties. Moments later, even though United would ultimately lose, both players scored in the shoot-out. There are solid precedents. The alternative is to put Jadon and Marcus on now and give this Italy side five minutes to score against unbalanced opponents. There is no choice without risk here, and no guarantees are available. But in light of the evidence, I am able to frame the decision that faces me as a choice between a calculated risk and a total gamble.

Incidentally, I am also aware that, along with Bukayo Saka, who came on earlier, I am skewing young in my selection of penalty-takers. Only Harry Kane has faced a scenario of anything like this magnitude before. In this moment, however, based on training, evidence and circumstance, it remains our strongest option.

So, totalling everything up as quickly as I can, I go with the calculated risk, leave a balanced team on the pitch and wait until the game is almost done before making my two substitutions.

If you're an England fan, I probably won't need to remind you what happened next. Kane and Harry Maguire scored their penalties, while Rashford, Sancho and Saka were unsuccessful. The night ended in anguish and disappointment for my players, my staff, me, and the entire country, and the long wait for a trophy continued. All of the team and I were, of course, heartbroken at the result. I knew that we had played at a high level across the tournament. I knew that our opponents in that final were exceptional: Italy were on a winning streak that would eventually see them go thirty-seven games unbeaten. Nevertheless, the gut-wrenching walk around a rapidly emptying stadium at the end of the shoot-out will stay with me for ever – a stark counterpoint for my memories of making the same walk, in a state of sheer euphoria, after successfully negotiating the semi-final against Denmark and having put an England team in a final for the first time in more than half a century.

The most shocking part of the evening was the abhorrent online racist abuse that Rashford, Sancho and Saka endured in the aftermath of the shoot-out. It never crossed my mind that they would have to deal with such an appalling scenario. The FA released a statement condemning this disgusting behaviour which had no place in football. I tried to offer the players solace in their shoot-out disappointment, and support in the face of such vitriol. I hated the fact that we had been united as a nation in the good times, but now in defeat 'race' had become an issue.

In the press conference after the game, I felt very strongly that I had to protect the team and especially the players who had missed their penalties. I wanted to be clear that I had chosen the takers – nobody volunteered, nobody refused to take a penalty, all were my choices, on the recommendations of our process. I basically wanted to take as much of the pain for them. I felt better equipped to handle it and I didn't want them to go through what I had experienced after missing in my own shoot-out in Euro 96. We won and lost together. As manager, I tried to shoulder responsibility for the loss, and then I faced the questions. Why had I made such late substitutions, literally placing younger players on the spot? Where were the likes of Raheem Sterling, a more experienced player who had put in big performances in an England shirt? How could I have got it so *wrong*? This was just a taster: in the days following the game I would absorb the anger and frustration of large sections of the media and English public.

Throughout almost eight years in my role as England football manager, every decision I made came under close scrutiny. When the national team is involved, it can seem that literally everyone has an opinion – and a right to it, of course. But it can become a cacophony at times, and it is always loudest after the match. At that point, looking back through the lens of the result, every move I made became somehow binary. 'He did x, and we lost. Obviously, he should have done y, and then we'd have won.' I understand the satisfying clarity of this kind of analysis but, of course, what doesn't get a look in here is the fact that I made my decisions in the moment, based on evidence that supported the best outcome.

Inevitably, though, I, too, reviewed my handling of that Italy final. Naturally, in the face of such widespread criticism, it was only natural that some negative thoughts crept in. While I'd learned to insulate myself as much as possible from external noise during a major tournament, my inner critic still had a voice. On my own, I'd find myself in that internalised debate familiar to all leaders under pressure. Did I make the right calls? Could I have done things any differently?

In the end, the answer lay with the team. Consulting with the technical staff, I reviewed every decision I'd made, based on the data and practices we'd established. While nothing could change the outcome, in a game of so many variables, we confirmed that our process around penalty-taking had carried the highest probability of success at Wembley in 2021, just as it had in Russia in 2018. This had informed my decision not to include Raheem Sterling in the shoot-out. Without doubt, Raheem was an important player for the team. He scored many critical goals, but when it came to taking penalties his success rate was 33 per cent. On that basis alone, I believed it had been the right decision to favour players higher up the order we had established. The alternative, as I reminded myself, would have been to abandon an approach that we believed in and just thrown ourselves on the mercy of fortune. In my view, that wasn't leadership. That was gambling.

In fact, it wasn't even gambling. Soon after I took charge at England, we invited the professional poker player and motivational speaker Caspar Berry to talk to the team's coaches.

Our guest demonstrated to us that even gamblers have an evidence-based strategy – or certainly the successful ones. Caspar said he never made a move on impulse. Nor did he dwell on what had happened in previous rounds or concern himself with what might come later. Instead, he focused on the immediate situation in front of him and the information that he had.

To illustrate, Caspar revealed that when he played at the casinos in Las Vegas, invariably he'd be sharing the table with tourists. He knew that even if the holidaymakers had been dealt a weak hand, in all likelihood they wouldn't be sensible and fold. They were in Vegas, after all. They'd come to gamble. So, for Caspar to stand the best chance of winning, he didn't need to take additional risks. He just had to stick to the game-plan and wait for the holidaymakers to gamble wildly and lose. Dealt a weak hand, he'd fold. Dealt a strong hand, he'd play. With the information that he had – in his hand and in the way his opponents were playing – the odds were always in his favour. Even if the tourists got lucky with a royal flush in some rounds, Caspar's approach would still lead to a successful outcome in the long run.

All of us left that talk fascinated – and planning a trip to Vegas ASAP. Seriously, though, there was an important strategic lesson for leaders in there. It was about making sure your decisions are rigorously based on the information available in the moment and sticking to the plan despite distractions. Faith in what you know, when people and random setbacks and random circumstances are urging you to throw caution to the wind, is a form of resilience. Of course, there should be flexibility to adapt to the unexpected, but that's very different from making changes on the fly. Yes, that one bold, unplanned change could make all the difference, but if it doesn't do so, then the temptation arises to throw in another change, and then another, and before you know it you're so far off the original plan that the team has lost its identity and stability, and you've merely introduced new levels of uncertainty and confusion. Under intense pressure, when facing challenges, the brave move isn't to veer off-plan. The brave move is to stick to it. It's a permanent challenge. But it's a challenge a leader has to rise to, standing by the evidence-based nature of your decisions, even when you face criticism subsequently from people who have the one piece of information that you lacked at the time: the result.

With my confidence in the process challenged but intact, we continued with our penalty approach in future training camps, monitoring and modifying as necessary. Where some players sought to perfect their technique from the spot with constant practice, we actually pulled back the repetitions by a degree with others.

Marcus Rashford was a case in point here. Marcus spent a great deal of time refining his penalty-taking. Such was his commitment that the goalkeepers in training began to work out his approach, and our feeling was this caused him to become too precise with his shots. Observing this, as well as analysing the numbers, we concluded that players could be more successful taking fewer penalties but with a greater focus on making them count. A little more pressure, we believed, gave them an edge. We even brought an additional goalkeeper into training so the players weren't always facing the same one, which added more realism to the challenge.

In our preparation for Euro 24 in Germany, we again reviewed our process. Bukayo Saka was older and more experienced in taking penalties than he had been at Euro 20, for example, but was it fair to place him back in the same position he had faced on that night at Wembley? In light of the racist abuse that he and the other two young black players endured after missing their penalties, his welfare was a serious consideration. Even so, every question we asked the players and ourselves around our shoot-out practices strengthened my confidence in them. As long as I had the buy-in from the players I selected to take penalties, in the knowledge that I had their backs, I believed our process would continue to provide the very best chance of success in that event.

The test of my convictions ultimately came in a game against Switzerland in Düsseldorf. This time the prize on offer was a place in the semi-finals of the 2024 Euros. Again, we had prepared thoroughly and with a view to controlling every controllable aspect of the process, including prepping the exact roles and positioning of all staff members in a run-through in a sports hall at Middlesbrough's training ground three weeks earlier. We established who should be where on the day and created strictly defined lines of communication to prevent crowding and over-briefing of the players in that volatile moment, and to replace the sense of chaos that often descends during the pre-shoot-out phase with a calm and ordered working environment.

In the closing minutes of added time, with Steve Holland

at my side and our list in hand, I reviewed the penalty-takers on the pitch. We had just lost our first pick when Harry Kane came off with cramp and fatigue. We replaced him with Brentford's Ivan Toney, who, though inexperienced internationally, was very high up on the list of penalty-takers: twenty-four goals from twenty-four penalties at club level. Liverpool's Trent Alexander-Arnold was another strong shoot-out candidate on the substitutes' bench. He possessed excellent technique and strong self-belief. I had twice seen Trent successfully take penalties for his club in cup finals under the same kind of pressure that we faced here, and he had been fantastically consistent in training for the shoot-out. I brought him on with five minutes remaining.

Just as in the Euro 20 final against Italy, then, three of our first five penalty-takers would be subs. What's more, once again, I had brought two of them on in the final phases of the game. I could hardly have been more boldly committing myself to the strategy. I was confident in my reasons but, even so, if we failed to go through now . . . well, I could write the headlines myself.

Thankfully, I didn't have to. My confidence, and our prep, was borne out. Every England player who stepped up to the spot showed tremendous composure and confidently converted their penalties. This included Bukayo Saka, showing supreme resilience by accepting the responsibility after missing against Italy, and reaping his reward. Ivan Toney even had the belief to deploy the 'no-look' technique; maintaining eye contact with the goalkeeper for what seemed like an age and waiting for him to commit to a movement before shooting into the other corner without looking down at the ball. His goal, ice-cool and assured, capped off the performance and fed a narrative that the national team had now turned penalty-taking into a strength.

I was delighted to think so, although, of course, the decisions I made in the game we had just won were based on a long-standing process that had been in place at Wembley four years previously, when the outcome invited nothing but criticism. Sometimes vindication is a long time coming – and a bit mysterious even then.

The 'challenge' mindset

Our work on the penalty shoot-out can be seen as a version in miniature of a broader transformational strategy for the way our England teams coped with pressure. It involved changing the mindset – from a 'threat' mindset to a 'challenge' mindset. It involved meeting pressure halfway, through intensive preparation and 'scenario planning', which I'll discuss in this section. It used innovative research in carefully calibrated dosages to yield improvement. It encouraged ownership, agency and self-belief to create composure and drive high performance under conditions of extreme pressure. And it set out to challenge and change the received narrative.

When I took over the national team, I watched back the unexpected 2–1 loss to Iceland in the 2016 Euros to see what we might learn from it. England had been clear favourites to win the game and we went ahead early, creating the feeling that this match was going to play out entirely as expected. Then came two quick goals from Iceland, and now our belief was rocked. At that point, quite visibly, the collective mindset switched from confidence to fear. *We can't lose this, not to a team as low as Iceland in the rankings.* It seemed to me that players stopped thinking clearly and lost their focus on the process. Instead, they started to worry about the outcome. You could almost see eyes developing far-away looks, and decision-making definitely started to suffer – shots taken from unrealistic scoring positions, simple passes given away. Instead of calmly trying to work their way back into the match, the players were now preoccupied almost exclusively with *the worst thing that could happen.*

I recognised this 'threat' mindset as a big hurdle for the England team to overcome. It dated back a lot further than that Iceland game. For decades our national team had fallen short of public expectation, creating a cycle in which disproportionate hope was followed by inevitable disillusionment, and there had been an escalating sense of dread around tournaments. As we saw earlier, the work on identity that I carried out with the team – talking more about writing our own stories, the stories of a modern England, rather than being perpetually burdened by the failures of the past – strove specifically to address this dread. The change in our communications with the media and fans was another way for us to relieve some of this tension by managing expectations. Ultimately, however, the team still had to go on the pitch and deliver. Supported by my coaching staff, it was my responsibility to prepare the players psychologically by creating the needed shift in mindset through our work on the training ground and in the messages I delivered in every conversation and meeting.

In every camp, the mindset I wanted us to instil was one of 'challenge' and what was possible, rather than one of 'threat' and what might go wrong. To that end, my players will tell you how often I told them that I expected them to make mistakes. If we weren't making mistakes, then we probably weren't trying things, and if we weren't trying things we might never know how good we could be. That was practically a mantra with me. All I asked after mistakes was that players put themselves straight back in the position to succeed or fail again.

And then, in games where we fell behind, the mindset had to be: how do we get back into this? How do we banish panic from our emotional repertoire and replace it with (a word we used a lot) composure? How do we become resilient enough that we are never beaten mentally, but only beaten ultimately by the clock?

In a 'challenge' mindset, challenges are framed as an opportunity for gain. To illustrate what a difference this outlook can make, let me describe a football club's treatment room in two different scenarios: positive and negative. At a club involved in a relegation battle – a negative scenario – the treatment room is invariably full. I know this from my experience at Middlesbrough. The players have experienced the kind of stress that leads to tightening muscles and suboptimal decision-making. Combined, this increases the chance of injury. There will be players, too, for whom the stress itself is too much. They might not admit it, but for them the treatment room becomes a place of safety, a space away from the line of fire. Towards the end of those seasons when relegation loomed, it was sometimes hard to get a willing team out onto the pitch.

Now let's compare the treatment room ahead of a positive scenario, like a cup final. It's invariably empty. Everyone is available, with some even masking injuries in order to have a chance to play. I swear I've seen players on crutches trying to accelerate their rehabilitation to make themselves available for a final. Yes, these are high-pressure matches, just as relegation battles are; but the pressure can be framed as an opportunity for gain. In the same way, if we return to penalties for a moment: looked at negatively, a penalty is a frighteningly extreme test of nerve offering a decent chance of humiliation. Looked at positively (and this is how some of the most reliable penalty-takers regard it), it's a golden opportunity to score a goal: twelve yards from the target, only the goalkeeper to beat, with a stationary ball, in your own time . . .

Switching the mindset from 'threat' to 'challenge' empowered us to frame high-pressure scenarios as positive opportunities for gain, rather than daunting occasions for fear. It was another way of taking the 'weight' out of the England shirt. And combining that mindset switch with a focus on preparation and scenario planning ultimately transformed our team's chances of success, taking us to two finals in eight years after that long, barren period and the heavy burden of its negativity.

I was intent on ensuring scenario planning was something

we devoted considerable energy to during my time with England. It was a topic I learned most about from the Army on my visits to Sandhurst. In battlefield planning, the military recognise that different scenarios might play out from the one they believe to be most likely. Their assumption is that no plan necessarily survives first contact with the enemy. With this in mind, they 'scenario plan', imagining as thoroughly as possible the potential setbacks that might occur within the original plan and rehearsing strategies to deal with them, using realistic deliberate practice.

The great thing about this method is that it breeds good habits – flexibility, clarity of thought, resilience in the face of setbacks – which endure even when a scenario occurs that *hasn't* been planned for. A classic example would be the mission in which the United States Navy's elite SEAL Team Six captured Osama bin Laden in Pakistan in 2011. There was a clear plan, they had reconstructed as closely as possible the buildings they were going to infiltrate, they had scenario-planned for multiple off-plan eventualities, and they had practised and practised. Consequently, on the day, when they ran into a problem they hadn't anticipated (one of the helicopters struck the wall of the compound and crashed), the fact they had prepared and planned so extensively for the need to come off the plan meant that they were supple enough to react calmly even in this circumstance and continued to make good, clear decisions under pressure.

At England, scenario planning gave us scope to adapt quickly and with composure to rapidly altering circumstances and to respond calmly when an event didn't go to plan. It allowed us to say: there's no drama; we've prepared for this, talked about it; we're all on the same page and we can pivot to a different approach. It's a change of plan but one that's still been pre-prepared and is based on evidence.

As a coaching team, we might not have been quite at the SEAL Team Six level, yet I would say we were as close as football could be, plotting out our best changes in the event that we went behind in a game, or ahead in a game, or had a player sent off, or faced an opponent down to ten players. Of course, no matter how many scenarios you plan in football, there will always be a new one that surprises you. But when this happens, you can be ready for the unknown, which in itself is a scenario you can prepare for mentally.

A moment I can point to where we benefited very clearly from our scenario planning was in the final minutes of injury-time against Slovakia in the round-of-sixteen tie at the 2024 Euros. We'd been 1–0 down since the first half, but we had been pleased with the way the players had dominated possession and mounted a steady fightback. Still, nothing had yet worked. Slovakia had continued to deny us and it looked like we were going home.

With one minute of time added on remaining, we summoned Ivan Toney from the substitutes' bench. It was a decision that raised eyebrows – not least the eyebrows belonging to Ivan himself, who naturally wished he had been on sooner and must have been wondering what difference we could possibly expect him to make in such limited time.

As I mentioned earlier, the right move often isn't to make a rash decision. Rather, the right move is to be patient and to stick to your evidence-based approach, waiting for the optimum moment when you have all the information at hand to act. In his book *Think Again*, Wharton professor Adam Grant demonstrates that while we admire people who are decisive, the research shows that they can make wrong, uninformed choices. They are too hasty. The most successful outcomes can come from individuals and teams who are willing to 'rethink': pausing, adapting and responding to the latest data and feedback. Well, in the case of Ivan Toney, we had waited for that moment. And now it was time to act.

We had held our nerve by keeping Kane and Bellingham on the pitch. There had been a call from some parts of the media and some fans to take those two off, but we held back from doing so because we knew they gave us the best chance of scoring (more on that in a moment). Ivan's introduction was more impulsive, but the reason we had the opportunity to make the substitution was because Slovakia conceded a throw-in deep inside their half. As we saw it, this was a moment we could capitalise on. It was far enough up the pitch for Kyle Walker to launch the ball all the way into the box. And now, if we moved quickly, we could send on the perfect player to be in the box for it. Ivan had a formidable physical presence and possessed strong and quick skills in close quarters. This was our last chance to disrupt Slovakia's increasingly creaking defences.

In training the day before the match, we had walked through the long throw as a set-piece for emergencies and identified how individual players could make a difference. Long-ball was not the route we would be generally aiming to take, but in moments like this we would go that way. It was scenario planning, for precisely this scenario.

On the touchline I told Ivan: 'You think you haven't got time to affect the game, but I'm telling you now, you have. We're not dead.'

I'm not sure, even as he ran directly into the penalty area, that Ivan believed me. But, as Kyle's throw-in sailed in, Ivan found himself with an extra marker. In the scramble, thinking on his feet, he drew a defender away from the penalty spot. Now with an additional two yards of space as the ball arrived, Jude Bellingham dared to perform a stunt that only a player of his class could successfully pull off: scoring from an audacious overhead kick that flew into the net and sent the game into extra-time.

Almost as soon as play resumed, Ivan showcased his determination, strength and awareness to deliver a precision header for Harry Kane's winning goal. Having been on the pitch for just two minutes, a fully briefed substitute with the right mentality had helped us effect the most dramatic turn-around. The game ended 2–1 and we went through.

I was, of course, ecstatic at the win, but I was also immensely satisfied at what the performance signified for all of us who had been working on this England project. Over a period of years, we had concentrated on instilling resilience in this group of players and a 'challenge' mindset. We had sought to help them deal better with setbacks, like conceding the first goal in a match. We had been coaching the players to stay composed and to focus on the process. We had been encouraging them to be flexible and adopt the idea of scenario planning. Ivan Toney was one example, but we would go on to do the same later in the tournament in our semi-final game against the Netherlands when we brought on Ollie Watkins. We thought he could exploit the space behind the defenders better than Harry Kane could at that point, and so we made that late change. We were lauded for that decision, whereas holding fast to an existing line-up rarely wins plaudits. But we had reassured the team too of the importance of sticking to our convictions and of ignoring outside pressures – to keep playing the way we wanted to, to keep utilising the best systems and the best players on the pitch to win. Playing this way can open you up to criticism by appearing to be intransigent. But it's often the best thing to do.

The final reason I was pleased with the Slovakia game was that during the course of all of our preparations we had endeavoured to cultivate a never-say-die attitude that would keep our players pushing to the end of any game. This attribute, along with all of the qualities above, had been displayed by our team that night against Slovakia. I was extremely proud of how far we had come.

Stress management

'Nobody performs better under pressure.
The best just maintain their level better.
The "edge" is by not doing worse.'

Hank Weisinger

We talk a great deal about 'pressure' but I always say to people that nobody is physically standing over us, pressing down. So what, actually, are the factors that produce the physical and behavioural responses that we all recognise as 'under pressure'?

I once attended a coaching seminar on this subject by the American psychologist Hank Weisinger, whom I quoted above. Among many brilliant observations, he listed several factors that contribute to the feeling of pressure:

- The demand to succeed
- Uncertainty of outcome
- Desire for a positive outcome and/or aversion to a negative outcome
- Perceived responsibility for results
- Consequences, loss or gain

I would say that all of those conditions were in operation, and very clearly, every time England played. I would also add that the public nature of our work had an enormous further bearing. There's a reason that public speaking is perceived to be the most nerve-racking of tasks. It brings with it the possibility of humiliation in front of others. Well, there can't be many situations more prone to public-speaking-style fears than playing for your national football team in a major tournament, with thousands in the stadium, and hundreds of millions watching around the world including, most likely, everyone you know and have ever known. So, a huge part of the challenge in managing the national team involved psychologically priming the players, as well as myself, for the inevitable and constant pressure created by this unique form of exposure.

My notion here was that we could make pressure work for us if we could reframe it as a positive driver. As a young player, I would need to work hard at calming my nerves before a big match. As I became more experienced, I could draw on a greater store of self-belief: I'd been there before, I knew what was required, I had demonstrated the ability. At that stage, a surge of adrenaline that had once felt out of my control could get me into a good place. It sharpened my attention, helping me feel alert and focused. Indeed, the older I got as a player, the more I had to work to get mentally right for the 'lesser matches' with little jeopardy riding on them. Without feeling so naturally pumped up at the prospect, I had to consciously get myself into the same heightened state, otherwise I risked underperforming.

Ultimately, my career on the pitch showed me that there could be a positive relationship between pressure and performance, and I sought to instil that in our players, getting them to expect and embrace the pressure rather than to resist it or fear it.

Meanwhile, our preparation and scenario planning were designed to equip us with the necessary clarity and composure to perform effectively when pressure had us in its grip. Those things would ideally give us the foundation we needed to be thinking clearly under pressure (T-CUP), to borrow the maxim from Clive Woodward's golden era of England rugby. It was true for the players, and it was true for me as the leader on the sideline: the key to coping with pressure in a developing game was staying 'in the moment' rather than worrying about possible outcomes or other situations yet to arise.

Whenever I discuss leadership with groups of business executives, I'm regularly asked how I personally coped with the constant strain hard-wired into the role of England manager. From their own lives, perhaps, they recognise the stress that comes with the constant demand for results, along with the complexities of leading a team of high-achieving people. In addition, they seem to be curious about the weight of the additional expectations and scrutiny that came with the particular role I held.

I find myself explaining that my attitude changed. While battling to avoid relegation at Middlesbrough, I was determined to project a show of strength. As manager, I tried to demonstrate that the pressure we were under didn't affect me. In reality, I worried about it constantly and so the way I presented myself became something of an act, and almost certainly an unconvincing one. I was new to the role and I was having to learn at pace. I'm pretty certain that the strain will have shown itself to the people I was leading.

With more experience of facing pressure, and with confidence in the role, I was better prepared for the moments of difficulty with England. The preparation of the team was detailed, with added scenario planning as well. I knew what was required to steer a group of people through difficult times. I knew the moments to address the whole group, when to demand more, when to empathise and how to find the right ways to challenge, so as to retain confidence without accepting lower standards. I also wasn't frightened of showing a vulnerable side. In talking with England players, I would often be frank about the challenges I'd faced in the past that ultimately proved to be learning experiences. I think it helped the team identify with me. Being authentic is, as we have discussed, a crucial quality in leadership, and experience gave me the courage to lean into that. I'm certain my communication was more powerful and believable because I had more confidence in my ability to navigate through events. I'm not certain you can fast-track that process of learning to lead, but it's perhaps reassuring to younger leaders that nobody has all the tools when they start out. Some experience gained is due to a painful process of learning through failure. We probably wouldn't choose it but we're definitely better leaders for it.

As for managing my stress levels and my own energy and resilience under pressure, I've attended an awful lot of presentations in this area, and I've always gone along in hope, waiting for somebody to stand up and hit me with something life-changing. Yet all the research points to the basics: sleep, nutrition and exercise. Hardly big news and yet how many of us really commit to being disciplined about those basics?

No doubt advances in technology will continue to make managing our well-being and energy easier. Based on my own recent experience, however, I'm not yet ready to outsource the responsibility for that completely. During Euro 24 my staff and I were each given a smart ring – a wearable device to track our sleep, heart rate and general levels of stress. I was particularly interested to see what my smart ring had to tell me on the morning after our penalty shoot-out win over

Switzerland – a high-stakes moment in my managerial career that had arguably knocked years off my life.

Eventually the notification came through from the app on my phone. It read: *Yesterday was a perfectly normal day for you in terms of stress. Does that seem right?*

As much as I'd like to say the smart ring had detected a strength in my leadership character that I had underestimated, in reality it reminded me that the most effective monitor when it comes to maintaining our welfare in a high-pressure environment will always be ourselves.

SUMMARY
When the Whistle Blows
On turning pressure into performance

- Great leaders recognise that pressure is a privilege that comes with the position. They prepare for it and normalise it to fuel their team's performance.

- Look to control the process rather than the outcome when performing under pressure or when the stakes are high. Instead of worrying about what can go wrong, shift the mindset from 'threat' to 'challenge' and reframe the narrative: what can go right?

- Fear often comes from uncertainty. A clear plan, with clear roles and clear expectations, breeds confidence in high-pressure moments.

- Communicate with precision. Bombarding your team with too much information in times of stress will jeopardise their performance. Only share the essential details they need to deliver at that time.

- Prepare for the unexpected. Scenario planning won't cover every eventuality but it will improve your team's adaptability and composure when things go wrong. Life, sport and business are all predictably unpredictable. You need to be ready for the uncertainty when it comes.

- Psychological safety matters. If people know they will be supported regardless of the outcome, they will be free to optimise their performance without the negative impact of failure.

- Accountability comes with leadership. Even if others are to blame, if you own a decision you will shield your team from criticism and improve their chances of success in the future.

- When undertaking a review, focus on the merits of a decision, using the knowledge you had before the result was known. Hindsight can make everyone an expert, but it fuels opinion rather than fact.

- Prioritise your own well-being in order to manage the pressure and stress of leading others. Maintaining the fundamentals of sleep, nutrition and exercise will deliver benefits way beyond the energy and discipline required in keeping a consistent routine.

CHAPTER 9

Holding the Line

On leading through adversity

Football in the time of Covid

'Take what you need.'

That was the advice from our technical director, Les Reed. It was mid-March 2020 and the government, scrambling to react to the rapidly rising cases of the Covid-19 virus in the UK, had just announced a stop to 'non-essential contact and travel'.

I took a look round my office. We were just three months out from the European Championship, with preparations in full flow. What did I need? How was this even meant to work? Eventually I picked up a whiteboard, walked out to the car with it, loaded it up and headed home.

It was becoming rapidly apparent that the chances of an international football tournament taking place that summer were shrinking. Indeed, those chances were now the product of our wishful thinking as much as anything else. A few days earlier, I had been at a planning meeting for the two March internationals, scheduled for the end of that month. The meeting had been held at Wembley, rather than at St George's Park, which was unusual but then so was the agenda, which was dominated by updates on national case numbers and the logistics of cross-border travel at this time, and with input from Whitehall. One of our matches was against Italy, the European country hit earliest and hardest by the coronavirus pandemic and where the first national lockdown had just been announced. I left that meeting thinking, there is no way this game goes ahead.

Sure enough, on 13 March, all Premier League football was suspended, along with our two internationals. Two days later, I was driving home with my whiteboard. And the day after that, Uefa announced the postponement of Euro 20 until the following summer.

It was bitterly disappointing. For months our thinking had been laser-focused on the summer and our anticipation had been rising, along with a genuine feeling throughout the organisation that we would be in a good position to do well in that tournament. And now something had come along to dwarf all of that – a global emergency, no less – and make it look an entirely irrelevant concern. It was an eerie and frightening moment. I should have been getting ready to greet the players as they arrived for the March camp. Instead, I was at home, writing an open letter for the FA website containing phrases I'd never envisaged having to compose as an England manager.

For everyone in our country, the primary focus of the present –
and the coming months – is undoubtedly to look after our

families, support our communities and work together to come through what is clearly the most extreme test that we've faced collectively in decades. On behalf of all the team and staff, I would like to take this opportunity to send our sympathies to those who have lost loved ones already. Our thoughts are with you and with those who sadly will suffer similarly in the coming period.

That letter was published on a Friday. The following Monday the government announced the first full lockdown and life immediately changed for all of us.

The positive reaction to my letter initially surprised me. However, it soon became clear to me that in a time of such uncertainty and, for many, loss, people were seeking reassurance and comfort from leaders around the country. Two weeks later, at the beginning of April, like millions of others I watched as the Queen stoically addressed the nation in a special broadcast from Windsor. As she closed with the memorable and soothing words 'We shall meet again', I thought to myself: *Here's someone who's really in charge. She's lived through worse than this. She's calm. We're in good hands. Everything will be OK.* Of course, my own modest letter couldn't begin to compete with the gravitas of such an address from Britain's longest-reigning monarch. But I felt I had done the right thing because I knew the national football team connected with so many people on an emotional level, and as its manager I had a duty to reach for the right words in that moment, as I would try to do at other times during my tenure at England. It had felt important for me to promote unity and composure at a time when everyone's world was being turned upside down.

Like everyone, I now found myself operating in a new reality, with huge and unfamiliar challenges. That said, I should stress that in writing about those challenges here, I do not compare my own adversity to that faced by so many others. I recognise how lucky I was. Doctors, nurses, care workers and countless others faced hardships and dangers I could only imagine, and I have nothing but awe and admiration for them. Like millions of others, my family and I stood outside on Thursday evenings banging pots and pans in appreciation of NHS and frontline staff. My intention in this chapter is simply to highlight the complexity of the leadership decisions and challenges I faced in a high-profile role, in the hope that readers might take something from them, and how I tried to use my platform responsibly to support wider society where I could.

But in effect, I was trying to run the national football team while working from home. And as my FA role also involved advising colleagues on everything from grass-roots football at one end of the spectrum, to global relationships with Uefa and Fifa at the other (and plenty in between), I was trying to do that as well. What with all these diverse aspects of the job, 'working from home' pretty quickly came to feel more like 'sleeping in the office'. Until that time, I'd never been on a video conference call. Within days of restrictions coming into force, I found myself utterly dependent on them via my laptop, hopping from a call about budgets, to a call with the national junior coaches, to a call with one of my players, and back to budgets again, as we all began to consider the full implications of this unprecedented situation.

As for any organisation, business or enterprise at that time, the inability to function as normal had immediate financial concerns. St George's Park found itself with hundreds of budget decisions to make and it was instantly clear we were going to have to lose personnel and projects. Because I had been in the organisation longer than nearly everyone in the St George's Park leadership team, I wanted to stay across these decisions. I knew why budgets had been allocated originally, and I knew the potentially devastating risk of cuts in certain areas, not least the development of our junior teams, so I wanted to have as much input as possible here. Nevertheless, international junior camps were getting cancelled because of the cost of running them with testing and medical restrictions in place, and because of the impossibility of getting teams to travel from anywhere apart from Scotland and Wales. We lost what had been shaping up to be a fantastic football skills development initiative for schools. We also lost some good coaches in this period for the simple reason that there were suddenly no camps, and therefore fewer opportunities for them to work. I volunteered to take a salary reduction because I felt it was the responsible thing to do.

Nobody enjoyed this enforced restructuring process. The conversations were difficult and the impact on morale was palpable, even down the line on a video call. In that environment, it was very hard to project positivity. At the same time, in disorientating circumstances, any team will inevitably look to the leader for exactly that. I felt a need to try to closely support the coaches of the national junior teams to keep them engaged and reassure them during all this uncertainty. To that end, I took charge of the remaining coaches and we set up some of the research projects that we'd wanted to do before but hadn't previously had time to undertake. We studied best practice in aspects of the game such as defending crosses, building play from goal-kicks, attacking-third play, and strategies for pressing. The coaches worked in small groups and then reported back their findings to all of us so that the whole department could benefit.

Meanwhile, at senior level, we did a research project on the last five winners of international tournaments, looking at all the areas of the game listed above and also seeking key findings in areas such as how many players they used, their tactical formations, their goals from set-plays, whether they pressed high or defended deep, and so on. As for the regular calls and even the online quizzes that became a part of life in lockdown, I made sure to be involved. With such limited contact, my communications with the team had never been more critical. Even though I suspected there was plenty of googling for the answers!

When it came to the players, responsibility for their welfare fell to their respective clubs. Even so, it was important to me that we stayed in touch. I arranged a video call with my squad members in turn. Even with thirty or so players to contact, I wanted to give each one the time and focus just to check in and talk about the reality we found ourselves in. I had definitely messaged players before, but the purpose of a Zoom call was to give each individual the opportunity for a lengthy, personal discussion. I wanted to tell them where they sat in my thinking for England, and to find out how they were coping with the unique challenges of Covid. Ultimately, I wanted to offer them my ear to listen at any time; my Zoom door was always open. Of course, you can only ask the questions, and not everyone will show vulnerability and let you 'in'. Some players opened up quickly, others needed more time; and a few were strikingly candid. Away from the spotlight, they were young men dealing with the same fears and uncertainties as everyone else. I felt at that particular moment, I could perhaps be someone from outside their football club, a confidant of sorts, who could help advise them without immediately affecting their selection for the weekend. Our conversations were wide-ranging, and often lasted up to an hour. We all had a sense of perspective on the situation: football had to bow to public health, and even thinking about the game seriously during a time of national crisis seemed somehow wrong. Nevertheless, it was our responsibility to be ready to return to action when that became possible. It was a difficult line to walk.

These conversations also sharpened my awareness of the responsibility leaders have to put other people's needs before their own. I won't pretend I always managed it – there were moments when I found myself dwelling on my own frustrations or fatigue. It was mentally exhausting. But, on the whole, by focusing on the needs of the players and staff, I felt I was able to get my priorities right most of the time. Leadership in adversity isn't about being flawless; it's about recognising when others need you, and stepping up for them as best you can. And when it all became too much, I knew there was always time for a simple walk in the park to clear my head and reset.

I also realised in that period just how vital it was to recharge and re-energise if I was going to lead effectively. Leadership can feel lonely at the top. You can give your energy in service to others, but you also need to find spaces where you can talk honestly to yourself. For me, that meant leaning on my family, a close circle of friends, and mentors I trusted. At various times, I have had a personal coach who has served as a sounding board and helped me to clarify my thinking. That was useful, but so too were conversations with other leaders in the same position. I would regularly join Zoom calls with head coaches from different sports, all over the world. These weren't formal seminars but open conversations: sharing challenges, frustrations, and specific approaches to supporting players through circumstances none of us had ever encountered. Covid had no geographical barrier and no respect for sport – it united us all in difficulty. People were willing to open up, to show vulnerability, and to admit that they didn't have all the answers. That honesty, and the sense of solving problems together, was immensely reassuring. To know that other leaders of high-profile teams were wrestling with the same unknowns, and learning as they went just as I was, gave me the strength and perspective to carry on.

Getting back to 'playing'

Our first window of opportunity opened in September. The Premier League had completed Project Restart, which saw the remaining fixtures of that season take place in June and July. At that point, I was one of a very small number of people who were allowed to attend games – a truly peculiar experience under lockdown conditions, sitting ten yards from everyone else in an almost entirely empty stadium, being able to hear every player on the pitch, and then (one plus, at least) not having to spend an hour stuck in the car park afterwards. The combination of absent traffic and staggered kick-off times, arranged for television, enabled me quite regularly to hit two games in a day, and on one memorable occasion, I managed to clock up three.

July was a later finish than usual for the league, which put a squeeze on the time available for international meet-ups before the start of the following season, which was delayed until mid-September. Our international week, with two games, was tucked in just before that. In a world without financial consequences, those matches wouldn't have gone ahead. But cancellation would have meant penalties from television companies and sponsors, all of whom had been under the same financial pressure as everyone else, and would have been hugely damaging for Uefa, Fifa and every national federation. So the games went on.

It proved to be a mounting nightmare. The first obstacle we ran into was the reluctance of the clubs to release their players. Manchester United and Manchester City had taken part in the latter stages of the Europa League and Champions League, held across one week in a central venue after the finish of the Premier League, so those clubs were rightfully keen that their players should be resting up. But I don't think any club was happy to surrender their players in these circumstances, right on top of the new season. In any case, no deals could be done. Allowing the players of one club the extra rest would have been regarded as unfair on the others and I'd have been accused of preferential treatment. And in my experience, nothing makes a club manager more irate than the feeling his rivals are being given an advantage. Anyway, I stated our case firmly: we had Nations League games to play. In our group, we would face Iceland along with a strong Danish side and Belgium, who were the top-ranked team in the world at the time. So it was important for us to field our strongest side.

A couple of days before the camp, another complication emerged when Harry Maguire was arrested in Mykonos following an altercation outside a bar (at the time of writing in September 2025 he is still awaiting a retrial). My feeling was that as the player hadn't been charged with anything at that stage, and the case seemed vague, we should support him by picking him. These calls are always more complicated with England than with a club. The bar for scrutiny is higher and so, when I named my squad, I received an absolute grilling over Harry's inclusion. I was also heavily questioned over the selection of other United players, and City players, who needed a rest after their European exertions, and over my non-selection of other names, some of whom had actually tested positive for Covid at the time, though I wasn't allowed to say so. In a nutshell, it was a typical England manager's press conference, where you take a battering, can't give all the details in your own defence, and infuriate supporters up and down the country.

Sure enough, three hours after I announced the squad, Harry was charged and I had to remove him – not because

I was prejudging him, but because I felt the attention his presence would attract would be too much in these circumstances. Cue more 'England Manager Laughing Stock' headlines.

In the squad that we eventually assembled, all of the players arrived short of training and match time, and below their best physical level. Seven were recovering from Covid. They were available to us but had been unable to train properly and could only safely play sixty minutes here, or thirty minutes there, as you would in pre-season, to avoid injury. In other words, we were going to be playing competitive matches but under typical pre-season conditions.

Moreover, the rigorous Covid testing protocols that were in place brought both an administrative burden and a constant feeling of uncertainty. All players and staff had to be tested the day before travelling to games, and then again the day before each match. Every morning we waited for test results in order to know who was available to train, and it was only on the morning of the match that we knew who was available to be picked.

Then there were the social distancing measures. Meetings were held in the conference area of St George's with everyone sat a yard apart. The medical room and gym had also been moved into that space because it was the only room large enough to meet the restrictions. At mealtimes, we were obliged to sit two per table, with Perspex screens between us, which just amplified the sense of isolation. It was always my desire that the players should feel confident and relaxed with one another so that when they played, it would be with freedom and belief 'in' each other, but this necessarily sterile atmosphere hardly encouraged that. The limitations meant that the environment all week allowed little freedom at all, just rules and constraint.

We had special international dispensation to travel to Iceland but that included having to drive straight from the airport to a clinic for everyone to be tested again. Those particular tests were administered using the longest swabs any of us had seen – and we had all seen a lot of swabs by this stage. As everyone took their turn having this giant instrument rammed up their nostrils, a good deal of apprehension fell over those sitting in line and waiting. I must say, though, that as the owner of a nose that can take a larger swab, I was in a position of some advantage.

At the stadium, we were allocated two small changing rooms, each restricted to five people only – not especially useful. The subs changed in those. The players changed in a hall, with a curtain down the middle, behind which were our opponents, also getting changed. No secret team instructions in this setting.

Finally, a game of football took place. The pitch was dry, the weather warm and a handful of fans watched from a hill overlooking the stadium. We had a goal wrongly disallowed for offside (no VAR in operation), which might have settled everyone down. Instead, Iceland were dogged and we were unsurprisingly lacking in rhythm and struggling to create chances. Just to compound things, Kyle Walker picked up a second yellow card in the seventieth minute and was sent off. We finally got a break with an eighty-ninth-minute penalty, which Raheem Sterling squeezed in, only to concede a penalty at the other end almost directly from the restart. Thankfully their centre-forward skied it and we took the points.

This was definitely the match that started the high-level negativity externally that beset us for the rest of my tenure. The media were unimpressed, and like everyone else during that game they were at home watching the match unfold on TV, not physically in the stadium as usual. I suspect they were probably influenced as much by the commentators' words and by the social media reaction as by anything else. Everybody was watching from their sofa, mid-pandemic, frustrated and wanting entertainment but getting a laboured victory over Iceland instead. Just as it was hard for the players to perform in such a sterile atmosphere, the lack of crowd reaction made the game harder to enjoy from a spectator's perspective. It was lose-lose.

We returned to our hotel, where we were staying over the weekend before flying to Denmark, and took a welcome moment to draw breath – at least for thirty-six hours. At 6 a.m., I was awoken by a knock on the door from our head of security, who informed me that, during the night, two of our players had breached the quarantine rules. Icing on the cake, really. I had no choice but to send both the players straight home.

We flew on to Denmark for our second match, amid all the restrictions and protocols and now with a disciplinary storm to throw into the mix, one which required us to explain ourselves to the government back home. By the time we had counted how many fit players we had left, and how many minutes we could play the others for, we decided our best option was to switch to a back three. This at least allowed us to look at some new players and an alternative system, but I can't pretend it wasn't forced upon us. Having announced the team, I found myself berated for not fielding enough attacking players, slightly overlooking the fact that we'd just sent two of those home and couldn't start two of the others.

There followed another sticky performance and the game ended 0–0 – not disgraceful given that Denmark went on to reach the semi-final of the Euros, but it enabled the disgruntlement among the supporters to build. That dissatisfaction didn't go away even when we beat Belgium, the world's number one ranked team, at Wembley, and it surged again when we lost to Denmark thanks to a terrible penalty decision against us, compounded by a red card for Harry Maguire.

Prior to the pandemic we'd enjoyed a buoyant period from the 2018 World Cup through to the 2020 qualifying matches. We'd become the highest scorers in Europe and our reputation was expanding, only for it to be undermined by this block of matches in a period when it was hard to know what we'd be asked to adapt to next. It was altogether the least enjoyable phase of my tenure (although Germany in 2024 would end up giving it a run for its money).

There are these periods for any leader when you have to keep a tight rein on things, but also roll with the punches a bit. Your resilience comes to the fore and you have to make the best decisions you can with the information to hand. You can't bemoan your bad fortune and drag down those around you. Instead, you've got to find the best solutions, look at the situation as an opportunity for people to grow, and hope to come out stronger for it all in the end. I know that some coaches and organisations, such as Eddie Jones when he led England's rugby team, have felt the need during camps to deliberately throw 'curveballs', intentional moments of disruption and chaos that test the staff and prepare them for tougher challenges ahead. Well, at England's football team, we consistently got those curveballs for free. The bigger test would have been a seventy-two-hour period of calm. Then we definitely would have started to worry . . . If nothing else, that September 2020 camp provided me with a great case study for aspiring managers when I presented it to coach education courses where I had been asked to provide something about the complexities of running an international team. Especially during times of adversity.

Finding positives in adversity

The selection difficulties I faced throughout our Nations League matches were complex and compromised our preparations. We continued to be plagued by players dropping out due to contracting Covid, and the knock-on effect that had on their ability to train and to be ready for matches. At the same time, these squad issues gave me the chance to try out new players. Bukayo Saka made his England debut in this period, as did Phil Foden and Kalvin Phillips. With Euro 20 rescheduled for the following summer, it strengthened my hand somewhat as we turned our attention to that tournament.

While Covid restrictions underwent a period of flux throughout our preparations, our training camp plans were still largely undertaken online. As an organisation we'd had time to learn how to make the most of remote working, but it wasn't the same as being together as a group. Our energy could falter without regular contact, and the culture we'd worked so hard to promote just didn't feel so alive. Technology was invaluable, but the longer the restrictions went on, the clearer it became to me that there is no substitute for being in the same place as your colleagues. For younger people especially, who are still learning, sharing ideas and finding their feet, the value of being physically together cannot be overstated. Working side by side allows knowledge to flow, sparks new ideas, and nurtures the kind of team spirit that is hard to replicate on a screen. That's not to dismiss remote work altogether – it has its place – but leaders in any field need to be mindful of what can be lost when physical togetherness is taken away.

At the same time, this adversity revealed how much potential already existed within the organisation. I was struck by how many people stepped up when circumstances demanded it. Often it wasn't the obvious candidates, but those who hadn't yet had the opportunity to show what they could do. I was genuinely impressed by their knowledge, strength, and willingness to go beyond the call of duty to find solutions. It was eye-opening to see leadership emerge from places you might not have expected, while some you assumed would naturally take the lead occasionally fell short. It reminded me never to pre-judge people, and reinforced the importance of giving everyone the chance to rise to the occasion. Difficult circumstances, while far from desirable, can bring out extraordinary qualities in people.

———

Staged a year late, Euro 20 took place at a time when the government began to ease restrictions. Set across Europe, the tournament saw a limited return of fans to stadiums, under social distancing guidelines, but their presence made all the difference. Within our camp we still faced disruptions to plans, losing Mason Mount and Ben Chilwell to isolation for five days after the pair chatted for ninety seconds too long in the tunnel with a Scottish player who subsequently tested positive. I was delighted when our doctor brought that one to my table . . . Not only did both players miss our final match of the group, against the Czech Republic, they were confined to their hotel rooms for the duration – an awful experience for them, as well as another unexpected headache. Even ahead of the final we lost Phil Foden to a foot injury as he was innocuously knocking a ball around at the end of training.

We can assess the impact of the pandemic on our performance in different ways.

My view from inside the operation was that we lost a little momentum during lockdown, perhaps inevitably given that we couldn't be together as a team for much of the time. We'll never know how England would have performed had Euro 20 not been delayed – had that momentum we had been experiencing in March when the lockdown happened been able to continue. That said, we discovered some new players and definitely established resilience that made us stronger.

To reach a first final in fifty-five years was an unbelievably emotional moment and it felt incredible to walk around Wembley after defeating Denmark and feel the energy of a nation rejoicing. Yet four days later, I was public enemy number one. Wrong tactical system, too late with the substitutions, wrong penalty strategy; the highs and lows of leadership in extremis.

Of course, I inevitably reflected on all of those decisions and whether different ones would have given us a different outcome. The reality is that my choices are the only ones that were played out. Everything else is a theory and, what's more, a theory without consequences. I've tried to demonstrate in this book the degree of careful thinking and planning that went into everything the team and I did. We were one moment, perhaps one penalty kick, away from immortality – and our penalty strategy, as you've read, was itself robust. In the final, should we have started with a back four in defence? Maybe, but we went a goal up after five minutes, with one wing-back crossing for the other one to finish the move. When a team goes a goal up, the dynamics of a game change and the decisions around substitutions become even more heavily loaded.

I have to accept that for all the incredible memories created and landmark moments reached during my time at England, not securing that elusive trophy means that people are entitled to discard the hundreds of good decisions I made, and to question my whole approach to the job. None of those people,

I would argue, know the complexity of some of the difficult situations I encountered, and few have offered detailed solutions beyond broad observations (though I'm still open to answers on a postcard). But being judged on binary outcomes and decisions is often the harsh reality of leadership, a truth that leaders across all organisations will likely confront at some point.

As we moved on from those Euros we had conceded just two goals in the whole tournament and were only behind for some fifteen minutes in total. Of course, we had work to do as we turned our attention to the future. But what a relief it was to put the Covid restrictions behind us and operate freely again.

I had, of course, never expected to lead the national team through a period of such turbulent circumstances. It was one of the most difficult and demanding portions of my eight years in charge – a challenge on both a professional and a personal level. Frankly, I found it gruelling to navigate the obstacles we faced, but it also reminded me of the importance of remaining optimistic in any unwelcome situation.

As a younger manager, if a player picked up an injury that ruled him out of a game, I would spend time and energy focused on what we had lost. With experience, I recognised a more effective response was to consider the replacements available and the benefit they could bring – to reframe the situation positively, as quickly as possible. That way, even in the face of situations that seemed uncomfortable, or even insurmountable, I was continuing to prioritise the needs of the team and trusting in the process we had put in place to help deliver the best possible outcome.

It was the same during the pandemic: I looked for the possible virtues and strengths of our 'new normal', and of the rearrangements that were forced upon us, even when it was a struggle to do so. We had to find a way to train and perform despite it all, and our resilience and resourcefulness alike were put to the test. But it made crystal clear to me the absolute importance of leadership at such times and the extent to which, in adverse moments, people seek reassurance and guidance from those in charge, even if they can't provide all the answers. Leadership in adversity, by definition, will involve challenges that are entirely unexpected and, in that moment, will require digging deep into your reserves, and staying true to your values, to rise to the task at hand. It is rarely about grand speeches. More often it is about small, consistent acts: being visible, staying calm, projecting belief, and showing others that you have their backs. People want to see a proactive leader, moving with purpose, but not making hasty or out-of-character moves that can quickly be undermined as a situation develops. They want reassurance – to know they're in good hands.

I stayed positive through the lows of those times in the belief that we, as an organisation, would eventually come through stronger for the experience. And I believe we did. And while I completely recognised that football was the least of the nation's worries when the pandemic began, I also witnessed how the sport became a symbol of unity and returning normality and a cause for celebration as restrictions finally eased. And that outcome, at least, it was good to feel a part of.

Politics and diplomacy

'How important is football given Qatar's human rights concerns?'

I believe the question came from a CNN journalist. It wasn't the first time I'd been asked it, though, and nor would it be the last. We were two months out from the 2022 World Cup at this point, but the broader questions had started during the Nations League games the previous year, and they would continue right through our stay in Qatar. Post-pandemic, I seemed to have shifted seamlessly from needing to make public statements about the relative importance of football and public health to needing to make public statements about the relative importance of football and human rights. Let no one say that international football operates in a bubble.

On this occasion, my answer got spun into a controversy – unreasonably, I would say, although the episode was a strong reminder to me that I couldn't be too careful in my phrasing in these media moments. One of several contentious subjects surrounding the World Cup in Qatar was the use of migrant labour in the construction of the stadiums for the tournament and alleged abuses of workers' rights on those projects, in which large numbers of people (exact figures were disputed) had lost their lives.

'I've been out to Qatar several times,' I said, during my response to CNN's question, 'and I've met with lots of the workers out there and they are united in certainly one thing, and that's that they want the tournament to happen.'

I thought it was a fairly neutral statement from me, designed to shift the conversation on to the football. But representatives of organisations including Amnesty International and Human Rights Watch were asked to comment on this remark and stated that while claims for compensation for preventable death and harm were still unsettled, it was inaccurate to suggest that workers in Qatar were 'united'. But I hadn't intended to suggest that they were. I merely meant that none of the workers I had met had told me they didn't want the football to happen, which was the case.

It was frustrating in the extreme to find my words taken out of context and used to generate unhelpful noise. Within the FA, our position all along in relation to Qatar had been that we needed to listen and educate ourselves. To that end, we had gone out of our way to talk to human rights organisations, lawyers and NGOs with specialist knowledge on the ground. As a consequence of those conversations, the FA had pledged its support for compensation for the families of workers who had lost their lives and for the construction of a workers' rights centre. I don't think our position was in any doubt.

But more broadly we had to be realistic about what was achievable by us, a football team who were trying to be respectful guests and ambassadors for England in a country over which we had no control, in a tournament that was going to take place whether we agreed or not. There wasn't much I or the players could do other than talk about the relevant issues with respect and open-mindedness, and put them on the table when we saw a value in doing so. We helped the players so that they would be as prepared as they could be to discuss the issues when they were asked about them, which they inevitably were for a whole year leading up to the tournament. I wanted to be sure they were able to use their voices in the right way, but I also didn't want them to be used with broader agendas in play. It was going to be complicated, and we were going to get criticised whatever we did, but we could only try to do our best.

It was the same with the issues around Qatar and sexuality. This World Cup would be taking place in a country where same-sex relationships were criminalised. We knew that we stood for inclusivity as a team and during the tournament we decided that our captain would wear the One Love armband, an idea proposed by the Dutch that gained support from six other European nations. It would be a non-confrontational statement of our values on that issue.

But then on the eve of the tournament Fifa announced that the consequence for teams wearing any politicised item of kit in Qatar, including the One Love armband, would be a sanction on its players in the form of an automatic booking. At that point, we reluctantly agreed to abide by the tournament rules. It was a decision I was disappointed to have to take – but I believe I did have to take it. There were pundits who said we should have stuck by our principles on this – sent Harry Kane out in the armband regardless and let him take the booking. I'm not sure what those pundits would have been saying if Harry had then picked up a further booking in the game and been sent off and suspended. And, assuming he stayed on the pitch, should he have worn the armband in our second game? That would have meant a second statutory booking and an automatic suspension for game three. We were at the mercy of the laws here, as stipulated by Fifa. What annoyed me was that the ruling on the armband came in just hours before our first game in the tournament. Fifa could, and should, have made their position clear so much earlier. Equally, I think it's also fair to say that the seven nations, ourselves included, should have sought written clarification much earlier in the process. Even Fifa's stance was complicated here. They had to apply rules around kit to 200-plus countries and there were obviously an enormous number of political and human rights issues going on in the world, so I understood their need to avoid setting precedents.

Still, given the prevailing culture, we were unhappy to think that some of our fans would feel unable to travel to Qatar simply because of who they are, or feel threatened or worried for their safety. The matter seemed to me to require clarification but, in another interview well in advance of the tournament, some of my comments were spun into a headline that suggested the hosts might offer some assurances that all fans would be safe to travel and enjoy the football. When this was put to a senior executive of the Qatar 2022 team, I could understand his angry response, especially as the media ambushed him at an event the Qataris were proudly hosting to shine a light on the positive tournament ahead. The executive felt that I had insulted his country and he publicly questioned how much I really knew about Qatar.

Rather than fuel the fire in the media, when his response inevitably got batted back to me for reply, I reached out to him when I arrived in Doha in April for the World Cup draw, and we met over dinner. I learned through our conversation that while there were obvious cultural and religious differences between our nations, he was of a younger generation that actually held very progressive views. There was a climate of change in Qatar, he told me, but it had to be handled with great sensitivity and couldn't be rushed. Listening to his account, I could appreciate why he had felt compelled to publicly challenge me, and in the same way I was able to articulate my own side, as the manager of a team and representative of a country whose culture was far more inclusive in 2022, although we all knew how long that had taken and how much was still to be done. As our conversation continued, we both opened up about our respective families and history in football, and it quickly became apparent that we had far more in common than the clash that had brought us together. We parted on good terms, with the shared sense that, despite our differences, we had established a solid basis for understanding. It once again impressed on me the virtue of listening to and respecting other people's points of view, and, from within your own position of integrity, being firm in your own opinion.

This was, to me, another form of adversity. Leadership is rarely only about what happens on the pitch or in the meeting room; it is just as much about navigating the scrutiny, the politics, and the diplomacy in the outside world, sometimes under the glare of the media and with the potential for misunderstanding at every turn. My job was to protect the players so that none of this distracted from their football, while ensuring that England represented itself with dignity. If my work behind the scenes meant taking the heat personally so that the squad could remain focused, then that was a responsibility I was prepared to carry.

Adaptability and planning

Even without these diplomatic issues, in terms of timing alone, Qatar 2022 was a unique challenge, requiring adaptability and resourcefulness. To avoid the extreme summer heat in the desert region, the tournament was staged in December instead of the traditional time of June and July. This meant it sat in the middle of our regular Premier League season. Only seven days would separate the players' last match with their clubs and our first game in the group stage. Only five of those days would be available for preparations. England's rugby players had recently had six weeks to prime themselves for a World Cup. I could only dream of that luxury. Still, the art, as ever, in challengingly unusual circumstances, was not to be distracted by dwelling on what was no longer possible, but to concentrate on the positive. At least our players would be arriving on the eve of a World Cup match-fit and not carrying the usual end-of-season fatigue.

By the time we arrived in Qatar, the tournament document containing our strategy had evolved significantly from the one that took us to the 2018 World Cup in Russia and its subsequent iteration for Euro 20. Having played seven matches in both tournaments, we had picked up valuable experience in terms of the physical and recovery challenges required to go deep into these competitions, as well as the associated logistical demands. In Russia, the immense size of the country had meant long travel times to and from stadiums, which had an impact on player recovery. In a small Gulf state like Qatar, no stadium was more than sixty minutes from our hotel. Although we still had some logistical challenges prior to the tournament, such as shipping equipment to our base camp two months before the finals began, we identified that the close proximity of the stadiums meant that we could streamline our operations and maximise our rest time between matches. It would also facilitate our delivery of what had become a mainstay of our tournament strategies: opposition analysis.

For us, this was the sporting equivalent of competitor mapping in business. Companies invest significant time and resources into understanding their rivals' strategies, tracking their moves, and assessing their strengths and weaknesses in order to sharpen their own edge. We took a similar approach. Since 2018, our approach to gathering, processing and delivering opposition analysis had only grown in sophistication. Going into Russia, we had focused our attention on the group-stage opponents and potential early-stage knockout rivals. It meant we had more limited time to consolidate analysis as we continued to progress to the semi-finals. We knew this was something we could improve upon. With our ambitions raised, we now doubled down, extending our preparation to cover every team in the tournament. The idea was simple: the deeper you go, the less time you have to prepare – so the more you can bank in advance, the stronger your hand.

To support this, we set up a remote scouting hub back at St George's Park. In the 'Mission Control' style of arrangement, national coaches monitored games on screens, tracking every team's strategies, line-ups, set-plays and tactical shifts, so that when the draw was finalised, we had a comprehensive bank of raw material, critical insights and visual aids to hand. At the same time, our scouts and analysts continued to attend matches in person, ensuring nothing was lost in translation. The proximity of the venues meant they could do so efficiently, and we could blend real-time insight with the depth of our pre-prepared work. In fact the proximity of games meant we all saved time, and while we all endeavoured to put that time to use, our kit man did reveal on a leisurely walk that he'd never have it so good again!

Strategically, challenges remained. Staging the Qatar tournament in December might have avoided the fiercest summer temperatures, but it was still punishingly hot. This influenced when we could train in the day, and required effective protocols on cooling, such as temperature-controlled pitch-side tents and a carefully calibrated hydration strategy that we could also deploy in matches. There was also the flipside of minimal travel, which was the fact that seventy team personnel now had to share the same hotel space for all five weeks of the tournament. Accordingly, we chose a hotel where we could essentially live outside a lot, and on one level, with no external guests, rather than check in to a high-rise hotel in Doha with great facilities but where we would be stuck living on two floors for most of the day, navigating lots of external guests every time we passed through reception.

We went, as always, to great lengths to make the hotel feel as much like home as we could. All of the leisure facilities were outdoors – pool, table tennis, basketball court and other games areas – while there were opportunities for casual collisions and an emphasis on togetherness at meal times. I can understand why all the tech companies invest significant brain power (and money) into their environments to foster team building because it definitely worked for us (and it didn't take a Google budget to do it).

No visits from Ed Sheeran, however, this time. (Ed had joined us for an evening during Euro 20 to sing some songs over a barbecue and a beer; our own private Ed Sheeran performance. Needless to say, it went down pretty well. He did the same for us at Euro 24 as well.) But we were very lucky when another music legend, and football fan, Robbie Williams dropped by to 'entertain us', which was more my vintage.

Thanks to Conor Coady, we also had 'Traitors' to play – our version of the popular TV game. All of the players were involved, taking the role of either 'traitor' or 'faithful', and all spending their downtime engaging in the deception, trying to eliminate their opponents or remain undetected. Even Robbie Williams joined in. Conor's innovation was so popular, in fact, that in future tournaments, such as Euro 24, the wider staff started playing too. Some colleagues took the game incredibly seriously, with notes being slid under people's doors at night and Marc Guéhi, the son of a minister, anguishing about having to lie if he was made a traitor! It was fantastic fun and more effective as a team-bonding exercise than anything we could have formally designed. It was also another example of the value of selfless, priceless squad members in the group — Conor, who started it all, never played a minute in Qatar but still played an absolute blinder.

Altogether, Qatar was an enormous undertaking in which we planned every imaginable detail long in advance to give the team the very best chance of success. We could always come off the plan — and would have done so at any point if it had been in our better interests. But you had to be aware, too, that even 'a day off' would be an enormous logistical headache requiring detailed collaboration. For instance, trying to find 'safe meeting places' for twenty-six players and their families, at short notice, could be a tall order. Similarly, booking restaurants, organising transport and planning security details all became complex operations, particularly in the middle of a city with thousands of football fans congregating in a very small area.

When Qatar 2022 got under way, we hit some of the finest form in my time as England manager. We scored twelve times in our opening four matches, with eight players getting on the scoresheet, and swept through to the quarter-finals. That meeting with France, the reigning world champions, summed up the fine margins in play at this highest level of knockout football. Two–one down and chasing an equaliser, we were awarded a penalty in the eighty-fourth minute. Harry Kane, who had already scored once from the spot in this match, stepped up again. This was a player you would back with your life to score in this scenario, and, at the very least, take the match into extra-time. But remember, even the best have a conversion rate just over 80 per cent. Harry missed and we were out.

We go again

After defeats, there will always be theories about what could have been done differently. There was little disputing that we performed well, though perhaps we lacked a tiny bit of belief at the start of the game – that touch of constructive arrogance that the really big teams utilise. I think you acquire that streak predominantly as a consequence of winning, something France could call upon, while we were still carrying the uncertainty of a fifty-six-year winning void. In very simple terms we conceded two goals that could have been defended better and we missed a penalty that would have taken the game to 2–2. As a team we recognise that individual actions will always affect these results, but there can never be any individual blame attached to these moments. Usually, the very players in the frame are the ones who have won us far more matches than we have lost.

Incidentally, the penalty was won when Mason Mount made a forward run and was tripped. I had just brought Mason on and, if the penalty had gone in, that would have been heralded as a decisive substitution. But the ball went over the bar and it got forgotten. The headlines were written. While France went on to reach the final, it was Argentina, in a game for the ages, who would win the tournament we had targeted for so long.

Had we failed to deliver? In simple terms, with the grand vision in mind as marked by the clock on the wall at St George's Park, yes. We fell short of winning the World Cup.

The heartbreak that the team and I felt in the aftermath of that game against France was real. We were utterly laid low. And yet I had to hold firm to my knowledge that by all other measures we had made invaluable progress. When I reflect, it's a tournament that seemed to pass so quickly – not the weeks of build-up after the season finished, as is the norm for World Cups; we had just seven days to meet, travel and prepare. Of course, we 'only' played five games in that tournament as well, as opposed to seven in all of the others, so we were home a week earlier too. Yet it was probably the tournament we performed best in, scoring freely, with strength in depth in the forward line and the emergence of a new star in Jude Bellingham.

In the end, Qatar reminded me that adversity doesn't only arrive in the form of crises like a pandemic. It can also come through unusual timings, unfamiliar environments, and the weight of expectation. We had overcome extremely challenging and disorientating circumstances to show resilience, character and togetherness. We had come a long way forward, and we could hold our heads up high.

I felt support and belief from my employers, the players and the fans. That meant the immediate task now wasn't ripping everything up and starting over; it was overcoming our disappointment, resetting our focus and going again. And therein lies the biggest outcome of conquering adversity. Through hardship and experience you develop a kind of armour and drive that can keep pushing you forward, no matter how hard things may seem at the time.

SUMMARY
Holding the Line
On leading through adversity

- Composure is the key attribute of a leader in times of crisis. If you can reassure the group with clear, empathetic communication, you will calm nerves and build confidence.

- Sharing your personal experiences of being in extremis will encourage others to do the same. This approach demonstrates self-confidence, rather than self-consciousness. A problem or challenge shared with the group can be immensely reassuring to others who might be reluctant to speak up, but who would benefit from doing so if invited.

- A leader's role is to embody hope and belief for the group, especially in the hardest moments. Draw on your personal resilience to give the group perspective and optimism when others don't see it.

- Adapt quickly and positively when things go wrong. Look for solutions, avoid complaining, and know that 'perfect' won't exist, so be pragmatic.

- Setbacks can reveal hidden leaders in your team, create space for innovation, and strengthen your group's resilience – better preparing you all for future growth.

- In uncertain times, the 'human' approach is more important than ever. Proactively engage with your team, deepen your understanding of them on a personal level, and offer them reassurance and guidance. Remember, people aren't numbers on a spreadsheet or magnets on a board. Sometimes, you can improve someone's life dramatically when they need it most, just by getting to know them better.

- When an event happens that might require disciplinary action, don't rush in or overreact when emotions are running high. Establish the facts, consider the consequences, and act with fairness.

CHAPTER 10

The Final Score

On what really endures

The bigger picture

England v. Spain, Final, 2024 Uefa European Football Championship, post-match press conference, Olympiastadion, Berlin, 14 July

'In 2006, you played your last game with Middlesbrough and started your coaching career. In 2016, you started your journey with England. What does that journey of eight years mean to you personally, and will we see you in North America in 2026?'

The question was a bit of a departure from those I had addressed about our performance. It came in the post-match press conference, which itself followed the trophy presentation, my time in the dressing room with the players, and then the usual six 'flash' television interviews and two radio interviews, which together had lasted an hour and took us to well past midnight. At that point, deflated, raw from the defeat and drawing on my last ounces of energy, I felt a powerful urge to answer: 'Nope. Count me out. That's it. I'm done.'

A month earlier, going into Euro 24, it had been quite clear in my mind that we had to win it. When I stepped up as England manager, the team were just outside the top ten in Fifa's men's world ranking. We rose to sixth place following the 2018 World Cup in Russia before moving into the top five soon after and then staying there. In that time, we had reached the semi-finals and a final of two major international tournaments.

But what we hadn't done was lift a trophy.

On this basis, I set myself the ambitious target of winning the tournament in Germany. To be clear: it didn't mean that I felt anything less than winning would necessarily constitute failure. Even as one of the favourites for the competition, we were given a 17 per cent chance of actually winning it before a ball was kicked. Tournament football is ultimately a knockout competition. A team has to peak for a four-week period. One moment can determine the culmination of two years' work. That's the reality, and yet the belief existed that, with the quality of our squad and our accumulated experience of big matches, we could now deliver.

My first step was to reinforce the belief in the players that we could win an international tournament, as this confidence can sometimes be missing in teams that haven't done so. We would do this by beating some of the top nations before the Euros. In March 2023, opening our qualifying games for Euro 24, and in our first match after the World Cup in Qatar, we travelled to Naples to play against the reigning European champions, Italy. Not only was the game critical in terms of points, it was also crucial for building belief – in our supporters as much as in our team. We had retained the goodwill of our fans despite being beaten by France in Qatar. But that was clearly on the line if we lost against the next tough team we played.

Happily, we put on an excellent first-half display against the Italians. In the second half, we went on to show great resolve to hang on for a 2–1 win even though we went down to ten men for the last fifteen minutes.

This was the kind of detail I believed could make the difference, particularly as it was our first win in Italy since 1961. When you get to the top of world football, and the latter stages of any competition, you are playing against the best. The players' technical ability, their fitness, their mentality and the tactics are all so finely balanced. It's small margins – such as the character we showed against Italy – that win a game or a tournament. We had now reached this level of performance. The players recognised our momentum but it was important that the fans shared the same belief. And it was particularly important in relation to my future. In politics, leaders can lose popularity simply because voters experience 'incumbency fatigue' and seek change. Even though the issues remain the same, people eventually crave a fresh face. Established leaders in business and sport can find themselves on notice for the same reason. I was well aware that the sense of unity and optimism I had brought to England could no longer carry the day on its own. Regardless of any progress under my watch, people would inevitably grow tired and even question my credibility if I couldn't take the team any further than I already had in a tournament. And if I pressed on regardless, and that criticism became intrusive external noise, I knew it could have a negative bearing on the team's performance.

After Qatar, I still felt I was the best man for the job. We had the team playing well, and there was belief from the players and the fans in what we were doing. It felt like we were still improving and I think it would have been destabilising to leave just before important qualifiers. I also felt I'd earned the right to have a crack at the Euros and not die wondering.

With one Euro final under our belts, and having reached the quarter-finals in Qatar, it was no longer possible for us to position the team as underdogs. That had worked very well for us in the past, with minimum performance markers to keep hopes in check. But now we had proven we could be contenders. If anything, it encouraged a return of that old belief in the media and among supporters that we were basically winners-in-waiting. We had to accept that pressure and deal with it. It was, after all, the consequence of our good work. But as we turned our attention to Euro 24, it became clearer and clearer to me that I would have to deliver a tournament win, or go. In the aftermath of a loss, I knew it would be hard to stand in front of the players once again and find the vigour to encourage them to take the 'one more step required' for the next tournament qualifying campaign. Even though I felt the players were with us as a coaching team (and stayed with us until the very end), I doubted they would be able to summon the requisite belief if they had to hear that message from me one more time. It was now or never.

Throughout the qualifiers, we remained unbeaten. Having won away against Italy in the opening match, we claimed a decisive 3–1 victory against them in front of a home crowd at Wembley. Our 7–0 defeat of North Macedonia at Old Trafford – including a hat-trick by Bukayo Saka – was a fabulous night. Around this time, with qualification looking highly likely, the FA, who were supportive throughout my time in charge, offered me an extension to my contract to take the team through to the World Cup in 2026. This was absolutely the way that good organisations should work. Internally, people knew that we were good at our job, they wanted stability, and they wanted to avoid being a hostage to fortune in the forthcoming Euros. Their view, correctly, was that one bad night shouldn't suddenly mean that the whole plan gets ripped up.

Signing on the dotted line would have provided me with security, from a career and a financial perspective. I could see all the upsides and gave some positive signs to my bosses. But something was niggling at the back of my mind. I remembered Fabio Capello signing a contract ahead of the 2010 World Cup and getting lambasted, actually putting the team under more pressure. While I felt the full support of the FA and the players, in football, the fans are still an important consideration in these decisions. Of course, there are times when you have to ride out a storm (I'd had a few of those) and boards should resist being reactive to the emotion of supporters, but when it comes to announcing a new contract,

I think there's got to be a feeling that everyone is on board with that. At this moment, I didn't feel everyone was. The fans were divided.

It was clear that every time we failed to win comfortably, there was a crescendo of criticism and derision. We got a draw in Ukraine, where we dominated the game but failed to create enough good chances. Although we earned a critical point, there was an adverse reaction to the performance. We went to Scotland a few days later, played really well, silenced a passionate crowd and an in-form team, winning 3–1 – and yet there was some criticism even then of the style. We were averaging more than two goals per game over more than ninety internationals. Only during Walter Winterbottom's period, and perhaps surprisingly Fabio Capello's, had England averaged better than that. The narrative was set: our, or 'my', style of play was negative, despite the facts saying otherwise.

We played North Macedonia away in our last qualifier, having already secured our place in Germany. We experimented, trying Trent Alexander-Arnold in midfield, a position we had real issues with in terms of depth of cover. We also gave Rico Lewis a debut, and Ollie Watkins a start in place of Harry Kane. The pitch was bone-hard, Rico unfortunately conceded a penalty, and we ended up missing some big chances in a 1–1 draw.

After the match, I gave a live TV interview where the desk was positioned directly in front of our travelling fans. While there was some applause when I walked across to take my place, there was also some abuse and chants of 'Attack!

Attack! Attack!', as if we'd instructed our players not to do this. It didn't particularly rattle me, but it did confirm something: that people were ready for a change. Signing an extension at this point clearly would not have gone down well with parts of the fan base.

I would need to be judged on the Euros. I was content enough with that, and we shelved the contract talks. It occurred to me over the following months that I was actually quite exposed: I had no contract after June. If it ended badly, I was out of work. To speak to a club during that period would have been unethical, so there was no way of lining up a future in management. Stay or go, it was all going to come down to our performance in Germany. I was happy to back myself and quite liked the fact there was no life raft. And if we won . . . well, might that actually be a good moment to leave anyway?

Our prep camp for the 2024 Euros troubled me in terms of the physical sharpness of a number of the players. We had numerous fitness issues, including Harry Kane and Anthony Gordon reporting with injuries. Two months out, nine of our eleven most capped defenders were sidelined. When we eventually named the squad, that department looked as much like a risk assessment as a form guide. Plus a long season had taken its toll. Declan Rice, Bukayo Saka and Jude Bellingham had each played more than fifty matches. Playing a high-pressing game with these issues, and in summer heat, would have been suicide. That approach (questionable anyway in a summer tournament) was a non-starter.

In the group stage in Germany, that high expectation from our supporters gave rise to a new level of discontent. Even though we would ultimately win our group, we couldn't find the rhythm that we had found in previous tournaments. I had to work overtime to keep the whole group focused and mentally on track.

Following our 1–0 victory over Serbia in the opening match, our 1–1 draw with Denmark earned us boos from the crowd towards the end of the game. We didn't handle that reaction well and started to lose our composure. Our decision-making began to suffer on the pitch, reminding me of the bad old days of playing for England when the shirt felt so heavy. In our debrief, while highlighting what we had failed to do tactically, I showed the players a still photo from the end of the match. Denmark were in front of their fans, celebrating. They had gained a point and were on two points for the tournament. In contrast, some of our players in the image were on their knees, some with heads in hands, a couple lying on the floor; all were reluctant to go over to our fans. This despite the fact we had also taken a point, and were now on four points, top of the group. In the worst-case scenario, we would finish third and be almost certain to qualify for the next round. Reminding players of the bigger context like this, and helping them to clarify their thinking, is crucial in tournaments. You are all in such a bubble and the external noise can drown you, create doubt and fear, and lead to disunity. I was working overtime to keep everyone thinking rationally, not emotionally. I was also very strong in pointing out that our body language at the end of that game was unacceptable. We should never show opponents any sniff that we are defeated; we should walk over to our fans, shoulders back, thank them and get off the pitch with our point gained.

I probably didn't expect that at the end of the final group match – a 0–0 draw with Slovenia – I would quickly be in a position to practise what I preached. Once again, we struggled to find the creativity to break down a packed, stubborn defence. Nevertheless, the draw was enough for us to top the group and get ourselves on the more favourable side of the draw in the knockout phase. However, there seemed to be little celebrating. When we went to the fans at the end of the game, plastic cups of beer were thrown in my direction. I had a choice: keep walking towards them, or stop and circumvent that area and head for the tunnel. In my view, walking away would have looked cowardly. Like I wasn't prepared to stand up to the abuse. So I deliberately kept walking towards the fans and kept applauding.

There are moments when the leader has to step up and absorb pressure in order to protect the group, or individuals within it. In the press conference after the game, I felt I had to speak out to give the team space. If the fans had seen enough of me, no problem, but they had to get behind the players. After thirty-eight years in football, I was hardened enough to deal with what came my way, and I was determined to stand strong and lead my players and staff through the maelstrom. But it was going to be incredibly difficult to win in that environment and I had to try to change it, even if it put me in the line of fire. My feeling was the fans were frustrated with the performances. They didn't really know why we weren't playing well, so the simple solution was that I wasn't playing the right players, or not making the right changes. Whatever their reasons, the one thing I categorically didn't want was for the fans to take it out on the players, because I knew that would have an adverse effect on them, no matter how strong-willed they were. Leave the players alone, come for me, was my thinking. After the press conference, I returned to my coaching staff where the dark humour that keeps you going in these difficult moments kicked in. Someone offered to pour me a glass of wine 'rather than throw one at you'.

That night was probably the final confirmation in my mind that this would be my last tournament as England manager. I resolved to keep my counsel, and not give anyone a sniff of what was going through my mind and what I was planning to do.

The end could easily have come sooner than I wanted and in a most horrible way. Going behind in the round-of-sixteen game against Slovakia, a team we were expected to beat, exposed us to another immense psychological as well as tactical challenge. The players responded. We won that dramatic match 2–1, as we have already relived in these pages. In the process we re-instilled precious belief into the squad and staff. But I knew what the reaction would have been from our fans and the media had we departed the tournament in disappointing fashion, or failed in the penalty shoot-out against Switzerland in the ensuing quarter-final, with young players and substitutes centre-stage. Our dominance in that shoot-out, as we explored earlier, was simply thrilling. Yet the threat of uproar never seemed far away.

Our semi-final against the Netherlands was one of the most tactically challenging games of my entire spell. We had to make a sequence of small adjustments to counter their tactics during the game. We played well and deserved to win. Moreover, after all the criticism levelled at me over substitutions, one sub created the chance for another sub to score the winner in the dying seconds. I was ecstatic. For about twenty minutes . . .

Having walked off the pitch, I enjoyed five minutes with my staff, watching the players celebrate in the dressing room. But then I found my mind going back to Euro 20, and Denmark at Wembley – our last semi-final victory. And I remembered how amazing that had felt, and how quickly it all turned. I knew any euphoria, and all the credit earned, would be gone by Sunday if we didn't win. Everything was conditional.

Something else I realised at that moment: that this struggle to enjoy the wins had been something I had been noticing more and more as time passed. And if you can't enjoy the wins, frankly what's the point? Again, it hit home to me: even if we won the Euros, there was so much I didn't want to face any more.

So there we were, playing Spain in a contest to decide the trophy – our first final away from home in England's football history. Apart from close family and Steve Holland, only I knew this would be my last game in charge of the team. It was a bittersweet feeling and yet, like the players, my focus was entirely on the win. I had every confidence in the team, even though we hadn't played anywhere near as well as we had in Qatar. That was where I believed we had given our best performance of the four tournaments in my time as manager, even though we had returned home at an earlier stage. In Germany, what we had shown was remarkable resilience and spirit in finding a way to win in some very tight games – the culmination of all the work we had put into building our culture and learning from the big matches we had won and lost. In the midst of huge pressure and criticism throughout the tournament, we came from a goal behind in every knockout round, and now we'd arrived at a reckoning. Despite our disappointment that we had rarely found the level of performance we wanted, given all the challenges we faced, I actually felt that I had managed better in this tournament than I had in my previous three.

You will know how it ended. It's where this book opened. Once again, we had come tantalisingly close to making English football history. As Spain celebrated with their fans and fireworks soared into the sky above the stadium, my heart went out to our players as much as the fans.

'. . . and will we see you in North America in 2026?'

When that question finished, I took a moment to gather my thoughts. I already knew the answer. I had had eight years of these conferences. I had reached the point where it was a real challenge not to sit there and peer out at the faces, many of which hadn't changed in all that time, and just remember all the criticisms and the personal comments that had been made. I really wouldn't be missing this aspect of the job in future. But I had to stay in control, retain my dignity until the end. I had a responsibility. Like any leader, I couldn't blind-side my employers with this information. I had to tell the FA first, in the right way, before making it known.

I looked out wearily through the lights.

'We came here to win,' I said, eventually. 'We haven't been able to do that.'

The difference made

At the time, the players were still pressing for the coaching team to stay on. With support for me to remain from the FA, it would have been perfectly feasible for me to sign another contract. From my perspective, however, I felt that my presence really had become divisive among the team's fan base. There's no doubt in my mind that the situation had been enflamed by elements of the media. Whether any of that was fair or not was irrelevant. It was starting to inhibit the team and that was the reality of the situation.

That evening, back at England's hotel, I informed the FA that I wouldn't be renewing my contract. As the players reunited with their families, I took the time to speak individually with my bosses. Thanking them for giving me the honour of leading the team for eight years, I then set out my reasons why it was time for me to step down. I had no desire to become a distraction. Even though we had come within reach of achieving greatness, I would be facing another two-year cycle where my will to win would be met with widespread negativity. This could come at a cost to the team and to my own personal energy.

England had six weeks before their next matches — a set of Nations League games where they would face no team in the top thirty in the world — and they were still more than six months away from their next tournament qualifier. So the FA had ample time to appoint a replacement and presumably they had succession plans in place anyway.

A few days after the team returned home, the FA announced my resignation. The public response was largely one of understanding and respect for my decision. I have to say I was heartened by that. It was almost as though some kind of pressure valve had been released and it allowed people to reflect on the broader achievements across the eight years. I felt like I was given the privilege of reading my own obituaries. Inevitably I was asked about my future. I believed I had more to offer in football, but the fact is tournaments at this level take a great deal out of you. Delivering the highest level of performance is demanding in every way, not just for the players but the supporting staff. It requires total dedication and absolute absorption, which can be exhausting. I now needed to decompress, which meant time with family and the opportunity to reflect in peace on the end of this chapter in my career.

Despite coming so close, the fact remained that we hadn't won a trophy since 1966. In a sport defined by winning and losing, that could be deemed a failure. I completely recognise what the dream of an England tournament win means to people. I share it just as keenly. I prayed for it as a fan, I fought for it as a player, and I lived it for almost every minute of my eight years in charge, striving throughout to make it a reality. Ultimately that wasn't enough.

When I think of legacy, however, I'm aware that there's so much more involved in all of this than silverware. If I refer back to the one-page 'philosophy' document I set out at the start of my England tenure and that I mentioned earlier in this book (see page 90), it's a useful measure of perform-ance to answer the original questions I posed: Did we create memories that people will remember for ever? Did our players and staff enjoy the journey? Were the perceptions of the England player changed? Did we create a strong and enduring culture? Had we forged a winning team identity? Did we go about things in the right way and were lessons learned for life as well as for football? I'm proud to say that I think we ticked an awful lot of those boxes.

When I look back at my time as England manager, there are other questions I ask myself in areas that also matter to me. How did I make people feel? On and off the pitch, what standards did I set in shaping the values and culture of the team? How did I challenge players to develop and then perform collectively to the best of their abilities? What steps did I take to unite, inspire, support, protect and champion the team so they could play to their strengths? Ultimately, what difference did I make in leading a diverse group of individuals to a point where they had the best possible chance of success in the future?

Like any leader at the end of a journey, I can measure my impact by comparing what the organisation looked like when

I stepped up to how it looked when I stepped down. Fact: it was in a far better place. And if I were remembered as a decent person who led authentically, treated others fairly and did his best for the team and for the nation in his own way, then the fact that I oversaw the best period in English football for more than fifty years would merely be a bonus.

Recovery

In the weeks and months after Euro 24, however, following my resignation, I felt a weight coming off my shoulders that I hadn't fully appreciated was there.

There was definitely some relief at not having the normal work stresses of management – the travel, the meetings, the deadlines. Beyond that there was some respite from the additional intrusions that come from a high-profile role – the constant stream of speculation, the criticism, and the days when you find yourself the subject of totally fabricated stories in the media (although this last bit hasn't completely disappeared!). During camps, I would withdraw from consuming any media to keep my head clear. Even so, I would definitely notice my mood change when I accidentally glimpsed a negative headline or caught the start of a TV debate before swiftly switching channels.

Since stepping down, I've attended only a handful of matches. That's been a conscious choice. I'm still curious to see how players and coaches do, and how clubs are getting on. And I'm glad to be able to do so now without the risk of fans confronting and at times abusing me outside the stadium because I haven't picked a certain player, and without having to hide my reaction to a goal going in or a player making a mistake in case I'm picked up on camera. But it still doesn't feel comfortable. My obsession with football is on the back burner. My passion is on hold. My thoughts are quite distant. I'm at peace with that, although it's interesting to me that this is the way I have come to feel. As I mentioned earlier in the book, very few England managers have survived the role without sustaining enormous scars. Bobby Robson was probably the only one to go on from England to take big football jobs. The role chews you up. It puts your family through incredible stress – and I speak as the manager who experienced the best period in more than fifty years. Is this how all the others felt? In the England role, maybe survival is success enough, and the fact that I was able to leave on my own terms. I'm fortunate that the reactions I get from people in the street are generally warm. I can hold my head high and go out without a hat.

In every aspect of my life, in fact, I found myself benefiting from the period of decompression and recharging. After nearly four decades in football, it allowed me to begin considering what I want to do next.

I'm an ex-footballer and it's often struck me that football doesn't deal well with players in terms of help around future careers. When they start in academies, we talk to young players about the possibility of 'not making it' and therefore the wisdom of continuing with their education. This generally falls upon deaf ears. No youngster wants to contemplate 'not making it' and a back-up plan can feel like a life raft, indicating a lack of belief. In my opinion, we should reframe this conversation and say: 'If you are going be a footballer, then you need to plan for having a second career.' Because the one certain thing is, whether you are sixteen or thirty-six, there is going to come a time when you can no longer play.

Perhaps the hardest thing for any professional athlete to deal with is the transition to not competing any more. I believe that we should prepare them better for this inevitable step. Currently, so many are totally unsupported for that phase of their lives. As a consequence, they lose purpose, structure and a sense of identity. Some end up divorced, some end up bankrupt, or worse.

I was fortunate that I never had to face that transition; I was literally one day a player, the next day a coach. I had a brief period to reflect after I was sacked at Middlesbrough and worked in television. There, I continued my learning and enjoyed experiences I hadn't had the chance to enjoy previously, like going skiing and running a marathon. But now, in my mid-fifties, I have to decide whether it's time for a second change of career.

Of course, there have been opportunities for me to stay in football. However, having held one of the biggest jobs in the sport, there are very few roles that truly excite me. Indeed, there are probably none with the same sense of purpose as trying to improve football within your own country, which was the reason I originally joined the English FA. I'm not desperate to manage in the Premier League purely for the experience. I did that for three years when I was thirty-five.

So, while I would never say never to a return to management, it would have to be a very exciting proposition.

What I've really valued since leaving my last role has been a period of reflection. It's provided me with the chance to speak to a broad network of people, many of whom have experienced a significant career change themselves. In fact, this process started with a chance meeting with someone who had transitioned out of a role of even greater intensity and scrutiny than my own: the former UK prime minister, Sir Tony Blair.

We happened to be speaking separately at a business event and it seemed a golden opportunity to ask what his process had been, having stepped down from the biggest job of all. *Take your time* was his first comment. Pertinently, he then observed that I could expect lots of opportunities to cross my desk. With time on my hands, I might be tempted to fill my diary with any and every commitment on offer. But I should sift through them carefully, was the former PM's advice. Or, in the sage words of a friend: *when you're presented with an opportunity, if it's not a 'Hell yeah', then you probably shouldn't do it.*

Looking ahead – the challenges facing young people

Through conversations with friends, colleagues and mentors, I've been slowly piecing together the questions I need to ask myself in order to be able to shape the second half of my life:

What am I really passionate about? What are my absolute super strengths? What do I enjoy most? How much time do I want to devote to work, and what else do I want to do with the years ahead? Football inevitably features in many of those answers, but it is far from the only thing that interests me.

More and more, I have realised that what gives me the deepest satisfaction is helping other people to progress – especially young people with the potential to achieve extraordinary things. Even though my journey leading England has ended, I still want to be challenged. I still have ambition and drive. But most of all, I want purpose in what I do. Which is why I would like the next steps of my life to be dedicated to helping young people.

I've become acutely aware of the pressures young people face: through the experiences of my players, through my children and their friends, and through my work with the King's Trust. This is a generation whose developmental years have been shaped – and in many ways disrupted – by the rise of smartphones, social media, and the unprecedented inter-ruption of Covid. Jonathan Haidt, in his brilliant book *The Anxious Generation*, observes how the shift from a phone-free childhood to a smartphone-dependent one has created a mental health epidemic. Free play has been replaced by excessive screen-time, leading to social deprivation, disrupted sleep, fragmented attention and addiction.

When I had the honour of being invited to deliver the 2025 Richard Dimbleby Lecture, I chose to focus on this landscape, particularly the difficult path that many young men are navigating. They are clearly falling behind and wrestling with distorted definitions of 'success' sold to them online. Too often, there is a widespread absence of fathers or other strong role models they can depend on – teachers, youth workers, coaches, mentors – and into that vacuum step the wrong influences. There is urgent work to be done here.

To be clear, I recognise, too, the pressing challenges faced by young women, especially around self-esteem and mental health. But I also believe that if we can support young men to live more purposeful, constructive lives, the benefits will ripple outwards, positively affecting everyone.

The power of mentorship

In football, I saw the power of culture to build resilience. When players are encouraged to take pride in their identity and rally around shared values, motivation and belief grow. As they strive to be their best, setbacks and failures become lessons rather than barriers. They persevere, they bounce back, they keep improving – and in doing so, they develop self-belief.

That process isn't reserved for elite athletes. It is the foundation of true success in life. We need to encourage young people to embrace challenge, not avoid it; to stretch themselves, not settle for ease; to fail, learn, and go again. Fulfilment does not come from shortcuts or false images of success. It comes from resilience, service, character and growth.

One of the great strengths of sport is that it almost always provides a coach – someone who guides, challenges, supports and believes in you. I saw mentorship in action throughout my career. Over time, those I had mentored became leaders and mentors themselves. I knew their families, I watched them grow from uncertain teenagers facing setbacks to towering professionals with unshakeable belief.

But mentorship is not confined to football, nor to sport in general. It's a power that can be switched on everywhere. It can be a quiet word in a classroom, encouragement on a building site, advice in a kitchen, or a steady presence in a community hall. It doesn't require a job title or a salary – only time, care and consistency.

And the need has never been greater. Young people are more connected than ever, yet more isolated, bombarded with unrealistic expectations and warped values. In such an environment, even one mentor can be the difference.

We must flood young lives with positive role models: people who listen, guide, challenge, support and give back. And it's not necessarily complicated. Leadership in this area can be as simple as showing up, caring, and setting the right example.

Before delivering the Dimbleby Lecture, I wondered whether stepping into these areas might invite more criticism. But the overwhelmingly positive response to that broadcast reminded me that we should focus less on what might go wrong, and more on the difference we can make.

Since then, countless people have approached me with

the same questions: What can I do? Where do I start? How can I help? The truth is, there are already brilliant mentoring schemes, but too few people know about them – and too few young men access them.

This is why we need a wider, collective drive. We need to start a mentorship movement: government, charities, communities and individuals all working together to connect mentors with young people, and to make giving back an instinctive part of who we are as a society. Let's ensure that the future is shaped not by those who seek power for themselves, but by those who give of themselves to empower others.

Final reflections

My years with England taught me many lessons, as we have seen, but perhaps prime among them was this: that there is a fine balance between doing everything you can to win and 'winning at all costs'. The first is about excellence. The second risks sacrificing integrity. That distinction matters now more than ever.

In an age of twenty-four-hour news, relentless social media and the rise of populism, the concept of true leadership is under pressure. Authoritarian styles can yield short-term results, but they are rooted in obedience rather than respect – and each generation is less willing to accept that. Today's young people want something different. They want to know that their development is valued. They want psychological safety. They want leaders they can trust. That is why leadership today must be grounded in unity, empathy, integrity and courage.

The pace of change will only accelerate, driven by technology and AI. Leaders will need curiosity, humility, collaboration and the courage to listen. No one can be expert in everything, but everyone can learn from others.

Yet one thing will never change: leadership is always about people. My players were never magnets to be moved on a tactics board. They were individuals – flesh and blood, with their own hopes, dreams and fears. My job was to understand them, and, by understanding them, to bring out the best in them.

Earlier in my career, I worked alongside a leader who was outstanding in many ways but poor with people. When I raised this, my CEO's response was simple: 'The only problem with that is that human beings are the only species we employ.'

That truth has never left me. Guide, challenge and care for your people – and you will be on the right path. I know from my own journey that leadership is not about leaving behind trophies, titles or applause. It is about leaving behind belief – in people, in unity, in what we can achieve together.

I also know that true greatness in leadership can take many forms. It may be raising children with love and wisdom. It may be teaching a class, serving a community, running a business, caring for the vulnerable, protecting a nation, or even coaching an under-9s football team. What matters is not the size of the stage, but the strength of the purpose.

So my message to tomorrow's leaders would be this: embrace challenge. Stretch yourself. Fail, learn, and go again. Surround yourself with people who make you better; and in turn, lift others as you climb. Lead with kindness and humanity. Lead with courage. Lead with service. Because that kind of leadership is leadership worth believing in.

SUMMARY
The Final Score
On what really endures

- Protect your team from external criticism, noise or distraction. Leaders must absorb this pressure to keep the group's focus on what matters.

- Maintain composure under public scrutiny. Leaders must remain professional and controlled even at emotionally charged moments. Your organisation and people are your priority, and how you represent them, when the spotlight is on you, is important.

- Sustaining your optimal level of performance as a leader matters. If your energy, joy and sense of renewal are waning, then there is a high risk that your ongoing effectiveness may suffer.

- The hardest leadership act is recognising when your presence is no longer what the team needs. You must balance self-interest with self-sacrifice but always make your decision on the basis of future success for the organisation.

CONTINUED OVER

- How do we judge success? Of course, trophies in football, or profits in business, are important markers. But the values you stood for, the lives you changed and the progress you made should never be underestimated.

- True leaders today will already be shaping the leaders of tomorrow.

Appendix

'Dear England' by Gareth Southgate
The Players' Tribune
8 June 2021

Dear England,
It has been an extremely difficult year. Everyone in this
country has been directly affected by isolation and loss.
But we have also seen countless examples of heroism
and sacrifice. It's given us all a new understanding of the
fragility of life and what really matters. When you think
of the grand scheme of things, perhaps football doesn't
seem so important. And what I want to speak about today
is much bigger than football.

As we go into this summer, I know that there will be
a lot of emotion tied up in the Euros, and in this England
team. I can't possibly hope to speak for an entire country,
but I would like to share a few things with you, as we begin
this journey.

There's something I tell our players before every

England game, and the reason that I repeat it is because I really believe it with all my heart.

I tell them that when you go out there, in this shirt, you have the opportunity to produce moments that people will remember forever.

You are a part of an experience that lasts in the collective consciousness of our country.

We saw that during Russia 2018, with the street parties, the barbecues and with every drop of beer thrown into the air in celebration. When England play, it's not a few thousand – or even a few million – watching on subscription. You are representing more than 50 million people.

You remember where you were watching England games. And who you were watching with. And who *you* were at the time.

The first England match I really remember watching was in the 1982 World Cup, when I was 11. It was the first World Cup England had qualified for in my lifetime and I was obsessed. I had the wall chart, ready to fill in with every result, every goalscorer, every detail.

I rushed home from school for England's opener against France to see Bryan Robson score after just 27 seconds! To witness that as a young Manchester United-supporting midfielder whose hero was Robson . . . well, it's safe to say I was hooked.

Later that same year, I watched Luther Blissett get a hat trick in a 9-0 win over Luxembourg. That specific result might have been forgotten by many but it really stuck for me.

Every game, no matter the opposition, has the potential to create a lifelong memory for an England fan somewhere.

Why do we care so much?

Like with our own memories of watching England, everyone has a different idea of what it actually means to be English. What pride means.

For me, personally, my sense of identity and values is closely tied to my family and particularly my granddad. He was a fierce patriot and a proud military man, who served during World War II.

The idea of representing 'Queen and country' has always been important to me. We do pageantry so well in Britain, and, growing up, things like the Queen's silver jubilee and royal weddings had an impact on me.

Because of my granddad, I've always had an affinity for the military and service in the name of your country – though the consequence of my failure in representing England will never be as high as his. My granddad's values were instilled in me from a young age and I couldn't help but think of him when I lined up to sing the national anthem before my first international caps.

My belief is that *everyone* has that pride. And that includes the players.

What is sometimes forgotten is just *how much* it means to the players.

Players are fans too, after all. That's how it starts. It starts with kids sitting in front of TVs, with wall charts and heroes.

Undoubtedly, we're in a different era now, where footballers aren't as accessible to fans as they once were. They don't ride the same bus home from games, or meet in the pub for a pint and a post-match analysis.

But, despite all the changes in modern football, what cannot be questioned about the current generation of England players is their *pride* in representing this country.

This idea that some players don't know what it means to play for England – or don't care – has become something of a false narrative.

You don't need to dig deep to realise that.

You only need to see what I see when an under-15 comes into St George's Park for the first time, or when a senior player arrives on their first call-up. The pride for them, their families and their communities back home is *huge*.

The journey to earn an England cap is an incredibly difficult one, regardless of background or circumstance.

Only around 1,200 players have represented England at senior men's level. *Ever.*

It's a profound privilege. Don't forget, many of our lads started out at Football League clubs like Barnsley, MK Dons and Sheffield United. Their backgrounds are humble. For them to make it to this point as one of the chosen few in England's history . . . well, it simply doesn't happen without pride.

This is a special group. Humble, proud and liberated in being their true selves.

Our players *are* role models. And, beyond the confines

of the pitch, we must recognise the impact they can have on society. We must give them the confidence to stand up for their teammates and the things that matter to them as people.

I have never believed that we should just *stick to football*.

I know my voice carries weight, not because of who I am but because of the position that I hold. At home, I'm below the kids and the dogs in the pecking order but publicly I am the England men's football team manager. I have a responsibility to the wider community to use my voice, and so do the players.

It's their duty to continue to interact with the public on matters such as equality, inclusivity and racial injustice, while using the power of their voices to help put debates on the table, raise awareness and educate.

Social media has been a key resource in giving our players a platform and has been a positive tool in so many ways. In fact, I feel like this generation of England players is closer to the supporters than they have been for decades. Despite the polarisation we see in society, these lads are on the same wavelength as you on many issues.

That said, there are times when my parental instincts kick in. I can't help it. After all, I'm old enough to be a father to most of my players!

I see players scrolling on their phones straight after the final whistle and I think . . . *Hmmm, is that a particularly good idea?*

Reading abusive comments on Twitter or Instagram is never going to help performance.

There are genuine risks for our players online and I will always want to protect them, but I would never put rules on how or when they use their accounts while on England duty. I trust them and know they are mature enough to make their own decisions, to do what's right for their mental health and to keep being a force for good as we strive for a better society.

The last 18 months have put added pressure on everyone, I know. Venting that might have taken place while walking out of the stadium, or in the pub has been transferred online. I get that. However, there are things I will *never* understand.

Why would you tag someone in on a conversation that is abusive?

Why would you choose to insult somebody for something as ridiculous as the colour of their skin?

Why?

Unfortunately for those people that engage in that kind of behaviour, I have some bad news. You're on the losing side. It's clear to me that we are heading for a much more tolerant and understanding society, and I know our lads will be a big part of that.

It might not feel like it at times, but it's true. The awareness around inequality and the discussions on race have gone to a different level in the last 12 months alone.

I am confident that young kids of today will grow up baffled by old attitudes and ways of thinking.

For many of that younger generation, your notion of Englishness is quite different from my own. I understand that, too.

I understand that on this island, we have a desire to protect our values and traditions – as we should – but that shouldn't come at the expense of introspection and progress.

Regardless of your upbringing and politics, what is clear is that we are an incredible nation – relative to our size and population – that has contributed so much to the arts, science and sport.

We do have a special identity and that remains a powerful motivator.

In a funny way, I see the same Englishness represented by the fans who protested against the Super League. We are independent thinkers. We speak out on the issues that matter to us and we are proud of that.

Of course, my players and I will be judged on winning matches. Only one team can win the Euros. We have never done it before and we are desperate to do it for the first time.

Believe me.

But, the reality is that the result is just a small part of it. When England play, there's much more at stake than that.

It's about how we conduct ourselves on and off the pitch, how we bring people together, how we inspire and unite, how we create memories that last beyond the 90 minutes. That last beyond the summer. That last forever.

I think about all the young kids who will be watching this summer, filling out their first wall charts. No matter what happens, I just hope that their parents, teachers and club managers will turn to them and say, 'Look. That's the way to represent your country. That's what England is about. That is what's possible.'

If we can do that, it will be a summer to be proud of.

Yours,
Gareth Southgate

Acknowledgements

A big thank you to a fantastic team of people who have helped shape, challenge and refine my ideas for the book, and whose conversations and insight I am grateful for:

To my publisher, Ben Brusey, for your time, patience and wisdom in overseeing this project. To Matt Whyman and Giles Smith, for pulling together a lot of the content, setting up the structure and flow of the book, and for helping to articulate my thoughts into words with clarity and polish.

To my business partner Jimmy Worrall, thank you for the hours of reading, checking, prompting and challenging to keep standards high.

To Peter Ormerod, James Peacock and Stephen Small for your considered opinions, as well as Professor Alex Hill and Dr Dennis Vincent for your feedback on some of the early drafts of chapters.

I would also like to thank the team at Penguin Random House for their careful work getting the book ready for publication: Joanna Taylor, Jessica Fletcher, Emma Grey Gelder, Anna Cowling and Stuart Brown.

Sources and Credits

BOOKS

With thanks to the following authors, whose works were a source of knowledge and inspiration in writing this book:

Jim Collins & Jerry Porras, *Built to Last: Successful Habits of Visionary Companies* (10th Anniversary Edition, Random Houe Business, 2005)

Daniel Coyle, *The Culture Code: The Secrets of Highly Successful Groups* (Random House Business, 2018)

Reni Eddo-Lodge, *Why I'm No Longer Talking to White People About Race* (Bloomsbury, 2017)

Adam Grant, *Think Again: The Power of Knowing What You Don't Know* (Viking, 2021)

Jonathan Haidt, *The Anxious Generation: How the Great Rewiring of Childhood Is Causing an Epidemic of Mental Illness* (Allen Lane, 2024)

Richard Hytner, *Consiglieri: Leading from the Shadows* (Profile, 2014)

Michael Lewis, *Moneyball: The Art of Winning an Unfair Game* (W. W. Norton, 2004)

PLATE SECTION 2

Page 1 — image 1: Ryan Pierse/Staff for Getty Images; image 2: Stefan Matzke — sampics/Contributor at Getty Images; image 3: Robbie Jay Barratt — AMA/Contributor at Getty Images

Page 2 — image 1: Eddie Keogh — The FA/Contributor at Getty Images; image 2: Tom Jenkins/Contributor at Getty Images

Page 3 — image 1: Adam Davy — PA Images; image 2: Dan Mullan/Staff

Page 4 — image 1: Dean Mouhtaropoulos/Staff; image 2: Stu Forster/Staff

Page 5 — top and bottom images: Eddie Keogh/FA; middle image: courtesy of Gareth Southgate

Page 6 — top image: Lars Baron/Staff at Getty Images; middle image: Stu Forster/Staff at Getty Images; bottom-left image: Eddie Keogh — The FA/Contributor; bottom-right image: courtesy of Gareth Southgate

Page 7 — top image: BBC; bottom images: courtesy of Gareth Southgate

Page 8 — top and bottom-right images: courtesy of Gareth Southgate; bottom-left image: Ian Forsyth/Stringer at Getty Images

Index

GS indicates Gareth Southgate.
Page references in *italics* indicate illustrations.

INDEX